The Lives of Muhammad

The Lives of Muhammad

Kecia Ali

HARVARD UNIVERSITY PRESS
Cambridge, Massachusetts
London, England
2014

Library of Congress Cataloging-in-Publication Data
Ali, Kecia.
   The lives of Muhammad / Kecia Ali.
      p. cm.
   Includes bibliographical references and index.
   ISBN 978-0-674-05060-0 (alk. paper)
      1. Muhammad, Prophet, –632—Biography—History and criticism.
I. Title.

   BP75.3.A454 2014
   297.6'3092—dc23   2014009174

This book is dedicated to my children Saadia and Tariq, and to the memory of their sister Shaira (1996–2012). The standard biographies of Muhammad recount that seven of his eight children died during his lifetime. None of the miracles traditional sources ascribe to him impresses me more than his having survived such loss.

Contents

Chronology

Conventional dating (approximate) of key events in Muhammad's biography:

570	Muhammad's birth
580s	Journey to Syria with his uncle Abu Talib
595	Marriage to Khadija
610	Qur'anic revelation begins
615	Some followers seek refuge in Abyssinia
619	Deaths of Khadija and Abu Talib
621	Night Journey and Ascension
622	Migration to Medina
624	Battle of Badr
625	Battle of Uhud
627	Siege of Medina and retaliation against the Banu Qurayza
630	Conquest of Mecca
632	Muhammad's death

Introduction

For a man who lived fourteen hundred years ago, Muhammad has been in the news a lot lately. From the 2005–2006 Danish cartoon debacle to the 2012 uproar over the *Innocence of Muslims* viral video, media coverage has often explained Muslim outrage by referencing long-standing prohibitions on the depiction of the Prophet and sensitivity to any insult directed at him. By the time this book appears there may have been another flash-in-the-pan incident, with these same tired explanations proffered alongside a portrait of irrational and fanatical Muslim rage, contrasted with a rational, pluralist, democratic West.

Rather than plunge into these recent controversies, which reinforce an unpersuasive clash of civilizations rhetoric, this book approaches Muhammad as he has been portrayed over the centuries. It is a book not about the life of Muhammad but about the ways in which his life has been told.

Biographies of the foundational figures of world religions are inherently controversial. The faithful prefer one biography, those outside the fold offer competing accounts, and experts often insist on other versions based on prevailing scholarly views. Muhammad, alternately revered and reviled, has been the subject of hundreds if not thousands of biographies since his death in the seventh century.

Far from being uniform or unchanging, both non-Muslim and Muslim views of Muhammad have been diverse, multifaceted, and subject to dramatic changes over the centuries. This is widely known. Less well known is that since the nineteenth century they have become increasingly interdependent. In the twenty-first century, it makes no sense to speak of Muslim views of Muhammad in opposition to Western or Christian views. Instead, the images of Muhammad that contemporary Muslims hold fervently and defend passionately arose in tandem and in tension with western European and North American intellectuals' accounts of his life. At the same time, Muslim sensibilities and beliefs have affected the way many non-Muslim authors write his life. This book focuses on these interconnections, the circuitous routes that ideas about Muhammad have taken as they have circulated, and how these ideas have been shaped by shifting attitudes about human achievement, the nature and place of religion, and marriage and sexuality.

Interaction itself is nothing new. Muslims have always adopted and adapted material from their environments. Civilizational boundaries have always been porous, and were certainly so during the first two centuries of Islam's existence when the first accounts of Muhammad were written. The rapid evolution of his biography during the seventh and eighth centuries—shifting from biblical to Arabian motifs, merging the human and the heroic, engaging in contentious negotiations over identity and legacy—has its counterpart in the last two hundred years. Syriac Christian polemics against Islam motivated early refinements in Muhammad's biography.[1] Colonial-era missionizing by western European Christians had a similar effect. There is a striking parallel between the major and disruptive transformations wrought by the advent of Islam in late antiquity and the coming of European colonialism to Muslim-majority societies in Asia and Africa. Specialized scholars are working hard to discover what sort of biography of Muhammad and knowledge of Islam one can retrieve from its first two centuries. *The Lives of Muhammad* describes an equally massive set of shifts in the last two centuries.

Just as boundaries between traditions have always been fluid, so traditions have always been internally heterogeneous. The nature of prophecy, the status of miracles, and—in a more mundane vein—the roles of those close to Muhammad are perennial issues in Muslim thought. These are not just matters of disagreement between insiders and outsiders, but litmus tests that raise the question of who is to be considered an insider and what is to count as tradition. In the modern era, European and American accounts and ideas are pressed into service for intra-Muslim debates. Understanding the multiple, sometimes contradictory, accounts of Muhammad's life requires close attention to the ways in which writers read and draw on their predecessors and antagonists: differing from them, depending on them, appropriating and repurposing their materials—at times narrowly imitative, in other moments strikingly innovative, in what Virginia Burrus, a historian of early Christianity, has called "writerly acts of textual recycling."[2]

A book like this requires authorial choices if it is not to run, as medieval Muslim histories typically did, to dozens of volumes. Some decisions are large, such as what to omit. I have chosen, among other things, Persian poetry, the Danish cartoons—in fact, any and all visual depictions—and whole swathes of the globe, including sub-Saharan Africa and Southeast Asia.[3] Others are smaller, such as how to render foreign words and names, including that of the prophet. Earlier English-language authors generally preferred the French-inflected *Mahomet* but also wrote *Machomed, Mohamed, Mohammad, Muhammed*, and other variants, with little regard for consistency. *Muhammad* is now the usual English spelling, and I use it throughout except in quotations. Where I translate from modern French texts, in which *Mahomet* is standard, I use *Muhammad* to avoid accidentally imparting an archaic flavor. (One Indian biographer replaced *Mahomet* with *Muhammad* when quoting an earlier British work, "since the word Mahomet is derogatory.")[4] Texts also spell the names of people close to Muhammad in myriad ways. In quoting sources, I keep original spellings unless doing so seems likely to confuse readers. Otherwise, I use simplified versions of recurring names (for example, Khadija, Ali, Aisha, Abu Bakr). I usually skip the honorifics and blessings Muslim authors invoke at every mention of Muhammad and other prophets, and Muhammad's wives, close relatives, and associates. One becomes inured to these formulae when reading Arabic or devotional texts, but they distract those unaccustomed. Yet since their presence, especially in texts in European languages, tells about the intended audience for a work, I include them when it seems relevant.

I mostly dispense with diacritics in the body of the book, though quotes, notes, and bibliography retain full transliteration.

I draw primarily from English, Arabic, and French sources, occasionally dipping into works in other languages. I rely on published translations when appropriate; other translations are mine. (Where the nuances of the original language seem particularly relevant, I excerpt the key portion in the endnotes.) I do not read Persian, Turkish, or Urdu (or Dutch, Danish, or Latin) and am thus, like many before me, at the mercy of translators when I consult texts composed in those languages. Translations themselves have been of major importance in the production and dissemination of knowledge and ideas about Muhammad, reshaping works in revealing ways. I discuss such changes, too, as one more way in which Muhammad's *Lives* proliferate, entering new spaces, reaching new audiences, and contributing to the voluminous literature about a man variously known as the Messenger of God, the Arabian impostor, an arch-heretic, an antichrist, a false prophet, the founder of Islam, Mahound, God's beloved, a hero, a Great Man, and—in the modern era—simply Muhammad.

Chapter 1

The Historical Muhammad

The conventional narrative of Muhammad's life goes something like this:

Muhammad was born in Mecca in 570 CE to a father, Abdullah, from a poor but noble background. He belonged to the Quraysh tribe. Abdullah died while Muhammad was still in the womb of his mother, Amina. She in turn died when Muhammad was about six. He was taken in by his grandfather Abd al-Muttalib and, after the old man's death, by his paternal uncle, Abu Talib, who raised him with his own sons. These cousins included Ali, to whom Muhammad grew close. Once grown to young manhood, Muhammad accepted employment on a trade caravan to Syria for a wealthy older widow, Khadija. The caravan prospered; on his return to Mecca, she proposed to him. He was twenty-five and she was forty. They married and were, by all accounts, happy. Muhammad took no other wife. They had two or three sons, who died in infancy, and four daughters. He also freed and adopted a male slave named Zayd, whom Khadija had given him.

After some years of married life, Muhammad took to meditating in a cave near Mecca. When he was forty, in 610, he had an experience during one such retreat: Muslim accounts say that an angel visited him and ordered him to recite what became the first verses of the Qur'an. He sought solace and reassurance from Khadija. Once convinced that he was receiving revelations and not going mad, in part through confirmation from a local Christian, he began to spread the message slowly. Its key points were the oneness of God—a rejection of Mecca's rampant polytheism—and the coming of a day of reckoning when all people would be held accountable for their deeds. His preaching, with its egalitarian undercurrents, attracted converts among the disadvantaged and hostility from local elites, in part because his nascent religion threatened the economy, which depended on pilgrims visiting the Kaaba, a bastion of idolatry.

Hostility turned to persecution after the deaths in 619 of both Khadija and Abu Talib, who had protected him. He remarried—Sawda, a widow, and Aisha, the young daughter of his close friend and follower Abu Bakr. The latter marriage was not consummated until after his flight, in 622, to Medina, accompanied by his family and followers. In Medina, Muhammad led the community politically as well as religiously. His years in Medina were turbulent, with periodic flare-ups of trouble from insincere converts to Islam, alternating cooperation and bloody conflict with local Jewish tribes, and periodic raids and pitched battles with Meccan opponents. He married several more times, including his (adoptive) son Zayd's ex-wife Zaynab. He captured Mecca in 630, encountering little resistance. He died in Medina two years later, Islam already dominating much of the Arabian Peninsula.

Today, most biographies—whether in Arabic or English, whether by Muslims or non-Muslims—cleave to this outline, providing more or less detail as the genre demands.[1] Wikipedia follows this general order. So do newspaper reporters and textbook writers and documentary filmmakers and authors of popular biographies. Hostile biographers weave a tapestry of improper actions around this weft, while pious accounts supplement it with evidence for Muhammad's prophethood and the authenticity of the revelation entrusted to him by God. But important differences in tone notwithstanding, polemicists and apologists and journalists and many scholars follow its contours.

This ubiquitous narrative is relatively recent, though. Most of its particulars can be found in Muslim accounts dating back to the eighth century, but the arrangement of these snippets into a birth-through-death narrative, which pauses at marriages, battles, and revelation, only became standard a century or two ago. Before that, Muslim and Christian accounts differed dramatically, not only on the question of whether Muhammad was a true prophet but in terms of what information was relevant, how it should be interpreted, and what weight—if any—should be given to alternate accounts. Medieval European polemics commingled "information from Muslim sources and defamatory legend."[2] Fact and fabrication coexisted happily, in proportions that varied from place to place, time to time, and author to author. Some "pseudo-historical" accounts aimed at accuracy as part of a broader project of refuting Muslim doctrine. "Literary" presentations of Muslims and Muhammad served different purposes.[3] None was concerned with presenting a full narrative of his life.

Muslim accounts likewise varied, some telling an encyclopedic but roughly chronological tale, others selective, thematic, and devotional. All mixed miraculous events with daily interactions with family, followers, and foes.[4] These tales elevated Muhammad's stature. They also exalted particular factions, promoted distinctive theological positions, and even served as a bulwark against Christian and Jewish apologetics. The range of concerns manifested in most works was broad, but they did not revolve around historical accuracy or source reliability, nor did most explicitly engage with anti-Muslim propaganda.

This tailoring of accounts for various audiences should not be surprising. Stories always serve purposes. Narrative, writes Christian Smith, "arranges human actions and events into organized wholes in a way that bestows meaning on the actions and events by specifying their interactive or cause-and-effect reactions to the whole." What Smith says about narrative in general applies to biography in particular. By placing the events of Muhammad's life "in a single, interrelated account," biographers "always have a point, are always about the explanation and meaning of events and actions in human life."[5] The stories told about Muhammad's life have served a variety of purposes. At some point, however, the story itself—and its component parts—came to be called into question.

The Early Sources

Well into the twentieth century, scholars proceeded as if, in Ernest Renan's infamous phrase, Muhammad was "born in the full light of history."[6] Orientalists confidently claimed to distinguish a factual biographical core from the overlay of legend or the underpinning of political-sectarian bias.[7] Alford Welch pronounced the Qur'an "utterly reliable as a historical source, if it is properly interpreted," and drew from it a portrait of Muhammad's self-understanding.[8] But in recent decades, scholars have renewed their scrutiny of early Muslim history and turned a more skeptical lens on the textual record. The historian F. E. Peters has concluded that unlike scholarship on the historical Jesus, the "quest of the historical Muhammad" is unlikely to yield many certainties, because so little can be known for certain about the Arabian Peninsula of that era. Whereas the big wins of Jesus scholarship have to do with context, this is precisely what is missing from the sources for Muhammad's life.[9] Contemporaneous Arab sources are scanty, non-Arab sources are polemical, and Muslim sources are late and possibly untrustworthy. All attempts to radically rewrite the history of Islam face an uphill battle.

This, of course, has not stopped scholars from trying. Although the sanguine version of Muhammad's life story—an orphan of noble lineage challenging his tribe and the powers that be to proclaim God's oneness in an idolatrous wilderness—is widely accepted, there are reasons to question its accuracy. To begin with, Muhammad, "the praised one," sounds more like a title than a personal name.[10] And in an Arabia typically thought to have been suffused by paganism, it is odd that Muhammad's parents bore monotheist names: Abdullah means "servant of God" and Amina means "faithful one." One hypothesis, which requires only minor adjustments to the standard account, is that biographers whitewashed Muhammad's life to remove any pagan stain. And, indeed, the Muslim tradition preserves occasional traces of a Muhammad, who, before donning the mantle of prophet, worshipped in the manner of his people.[11] An isolated anecdote suggests that he once ate meat sacrificed to Mecca's idols.[12] Of course, most versions of the story tell precisely the opposite tale: even before his experience of revelation, he abstained from idolatry-tainted sacrifices.

Whether or not Muhammad ate the meat makes a great deal of difference to claims about his religious purity, but both variants reinforce the conventional view of Mecca as a hotbed of idolatry.

Other scholars, though, question this too, upending the standard narrative entirely. In 1977, Patricia Crone and Michael Cook published *Hagarism,* which, refusing to rely at all on Islamic sources, questioned the basic outlines of early Muslim history. Many of *Hagarism*'s suppositions have been convincingly refuted, and others more convincingly argued, but the basic questions it posed remain open: What can we really know about Muhammad, and how can we know it?[13] Did Muhammad exist? As to the latter question, though it is asked in the title of a new book by polemicist Robert Spencer, the answer, according to self-described "infidel" skeptic Cook, is an emphatic yes.[14] Even setting Muslim sources aside, early Greek and Syriac sources give sufficient evidence to remove "any doubts as to whether Muhammad was a real person."[15] Yet these same sources—themselves polemical—raise many other questions about Islam's early history. Scholars' theories are frequently incompatible. For instance, Gerald Hawting has argued that the Qur'an's references to idol worship and associating partners with God should be understood as intra-monotheistic polemic and not a description of an actual pagan environment.[16] Speculation of this sort understandably raises hackles.

Without seeking to discard the entire chronology and geography of early Islam, the historian Fred Donner argues that Muhammad's preaching was both apocalyptic and ecumenical, a movement of "believers" rather than "brand-name" Muslims.[17] Donner's view dovetails with other scholarship that sets Islam in a monotheistic context straddling the Red Sea.[18] He argues that Muhammad's community only later became a separate Arabo-centric religion—capital *I* Islam, rather than *islam,* the ongoing human phenomenon of submission to God. At stake in these debates are not just particular biographical details but the validity of Islam as a religion and the viability of early Islamic history as an academic specialization.

Even among specialists who accept that the early Muslim sources have their own complex agendas, debate rages about how or, indeed, if one can use them for a reliable account of Muhammad's life.[19] There is a stalemate in the field.[20] Some hold that traditionally transmitted texts are tissue of fabrications, mere "salvation history."[21] Repetition, no matter how frequent, does not amount to corroboration. Others—though not accepting faith claims about the literal truth of these accounts, or even necessarily agreeing with the conventional story—remain optimistic about the prospect of retrieving an essential historical nucleus to Muhammad's biography from extant or reconstituted sources.[22] One specialist asserts that "we should be able to reconstruct without fanfare an outline of Muḥammad's life that can withstand all but the most extreme scholarly criticism."[23] Writing for a general audience, another remarks, "If we were to restrict ourselves entirely to the undisputed facts of Muhammad's biography, we would run out of information after only a few pages."[24] This seems overly strict to him, and he proceeds to write an entire book; others, however, doubt one could fill even those few pages with indisputable information.

Two recent studies centering on Muhammad's life illustrate the major challenges faced by revisionist projects. One centers on Muhammad's death date; the other, his sonlessness. In *The Death of a Prophet: The End of Muhammad's Life and the Beginnings of Islam,* Stephen Shoemaker, a historian of early Christianity, revisits early Arabic and non-Arabic sources to argue that Muhammad may have lived through the conquest of Jerusalem in 634. When that conquest failed to bring about the large-scale conversion of its Christian and Jewish populace, the narrative of his life was rewritten to make Muhammad an Arabian prophet and to place his death before the conquest.[25] Like Donner, Shoemaker suggests that "during the century that elapsed between the end of Muhammad's life and the first recoverable narrative of Islamic origins," there was a "shift from an immanent eschatological belief focused on Jerusalem to . . . a sacred geography centered on the Hijāz."[26] (The Hijaz is the region of western Arabia encompassing Mecca and Medina.) In a different vein, scholar of early Islam David Powers argues that the doctrine of the finality of Muhammad's prophethood developed over a period of approximately fifty years following the Prophet's death.[27] After marrying, Muhammad had reportedly adopted a grown man named Zayd, making him the Prophet's sole male heir, his biological sons having reportedly died in infancy. Powers argues that Zayd's new status posed a challenge on two fronts: first, the issue of political succession, and second, the emerging doctrine of the finality of prophecy. Zayd would have arguably had a stronger claim to the caliphate than either Abu Bakr or Ali; more importantly, he would have been a prophet—compromising the doctrine that Muhammad was the last prophet. Powers argues that believers formulated two stories that, taken together, remove both challenges. One was the story of Muhammad's infatuation with, and eventual marriage to, Zayd's (ex-)wife Zaynab. Before marrying his (former) daughter-in-law, the Prophet repudiated Zayd, in accordance with a new Qur'anic passage declaring that "Muhammad is not the father of any of your men." The other story, that Muhammad appointed Zayd commander of a military expedition and sent him to certain death—and martyrdom—on a battlefield in southern Jordan, served to establish that Zayd predeceased the Prophet. Scholarly reaction to the books by Donner, Shoemaker, and Powers, like those of other scholars of early Islam, has been mixed, alternately appreciative and deeply critical.

For all their erudition, these scholarly squabbles have had little effect on how Muhammad's story is told and retold. This is so even though modern accounts of Muhammad's life by Muslims and non-Muslims alike claim to rely on historical sources, and debates over the reliability of early sources permeate even nonspecialist engagement with writings about Islam. To wit: an online reader review of a general-audience book, *The Future of Islam,* criticized the author, Middle East studies scholar John Esposito, for omitting discussion of the earliest extant Muslim biographical account (by Ibn Ishaq), which, alongside his "quite laudable" qualities, "reveals Muhammad as a man that slaughtered captives, robbed caravans, sold women and children into slavery," and performed a litany of other abuses. Another reviewer replies that Ibn Ishaq's biography may say these things but the accusations are "unwarranted and baseless" because a "matured and discerning" reader would not accept its claims at "face value." Not only was it written at least a century and a half after Muhammad lived, but in that era, it was typical for facts to be presented "in [a] highly emotional, embellished, fanatacised [*sic*] and exaggerated manner, primarily to appeal to the emotions of the listeners rather than to leaving hard historical records for posterity."[28] The reviewers' opposing stances on one source's reliability result in their divergent assessment of Muhammad's character, but both agree that one derives knowledge of Muhammad from early texts, properly read.

The reviews share, too, the unspoken assumption that the present and future of Islam cannot be understood apart from its origins, which are inextricable from Muhammad's life. Thus, debates about Muslim origins form an inescapable backdrop for the modern Muhammad, whose biographers, Muslim and non-Muslim alike, portray a figure of human rather than cosmic import. How did we arrive at the common version of his life we have now? When and how did the Muslim and non-Muslim accounts become impossible to disentangle—indeed, in some cases impossible to distinguish?[29] To begin to answer such questions, we must address the sources themselves.

In his history of Western life writing, Nigel Hamilton informs readers that Islam is "a religion that eschewed individual life depiction as insulting to the majesty of Allah."[30] By employing the Arabic name for God and avoiding the simple possessive—"the majesty of Allah" rather than "God's majesty"—Hamilton conjures alien-ness and archaism. *We*, like our classical Mediterranean forebears, value individual lives; *they* single out only the deity to set apart from the mass of interchangeable humanity.

As it happens, Hamilton is flat-out wrong. Muslims have a voluminous biographical literature. Indeed, in one scholar's estimate, "No premodern civilization has ever produced so many biographies or biographical sketches of its men and women."[31] Biographical dictionaries, which the historian Hamilton Gibb calls "a wholly indigenous creation of the creation of the Islamic Community," assemble notices for groups of people.[32] The earliest surviving collection is the *Tabaqat* (Generations) of Ibn Sa'd (d. 845).[33] In addition to its biography of the Prophet, it has entries for Muhammad's wives, relatives, and Companions—those Muslims who had contact with him during his life.[34] Its entries, "arranged more or less by religious importance,"[35] give genealogies and tell how people met the Prophet and when they became Muslim, in addition to other noteworthy facts. Later collections, of which there are many, focus on other groups: scholars of a particular city or intellectual subfield, notables of various types, or members of Sufi orders; each of these works contains hundreds or thousands of entries. Apart from these compendia, hagiographical works laud individuals, including founders of legal schools and local saints, or "friends of God." Rulers merited their own fawning biographies. Thousands upon thousands of pages depict lives singly and in aggregate. There are even medieval autobiographies.[36]

The Prophet stands at the center of these forms of life writing, often explicitly, otherwise implicitly. He is the paradigm of sanctity, the exemplar of manhood, the paragon of leadership, the model of devotion. His example is further fleshed out in the *sira* literature. The first such mostly continuous narrative is the "arabesque biography"[37] by Ibn Ishaq (d. 767), who lived a century before Ibn Saʻd. It was not a life story in the conventional sense. Its first book began with creation and the long lineage of biblical prophets, stretching back to God's first deputy on earth, Adam. Ibn Ishaq presented Muhammad as the culmination of that legacy, "plac[ing] Muhammad in the context of the history of the salvation of the world."[38] As Gordon Newby, a historian of religion, summarizes, "The form was universal history; the content was a mixture of Jewish Haggadah, Arab legend, and Christian martyrology; and the effect was hagiography and prophetology."[39] Ibn Ishaq's work survives primarily in a ninth-century epitome by Ibn Hisham (d. ca. 833). He viewed the entire first book as largely irrelevant and, more importantly, compromised by its extensive reliance on Jewish and Christian sources; thus, he cut it.[40] Ibn Hisham, like many later biographers, did not discard these models or stories altogether but emphasized authentically Arabian contexts, and specifically Islamic theological and political rationales.[41] This work in turn was very successful; one scholar observes, "In the edition of Ibn Hisham, Ibn Isḥāq's biography of Muhammad has acquired almost the status of a sacred book all over the world of Islam."[42] Yet it was not without its detractors, and the veracity of some of its stories was debated well before an Amazon.com reviewer took it on: "Muslim regard for his biography has never risen to the level of canonicity."[43]

The question of how to refer to the text has given scholars pause. Scottish Orientalist and Bengal Civil Service official William Muir referred to the work as *Hishâmi;* Michael Edwardes, working from the handwritten translation of a Hungarian-born, India-based scholar, completed in 1898 and given to the Royal Asiatic Society, refers to it simply as "Ibn Ishaq's *Life.*" He cut the text substantially, removing the poetry that abounded in the original and providing occasional connective paragraphs; a handsomely bound version appeared in 1964 from London's Folio Society.[44] Alfred Guillaume, in his 1955 English translation, attempted to segregate the two men's words, exiling Ibn Hisham's additions to the end of the work and restoring some of what he had excised by ferreting out portions preserved by other authors.[45] For better or worse, the text as it has circulated for over a millennium is an amalgam; I occasionally have recourse to the cumbersome designation Ibn Ishaq/Ibn Hisham but, where possible, follow the attribution in the Arabic text as to what content belongs to which man.

Roughly contemporaneous with this reconstituted biography are the "expeditionary" writings or "war memoirs" of the historian Muhammad ibn Umar al-Waqidi (d. ca. 822), for whom Ibn Saʻd served as scribe.[46] These recount Muhammad's military ventures, including minor skirmishes and major battles with Meccan opponents, and a protracted siege ending in brutal reprisal against a Jewish tribe.[47] Not exactly a biography, Waqidi's *Book of Campaigns* is full of stories about Muhammad, his Companions, and their neighbors and antagonists. Bernard Lewis describes writings of this type as "subjective and episodic, presenting a series of heroic figures and incidents without concern for chronology, sequence, or consistency—in a word, saga rather than history."[48] Its recent English translator describes it as "a work designed to show the role of Muḥammad as the chosen messenger of God whose work led to the fulfillment of the will of God in establishing his community of Islam. It portrays . . . his image as a prophet and his status as a statesman."[49] If Ibn Ishaq had taken biblical motifs and themes as his model, Waqidi "works within typical models of story-telling devoted to continuing and enhancing cultural notions of heroes and legends."[50] Arab intellectual historian Tarif Khalidi's comment about other biographical works applies to Waqidi: the agglomerating impulse records "thousands of . . . men and women whose life stories were intertwined with Muhammad's own. . . . It is as if some early Christian Gospel writer had decided to fill out the Sermon on the Mount and the feeding of the five thousand with the names and life stories of every single one of those who were present, together with some account, long or short, of their life and subsequent fate."[51]

Muhammad through the Centuries

Although these early sources, along with one or two slightly later histories, provide a canon around which contemporary controversies center—even among competing online reviewers—and which contemporary writers draw from, Muslim writing about the Prophet flowered bountifully through the centuries. Ibn Hisham and the rest were certainly known to scholars, but they did not determine or constrain the many and varied accounts of Muhammad's life and person, nor did they directly influence most lay Muslims. Muhammad's role as intercessor for Muslims on the day of judgment and his status as "the original light in creation," God's beloved, and the "perfect mirror of Divine Beauty," among similar attributes, "were far better known to the medieval Muslims than the historical facts of the Prophet's life."[52]

Though the facts of Muhammad's life may not have been the most important things to be known about him, some scholars pursued biography or *sira* seriously. In his *Images of Muhammad*, Khalidi divides Muslim biographies of the Prophet into three stages. First, in the late eighth through the early tenth centuries, there was the "*Sira* of primitive devotion," comprehensive in its impulse to preserve everything, including even "stories or anecdotes that may offend the sensibilities of Muslims." Khalidi argues that its "founding fathers"—the men mentioned earlier in this chapter plus historians Ahmad ibn Yahya al-Baladhuri (d. 892) and Muhammad ibn Jarir al-Tabari (d. 923)—"fixed the order of the *Sira* and determined much of its content for all later biographers."[53] Khalidi may overstate his case; Muslim authors through the centuries drew extensively on these thinkers but not uncritically. Indeed, in a second stage, "the Muhammadan *Sira* was subjected to critical assessment in order to prune it of superstition and heresy," resulting in a biographical tradition that was "canonical, moral, exclusivist, and rationalizing."[54] Though Khalidi refers to rationality and superstition, these biographies often presumed

"Muhammad's superhuman qualities—his pre-eternity, miraculous powers, and sinlessness"—as well as his suitability as "an object of love and devotion."[55] Khalidi's final stage, which he dates from the late nineteenth century, is "the polemical *Sira*, written largely to defend Muhammad's reputation against the attacks of the European Orientalists." It is this last period, and this genre, with which this book is primarily concerned. Not all present-day Muslim writings about Muhammad form part of "the polemical *Sira*." Other Muslim writings about Muhammad exist, including popular devotional works, compilations of *hadith* recounting his deeds, and works of guidance and reflection composed by lay believers and authorities of various sorts. Internal Muslim debates about who constitutes an authority, what role precedent plays, where it is reliably found, and who is qualified to interpret it are vibrant, vigorous, and sometimes vitriolic; these debates occur in sermons, online, and in a wide array of books, including biographies. To understand this modern Muslim approach to Muhammad's biography, we must know more about the millennium of writings about Muhammad's life that preceded it.

Like Christian writings about Muhammad, Muslim accounts of the Prophet's life were neither uniform nor static. Muslim thinkers engaged in subtle arguments and vigorous debate over such matters as the status of miracles and the relative prominence of various factions in Muhammad's community. Muslims told tales of the Prophet they required. Early texts depict Muhammad not as a psychologically unique individual but as a type, an exemplum, a manifestation, of a universal model. He represents an ideal: the "perfected human being" whose conduct people should try to emulate. Incidents and precedents drawn from his exemplary practice—snippets of life as reported, through authenticated chains of reporters, in accounts called *hadith*—overlap with bio-graphical retellings.

Birth and death inescapably bookend every human life, but not all life writing starts with the subject's birth or ends with her death. Muhammad's early Muslim biographies tend to start with his ge-nealogy; his immediate lineage includes noble Arabs but stretches back through biblical prophets to the first human being, Adam. Some accounts tell of a light his father bore, shining, until Mu-hammad had been conceived; in some versions, this light was car-ried from father to son through the generations until it passed to Muhammad. His pregnant mother was granted a dream-vision, announcing the birth of a son; a light shone from her—or from the infant, after his birth—all the way to the castles of Bostra in Syria. These stories echo and amplify Qur'anic stories and, in the case of the annunciatory dream, have obvious parallels in biblical accounts.[56] Just as European polemicists mixed fact and fancy in their catalogs of Muhammad's failings, so, too, Muslim authors alternated between what we might think of as empirical (if un-verifiable) fact—names, dates, kinship ties—and the aura of the miraculous, particularly surrounding Muhammad's birth. These events would form the centerpiece of devotional works associated with the *mawlid,* or celebration of his birthday.

Medieval Christian accounts say little of his birth but get mileage from his (usually humiliating and shameful) death. During the twelfth and thirteen centuries, Christians viewed Muhammad as "disgusting in life and, most of all, in the man-ner of his death."[57] Authors wrote Muhammad an undignified death—perhaps drunk or even murdered, in one account, by a cuckolded husband—and lingered on the dismemberment or desecration of his "smelly corpse"[58] by (unclean) animals, often pigs or dogs.[59] This "ignominious death . . . followed by the desecration of his corpse" aimed to engender disgust."[60] These themes persisted into the early modern era, repeated in fifteenth-and sixteenth-century English works, one of which had him "gnaven by swine" after collapsing drunk.[61] Authors sought to provoke repugnance and also to highlight "the permanence of the 'pseudo'-prophet's death in contrast to Jesus' escape from decay through resurrection."[62]

Other hostile accounts drew on Muslim sources to link Muhammad's death to the ingestion of poisoned mutton. The poisoning by a Jewish woman allows critics to view Muhammad as bereft of God's protection and therefore clearly not what he claimed to be: "notwithstanding the Intimacy he pretended with the Angel *Gabriel,* and the continual *Revelations* which he brag'd that he received from him, he could not be preserved from thus perishing by the Snares of a silly Girl."[63] Those Muslims who favored the account used it to prove his martyrdom at the hands of one of Islam's enemies: an additional blessing by God.[64] In this and many other details, Muslim accounts aimed to depict an exemplary death. How Muhammad died had implications for the community he left behind. Sunni and Shi'i versions differed as to whether he had died in Aisha's arms—the version followed in nearly all Western biographies—or Ali's, and whether he had called for someone to record his words on succession. Accounts also differed as to who washed his corpse, how it was shrouded, and who lowered it into the grave.[65] These details indicated intimacy with the Prophet; they also bore on questions of proper procedure for later Muslims to follow and were thus found in legal works as well as biographical ones.

In comparing Islam with Christianity, historian Chase Robinson suggests that religious foci determined the emphases of early narratives about Muhammad and Christ. It was Christ's death and resurrection, not "his birth or miracles," that held most significance for early followers; by contrast, "it seems that the earliest Muslims were principally interested in Muḥammad's charismatic career as God's prophet," not in "his childhood or career as a merchant."[66] (His gestation, birth, and infancy, including his fostering by a Bedouin woman, were central in *mawlid* texts, but less important in other sorts of works.) These elements "were central to their identity as Christians and Muslims" and therefore garnered the most attention within their respective communities. But "doubters and skeptics" questioned and probed, seeking stronger, more complete answers. Robinson writes that "having entered a market of competing ideas and polemics, early Christians and early Muslims eventually came to tell the *whole* story. What they could not remember they duly provided in the form of legends, myths, conjectures and reasonable guesses, all about things they had no real memory of, since they had not really mattered before."[67] Even though "by the standards of most historians, this is making things up," such details emerged in the eighth and ninth centuries to flesh out narratives.[68]

It was not necessarily Christian "doubters and skeptics" that Muslim biographers sought to convince, although interreligious debates and conversations were indeed taking place, and materials on miracles may have been oriented toward possible Christian audiences.[69] The primary audience for Muslim thinkers over the centuries has been other Muslims. Not as much effort was centered on the emerging sectarian divide between Sunni and Shiʻa as one might expect; Shiʻi authors focused on Ali and his descendants, the Imams, whom they believed were the rightful, though dispossessed, leaders of the community.[70] Sunni authors likewise praised the members of Muhammad's household, including Ali, Fatima, and their offspring, whom later Shi'a would venerate.

Rather than produce a sectarian Muhammad, the biographical tradition gradually shifted from a prophet in the biblical tradition to an Arab hero, suitable for the imperial context developing as Muslim rule spread throughout the near east, across the Mediterranean, and into Asia. The "progression from signs to miracles, from eschatology to history, from figurative description to the literal," happened as part of this broader hero-building project.[71]

Over the next centuries, images of Muhammad oscillated between emphasizing Muhammad's saintly qualities and focusing on his humanity.[72] But it was not only biographers who remembered and celebrated Muhammad. In each field of Muslim intellectual endeavor, the Prophet was a central figure to be reckoned with.

Scriptural commentators fleshed out their interpretations of Qur'anic passages with copious references to Muhammad's life. Where was he when this verse was revealed? What circumstance of his life prompted this passage? How did he understand and apply a particular edict? Tabari, whose *History* is a prime source for prophetic biography, composed a massive Qur'anic commentary that provides much material on Muhammad, as it elaborates the backstory for events the Qur'an describes only elliptically and allusively.

Jurists, too, drew on numerous specifics about Muhammad's life as they delineated norms to govern ritual, personal, and communal conduct. From the way he washed before prayer to how he treated his wives to what he liked to eat to how he commanded troops in battle, no detail was insignificant. Some material had direct legal effect. For instance, how many nights Muhammad allocated to his brides helped determine standard doctrines on the question of a new husband's duties. Because Muhammad's reported practice was central to ongoing debates among jurists, Joseph Schacht, a legal historian, suggested that "a considerable part of the standard biography of the Prophet in Medina" arose in response to these debates and is "without independent historical value."[73] Yet other biographical details yielded guidance rather than rules. His favorite foods and manner of eating provided material for pious emulation rather than legal rulings. The deep concern of Muslims with emulating Muhammad's behavior in every area of life meant that jurisprudence—an enterprise intertwining legal and ethical realms—was deeply informed by the prophetic model.

Pietistic movements developed alongside other forms of Muslim scholarly and popular activity. Storytellers and preachers recounted the lives of Muhammad and other prophets, combining entertainment and edification. Such stories could inspire a "mild asceticism" firmly grounded in law and ritual practice or, for others, lead to a preference for spiritual athleticism.

Sufi or mystical thinkers saw Muhammad not merely as someone whose balanced asceticism was to be imitated for the development of a virtuous character but as someone whose very existence suffused the cosmos with light, someone who served as a channel for grace and intercession.[74] The traditional response to quotation of the Qur'anic verse pronouncing Muhammad "a man like you" was to both accept and qualify this statement: "Yes, but like a ruby among stones."[75] Some mystical thinkers developed elaborate prophetologies, with Muhammad at their apex. Although allegorical and symbolic works of this sort were intended for the reflection of a small elite, this disposition toward the numinous was widely shared among premodern Muslims, including the idea that Muhammad was more than an ordinary man and that the universe contained more than was visible to the eye.

One type of vision widely believed to convey true knowledge was dreams. Sufis saw significance in dreams, but so did—and do—others.[76] As in many parts of the ancient and medieval Mediterranean, it was widely presumed that dreams were an accurate and important means for conveying information. They were available to pious laypeople, suggesting a breakdown of boundaries "between the exceptional few and the supposedly ignorant masses," though interpretation often relied (like legal queries) on expert guidance.[77] Some Muslims today continue to seek analysis from a spiritual authority; others post dreams to religious websites, offering them for collective comment and reflection. Dreams of the Prophet, perceived as a sign of the dreamer's piety, have always been particularly desirable, with various techniques employed to induce them. Such dreams were widely retold in hagiographical works about saintly figures, rulers, and scholars as a means of legitimation.[78] A widely quoted prophetic statement holds that anyone who sees Muhammad in a dream really sees him; Satan cannot take his form. Vision was a matter not only of the actual eyes but also of the "awakened heart."[79]

Dreams and pious emulation continue to shape Muslim belief and practice in many places and periods.[80] Yet a large swathe of Muslim thinking has been profoundly desacralized. This desacralization, contested in some quarters, is reflected in many biographies.[81] Although Muslims still put stock in dreams of the Prophet, unlike "true" dreaming's central role in Ibn Ishaq's biography, in which "dream accounts serve as narrative units . . . clearly integral to the themes of concern to the early transmission of traditions surrounding major events of the emerging Muslim community," contemporary biographers tend to pay it no mind.[82]

The demotion of dreams from a place of prominence is only one of many changes Muslim biographies have undergone. The ground for many of these transformations was laid by the Protestant Reformation, with its influential critique of authority structures, its assumptions about the accessibility of texts and the appropriate procedures for reading them, and the rise of vernacular scriptures. The composition of new sorts of *Lives* of Muhammad was precipitated, too, by European scholarship, beginning in the early modern era but developing under the aegis of Western European colonial power. German Jews and British Protestants engaged in the retrieval of early Muslim sources and, in doing so, shaped specialist, polemicist, and popular interest in Muhammad's life in the nineteenth century. From this point forward, Muslim *Lives*—engaged directly and indirectly with Western scholarship—are increasingly preoccupied with issues of achievement and historical significance. In order to understand these developments better, it will be helpful to know something about non-Muslim accounts of Muhammad up until that time.

Non-Muslim Accounts, from Late Antiquity to the Enlightenment

Nineteenth-century scholars were intent on discovering accurate, early information about Muhammad; their medieval counterparts were, for the most part, not.

During the first centuries of Islam's existence, many Europeans knew little and cared less about accuracy in their portrayal of Muhammad, whom they associated, as in the French epic *Song of Roland,* with paganism and idolatry. (As one might expect given their geographical proximity to early Muslims, Syriac Christian polemics against Muhammad were more informed than European ones, if no less hostile.) As paganism became less of a concern than dissent and heresy, Muhammad was refashioned a heresiarch, an antichrist, a false prophet, and, eventually, a fraud. John Tolan, preeminent historian of European views of Muslims, points out the "carefully construct[ed]" nature of such medieval accounts: "Rather than presenting an inept hodge-podge, these authors forge clever and coherent—although inaccurate—polemics."[83] Writers, often clergy, tailored their accusations to current local theological and social worries, using Islam as a foil to address their preoccupations. For instance, Embrico of Mainz wrote his Latin life of Muhammad at a time when clergy worried about heretical "wandering preachers." Muhammad appears as "a trickster and a scoundrel, not an Antichrist but rather an anti-saint." He "feigns holiness and performs bogus miracles through magic and sleight-of-hand, hoodwinking the gullible Arab masses into deeming him holy."[84] Equating the reviled prophet of Islam with "itinerant visionaries closer to home," Embrico tars both with the same brush. For a feat like this, Embrico needed few concrete details. Fewer still were required by Alexandre du Pont for his twelfth-century Old French *Romance of Muhammad.* Adapting a Latin clerical rejoinder, the poet deliberately tweaked Muhammad's story to provide details and themes that would meet a lay audience's expectations.[85]

Around the same time, a translation project sponsored by Peter the Venerable, the abbot of Cluny, sought to improve knowledge about Muslim doctrines to combat heresy more effectively.[86] Robert of Ketton translated the Qur'an into Latin. Though Ketton's 1143 translation was free from deliberate distortion, its title, *The Law of the False Prophet Muhammad,* makes clear its framing.[87]

(Muhammad's role as lawgiver was stressed on and off for centuries, to varying effects. At one end of the spectrum, a late-fifteenth-century English text emphasizes "the falsity and fakery of Mahomet's 'lawe,'" while at the other, Muhammad appears with other lawgivers on the U.S. Supreme Court frieze.[88]) Other texts provided further information about Muslim doctrines and history. Even as they increasingly drew on Muslim sources for tidbits about Muhammad, Christian authors told dramatically different stories from their Muslim counterparts.[89] Neither lay nor scholarly Christian narratives tried to understand Muhammad or retell his life in full. His life was interesting only insofar as it illuminated the beastly nature of Islam as a religion and Muslims as a group. Selected incidents of Muhammad's life appeared "in a way meant to ridicule and discredit his followers."[90] Such works followed, in a way, the classical Western biographical tradition of treating "the individual persons portrayed [as] moral exempla, which should be followed or avoided, as the case might be."[91] But unlike the accounts of illustrious men composed by Suetonius and Plutarch, there was a metonymic dimension to biographies of Muhammad: he was both cause *and* example par excellence of the failings of Muslims as a whole.

In places where Muslims and Christians had ongoing contact—such as the Iberian Peninsula, which Arab armies had conquered in the early eighth century and where Christian control remained patchy through the fifteenth century—texts condemning Islam and Muhammad were sometimes meant to reassure Christians of their religion's superiority. Chronicles of Muhammad's life sought to demonstrate "the illegitimacy of Muslim dominion" by proving him "a heresiarch and a false prophet."[92] At other times, the usually fruitless aim was to convert Muslims, either directly or by giving missionaries talking points "to demonstrate the superiority of Christianity."[93] A third function was to strengthen the "far from watertight" social barriers between Christians and Muslims by instilling "mutual repugnance."[94] Thus, Pedro Pascual's early fourteenth-century *On the Muhammadan Sect* "manipulates traditional anti-Muslim polemics, seeking to inspire in its readers hatred and disdain for Islam, in order to prevent them from crossing over to the rival faith." It also seeks to dissuade those Christians who "were ready to share their beds with the infidel." Although Muslims had been expelled from the Iberian Peninsula by the end of the fifteenth century, this gate-barring function was increasingly important as Muslim-ruled empires threatened Christian dominance in Africa, southern Europe, and western portions of Asia.

In Europe, from the fifteenth through the seventeenth centuries, one crucial way this happened was to portray Muslims— Muhammad chief among them—as monstrous. This might involve association with Jews, which "served a twofold polemical purpose, demonizing Judaism through its association with Islam, yet incorporating Islam into a grand Christian history through its connections with Judaism. Their shared monstrosity," Matthew Dimmock argues, "coalesces around two factors: the first, a continuing denial of the divinity of Christ . . . which transmuted in both cases into a responsibility for the murder of Christ, the second, the associated part both were to play in the events of apocalypse and revelation."[95]

The enemy within and the enemy without were two sides of the same coin. Especially after the start of the Protestant Reformation in the early sixteenth century, writers drew on Muhammad and Muslims for intra-Christian polemics. The accusations of debauched conduct launched against Muhammad had counterparts, sometimes even more virulent, against purportedly heretical Christians. The Protestant/Catholic split, a "bitter dispute of unprecedented geographical range and chronological endurance," prompted a "level of vitriol [that] was, if not unprecedented, then not surpassed either."[96] Islam and Muhammad played a crucial role. Generally, theological enemies were likened to Muhammad or Muslims, but occasionally Islam or Muhammad were compared favorably to the opponent in question, to make the enemy seem worse. As Tolan suggests, "European discourse concerning Muḥammad is often best understood as a deforming mirror."[97]

If Muhammad had been the antichrist for some medieval critics, for Protestant polemicists, so was the Pope. The connection with Muhammad intensified anti-Catholic insults. A sixteenth-century Swedish church painting shows St. Christopher rescuing the Christ child "from the water in which the Pope and Muhammad perish. . . . The drowning, nameless pope is humiliated by being associated with Muhammad and Islam."[98] A Swiss tract from the same era against a Catholic monastic order bears the title *The Franciscans' Qur'an*.[99] Catholics, too, used Muhammad and Islam to denigrate Protestants, equating Martin Luther and other errant pastors to Muhammad and comparing "Calvinist and Muslim treachery."[100] Sixteenth-century French scholar Guillaume Postel put it particularly bluntly: "The spiritual sons of Luther are the little bastards of Mahom."[101] As Jonathan Lyons observes, "Each side in the European struggle over the Reformation sought to tar the other by rhetorical association with the violent and dangerous 'Turk.'"[102] Yet anti-Catholic and anti-Muslim sentiments were more consistently interwoven, perhaps because Luther himself had penned a condemnation of Islam and its prophet.[103] These associations between Muhammad and the Pope, sometimes styled twin antichrists, persist well into the nineteenth century.[104]

Not only could Muhammad be marshaled to criticize Christian enemies, but he could also be linked rhetorically to Muslim political and military opponents. Renewed fears of Ottoman military advances led to villainous portraits of Turkish emperors. They were likened in their bad qualities to "the Arab pseudo-prophet Mohammed," to whom Philippus Meyerus's 1594 poetic Latin life assigns ruthlessness, cruelty, and a "diabolical combination of political astuteness and military strength." Other "dubious qualities in which the Ottoman sultans were perceived to emulate the founder of their religion were an extravagant lifestyle and sexual debauchery."[105]

The Ottoman threat revived the theological quandary Islam had posed centuries earlier for figures like Peter of Cluny. If Christianity was the true religion, why were Muslims enjoying worldly success? One answer was that God was punishing Christians for their failings; the catastrophe of Muslim military victory and widespread conversion to Islam was not because God had switched allegiance but because Muslims, just like Christians, were subject to God's broader plan.

This plan of God was under threat, too, from enemies closer to home. The early modern era, approximately from the Reformation to the French Revolution and the rise of Napoleon at the end of the eighteenth century, saw a series of intellectual and religious movements that challenged long-held ideas about God, humanity, and reason. The Enlightenment sought to replace irrationality and superstition with rationality. In addition to the Enlightenment's hostility toward religion generally, there was criticism of central Christian beliefs, including the Trinity, and widespread concern with religious fraud. Given that, as Ziad Elmarsafy notes, "the Enlightenment holds a privileged position in the making of modernity writ large," the shifts it engendered were deeply influential in how Muhammad's biography came to be written.[106]

Imposture was the early modern era's characteristic preoccupation. William Bedwell's 1615 *Mohammedis imposturae; that is, A discovery of the manifold forgeries, falsehoods, and horrible impieties of the blasphemous seducer Mohammed* leveled the charge of fraud, which picked up steam as the seventeenth century wore on.[107] By the turn of the eighteenth century, three overlapping bodies of literature converged on the idea of the false prophet: Orientalist scholarship, Enlightenment thought, and Christian apologetic and polemic. As theology ceded some ground to secular humanism, some tried to set all religions and their founders on the same playing field, while others worked to exalt one religion by denigrating others. It was precisely this recognition, in some spheres unwelcome, that there were competing "religions" and not merely distortions or usurpations of the one true faith that marked the shift from medieval to modern ways of approaching Others. In the developing study of world religions, European scholarship on Islam was influential in forming the category of religion. Historian Guy Stroumsa argues that prejudices against Islam changed in the seventeenth century, allowing the "gradual emergence of a new, more open attitude that was most significant for the birth of the modern study of Islam."[108] The entry on Muhammad in Barthélemy d'Herbelot's *Bibliothèque orientale* begins, "This is the famous Impostor Mahomet, Author and Founder of a heresy which called itself Religion, and that we call Mahomedan."[109] Oxford Arabist Edward Pococke (1604–1691) applies Maimonides's notion of the false prophet to Muhammad, though he also holds that

"Muhammad should nonetheless be considered a remarkable man who brought moral reform to his people."[110]

Enlightenment thinkers extended the criticism of false prophets far beyond Muhammad, considering all religions equally false. The existence of and proofs for prophecy in general had been a significant topic of debate among philosophers and theologians for centuries, and Muslim figures had joined the fray between the ninth and eleventh centuries, with rationalist figures arguing that claims of revelation did not survive logical scrutiny. Defenders of Muhammad's role often found themselves laying the groundwork for their claims about him by arguing for the authenticity of previous prophets.[111]

The famous treatise on *The Three Impostors*, which the historian George Minois has called "an aggressive work, a frontal attack upon religion,"[112] takes the anti-revelation view to its logical end. This book was born of rumor and innuendo; a thirteenth-century pope accused the Holy Roman emperor of the time of having written a book condemning Moses, Jesus, and Muhammad. The emperor denied the accusation, but the shadow book persisted for four centuries: "nobody had seen it, nobody had read it, but almost everybody believed in its existence." Eventually, "it became such an obsession that it ended up by existing."[113]

Its basic premise was that Moses, Jesus, and Muhammad and their religions were equivalent, "full of hoaxes, trickery, and illusions that knock out critical thinking and cause senseless massacres." Their Gods were false, and the prophets, frauds. *The Three Impostors* was undoubtedly quite a different work than it would have been had it emerged from "virtual" to tangible existence two or three centuries earlier. Still, its references to central Christian,

Jewish, and Muslim figures continued the "triangularity of religious discourse" at evidence since the late seventh or eighth century.[114]

Whereas some antireligious tracts argued for the essential sameness of all religious teachings and religious founders, other thinkers clung to a bright division between true religion on the one hand and falsehood on the other. One Catholic cleric, for instance, sought to rehabilitate the reputations of Moses and Jesus but affirmed that Muhammad and Zoroaster had been impostors.

Accusations of fraud could also be levied against dissenters within a tradition. A concern with "simulation and dissimulation, pretending to be what one was not, concealing one's real identity and convictions," was everywhere. Writing about a seventeenth-century Catholic Italian laywoman, Cecilia Ferrazzi, Anne Schutte notes that the inquisitors who prosecuted her did not begin from the assumption that women (or anyone) claiming certain kinds of spiritual distinction were possessed or inspired or "deluded by the Devil," as would have been the case two centuries earlier. But "If the Devil could not have inspired them . . . they must be held responsible for fabricating, consciously and deliberately, evidence of a holiness they did not possess."[115]

Similar concerns guided the most famous early modern treatise on Muhammad: Humphrey Prideaux's *The True Nature of Imposture Fully Display'd in the Life of Mahomet*, published in 1697. Prideaux was an Anglican clergyman, serving as dean of the cathedral in Norwich, then England's third-largest town. Not himself an Oriental scholar, his treatise was "a pungent and polemical compilation of the oriental translations and researches of others."[116] Prideaux's book straddles two worldviews. It echoes medieval accusations that Muhammad is an antichrist while debunking several popular legends and rejecting the enduring accusation that Muhammad was demonically possessed. Instead, Prideaux charges Muhammad with deliberate fraud.

Prideaux's treatise on Muhammad was mere preface to the real point: the accompanying refutation, long since fallen into obscurity, of Socinianism. Precursors of the Unitarians, Socinians levied radical criticisms of Trinitarian doctrine, prompting obvious comparisons to Islam and Muhammad. In the twenty-first century, Unitarianism has a reputation as wishy-washy liberalism. Prideaux, though, perceived Socinians as a major threat to his preferred kind of Christianity. The upstart Christians who were Prideaux's target were among those who viewed Islam and Muhammad positively—at least to a point. Muhammad's reformist monotheism was sufficiently distant that it could be used to critique Christians closer in for their irrationality and convoluted doctrines. Prideaux, too, used Muhammad to make his point because he was not admired by those Prideaux was attempting to persuade.

Within a century of Prideaux's polemic, shifting geopolitical realities sometimes enabled a more generous and nuanced appreciation of Muslims and Islam. Although "in regards to western views of Islam, the eighteenth and nineteenth centuries must be considered a prominent cultural and historical frontier,"[117] there was no clear transition from hostility to admiration. For one thing, earlier centuries' views of Muhammad were not entirely negative. Close study of earlier texts typically reveals more nuance than broad generalizations about Western portraits of the Prophet usually admit; even Théophane le Confesseur's early ninth century *Chronographie* treats Muhammad and Islam with relative "sobriety and objectivity."[118] Early modern English texts contain more than "unchanging and relentless vitriol towards the Prophet."[119] Nor were generally positive eighteenth-century texts entirely praise filled.

Grand claims have been made for the originality of various texts' positive presentation of Islam and Muhammad. For instance, the Comte de Boulainvilliers 1731 *Life of Mahomet*, which praised Islam and its prophet "above all [as] a way of denigrating Christianity and favoring deism," has been called "the first frankly pro-Islamic text produced by European culture" and "the first genuinely sympathetic western biography of Muhammad."[120] Thomas Carlyle's "The Hero as Prophet," a century later, most commonly receives such accolades, with one scholar calling it "startlingly revisionist."[121]

Even if these declarations overstate the newness of the authors' approaches, failing to recognize traces of more inquisitive and less condemnatory work scattered through earlier European accounts of Muhammad, the seventeenth and eighteenth centuries did mark a change. Opposed approaches to the study of Muhammad and Islam came to coexist: recognizably positive, or at least deliberately non-hostile, alongside harsh condemnations. Scholarship on Arabic and Islam in western Europe played a key role in this process. To give just a few examples, André du Ryer published a French translation of the Qur'an, which was in turn rendered into a "less learned" but more widely read English version in 1649.[122] The next year, Pococke published *Specimen historiae Arabum*, a Latin edition of a medieval Muslim history, which included a brief sketch of Muhammad's life; it remained a vital resource for scholars into the nineteenth century.[123] This spate of publications continued into the first decades of the eighteenth century, with Boulainvilliers; Jean

Gagnier's 1723 translation of a medieval biography, followed by his multivolume *Life;* and George Sale's 1734 English translation of the Qur'an.[124]

Accompanying this growth of scholarly interest in Arabs and Islam was a shift in European perceptions of Muslims. In contrast to the beginnings of "the European relationship to the Orient . . . when . . . that relationship was one of anxiety and awe on the part of the Europeans,"[125] by the eighteenth century, "Fear of the Turks gave way to contempt, fascination, and a sort of cultural and historical tourism."[126] (French Marxist scholar Maxime Rodinson, whose 1961 biography of Muhammad was stricken from syllabi at the American University of Cairo, viewed the rise of "romantic exoticism" as the result of "a change within Western sensibilities" rather than as the outcome of changes in broader relationships between East and West.)[127]

Although serious scholarly work on Oriental languages and texts had begun centuries earlier, including that by monks intent on refutation of rival dogmas, it increased commensurately with European colonialism in Arab and Asian lands. Johann Fück divides European scholarship on Arabic and Islam into two periods. From its twelfth-century monastic origins through the late eighteenth century, with "rare exceptions" a "'Christian agenda'" governed such work, though for many scholars, a nominal profession of Christianity was sufficient to allow their work to have "fundamentally neutral content."[128] From then on, "modern scholarly studies of Arabic" came to dominate within a university system.[129] Most German researchers involved in the study of Arabic, Islam, and the Middle East worked in Oriental-language positions. Their research was "distinguished not only by an impressive number of outstanding scholars, but also by a heavy and persistent focus on issues of language (in its classical form) and the early Islamic period."[130] In British universities as well, the study of Oriental languages, including Sanskrit and Arabic, ramped up dramatically.

Fascination with the East was by no means limited to universities. British and continental writers were drawn to partly known, mostly imagined exotic realms. The Romantic era, which spanned the last quarter of the eighteenth century and the first half of the nineteenth century, radiated out from Britain to affect much of Europe and "saw a crucial transition between an Enlightenment world view and the values of a modern, industrial society."[131] Romanticism was "a literary movement, and a profound shift in sensibility."[132] Early modern thinkers tried to unmask the impostor; Romantic thinkers instead aimed to reveal the genius. Concern with inner and outer, which had been focused on revealing the true hidden beneath the false, shifted to individuals' interior lives, not outward forms. Genius was the animating core of the Romantic vision, and its "prerequisites," in one early articulation, "were originality, passion, and enthusiasm."[133]

Ideas about genius and inner nature affected biography, a genre enjoying new popularity in Britain. Muhammad's biographers aimed to convey something of his "personality," as biographers did more generally. Beyond this concern for capturing a certain individual essence, biographers focused on Great Men and their Important Deeds. Military heroes (and antiheroes) figured large in the European imagination, and biography increasingly conveyed this information to a reading public. Philip Almond sums it up succinctly in his survey *Heretic and Hero: Muhammad and the Victorians:* "The Victorian penchant for great men coupled with the Western fascination for an exotic east engendered a sympathetic environment for the rehabilitation of Muhammad and Islam."[134]

As the next chapter will show, "rehabilitation" is too simplistic. Medieval obsession with disgust gave way to a modern scrutiny of deeds; concern with legend became preoccupation with fact. At the same time, churning away in the background were old ideas about Muhammad's calculating formulation of a false religion— and the even older notion, expressed in the view of an American clergyman who also served as Harvard's president, that "Muhammad had received his revelations straight from the devil."[135]

Chapter 2

A True Prophet

Orphaned of father then mother, bereaved of the grandfather who had taken him in, young Muhammad passed into the care of his paternal uncle Abu Talib. Not long thereafter, when he was nine or a little older, he accompanied his uncle on a caravan journey to Syria, during which he was miraculously shaded from the harsh desert sun. The caravan stopped at a monastery in Bostra, but Muhammad remained hidden until a monk asked Abu Talib to produce him. The monk, Bahira, questioned Muhammad closely and saw the seal of prophecy between his shoulder blades. Before sending him on his way, he predicted Muhammad's future greatness and warned Abu Talib to protect him from those who would harm him.

Muslim tradition views this encounter with Bahira as but one in a series of supernatural and non-Muslim affirmations of Muhammad's special status and future promise.[1] Extraordinary occurrences punctuated his life. Radiant light spilled from his father's forehead before his conception. His mother dreamed of illumination. Angels came and washed a speck from his breast when he was a boy in his foster mother's care. Classical sources elaborate at length on these portents, which surrounded Muhammad's birth and childhood with the luminous aura of the divine. Like the monk's recognition of the "seal of prophecy," which foreshadowed eventual confirmation of Muhammad's revelation by Khadija's Christian cousin Waraqa, these events indicated divine favor and linked the nascent faith to the tradition of biblical prophecy.

The Bahira story has a distorted reflection in early Christian works, which often unspooled from this fateful encounter. In Syriac sources, a renegade monk usually called Sergius plots with Muhammad to deceive his compatriots. In European sources, the monk was often Nestur or occasionally Arius, attesting to the intertwining of ideas about Muhammad with Christian heresies.[2] Rather than serving as independent witness to Muhammad's legitimacy, as he does in Muslim accounts, the monk, sometimes alongside Waraqa or other Meccan Christians, is complicit in his scheme.

Early Muslims used biblical categories, proof texts, and miracle stories to affirm Muhammad's prophethood and the superiority of Islam, just as Christian opponents of the growing Muslim tradition used the same texts to affirm the opposite.[3] Early followers compared Muhammad to other prophetic figures in a bid to legitimate Muhammad in prevailing terms and, later, to prove his superiority. Once Muslim success was a fact, adherents of other traditions recast their foundational figures in Muhammad's image: Zoroastrians reimagined Zoroaster as a lone bearer of scripture.[4] The images of Muhammad held by Muslims altered and accreted, as did the images held by Christians—both Arabs who lived alongside Muslims and those in Europe who had never met one.

The question of the relation of Muhammad to other religious traditions, particularly Christianity, remained central even as medieval concern with heresy became early modern preoccupation with imposture. The Enlightenment critique of religion, the growth of academic Oriental studies, and the rise of colonialism led to increased connection between Muslim and non-Muslim accounts of Muhammad's life. A steady trickle of books on Muhammad had appeared in western Europe during the seventeenth and eighteenth centuries, but the number of publications increased dramatically in the nineteenth century. In England and America—increasingly a locus of missionary fervor—popularizers supplemented scholarly publications based on newly available early Arabic sources with books and tracts targeting missionaries and general audiences. Although perennial themes persisted—miracles, sex, violence—non-Muslims posed new critiques of Muslim accounts and, even more fundamentally, focused attention on historical accuracy. The quest for correct information about Muhammad had precedent in the work of early clerical opponents of Islam, who aimed to know Muslim doctrines the better to refute them. In this era, however, a set of questions about historical fact came to dominate Western approaches to Muhammad's life. Their preoccupations intersected with those of Muslim religious thinkers, traditional scholars, and Western-educated reformers. In a series of exchanges, mostly occurring in English, among British scholars and missionaries, Indian Muslim elites, and Hindu reformers, new visions of Muhammad were hammered out.

The Original Sources

The battle over Muhammad's image was fought on the contested ground of history as preserved, more or less reliably, in "original sources." Despite significant disagreement over what kind of man Muhammad was and how he fit into narratives of biblical prophecy and world history, a set of largely implicit agreements came to govern claims about his life. Early texts gained new prominence; new methodological presuppositions fundamentally reshaped the way Muhammad's biography was written.

Historical chronicles and biographical dictionaries, like more straightforward biographies, use complex organizing principles and coded language to assert authoritative versions of events, even as they include information that is unlikely, contradictory, or unflattering. Today, those who study these texts tend to analyze the literary practices behind them, seeking to understand how their subjects, including Muhammad, were understood by those who wrote about them, fully aware that in many sources "the lines between outright history and devotion are blurred."[5] In the nineteenth century, however, scholars influenced by scholarship on the historical Jesus (and the historical Buddha) were primarily interested in ferreting out what was "true" or "untrue."

European biographies written in the previous century had relied on a small number of primary sources, including Jean Gagnier's 1723 Latin/Arabic edition of the biography of the Prophet by the Syrian Abu'l-Fida (1273–1331). That Abu'l-Fida's text became so central owed to the vagaries of manuscript circulation rather than any preeminence for medieval Muslims. Print made it available to Arabists who had no comparable manuscripts to consult; Latin made it accessible to scholars who did not read Arabic.[6] The Episcopal cleric William Murray published an English version for subscribers (*The Life of Mohammed Translated from the Arabic of Abulfeda*), probably in the 1820s, accompanied by a scathing introduction and conclusion, together equaling the length of the translated source.[7] It found some use in the hands of Christian apologists but did not supplant Gagnier's Latin version.

Though Abu'l-Fida's text had not previously enjoyed great renown, it shared features with important medieval texts, such as the chronicle of Ibn al-Athir (d. 1233), on which it depended heavily, and through it, the standard early biographies.[8] Such chronicles, in which Muhammad's life was only one element, were eclipsed in popularity among Muslims by highly stylized meditations on Muhammad's perfection, including devotional texts composed for celebrations of his birthday, which spanned the popular and the scholarly. One scholar notes that "among Muslims, the popularity of Muḥammad's biographies is based not on the historical evidence that they include but on their didactic, edifying, propagandistic, and entertaining features that address the needs of readers and listeners on various educational, psychological, and artistic levels."[9] This is certainly true for the premodern period, when "softer-edged Prophetic biography" was "in near constant demand by literate Muslims at large."[10] The *Shifa'* of Qadi 'Iyad, an Andalusian contemporary of these historians, was "an immensely popular compilation—indeed, arguably the single most popular Prophetic biography of the entire tradition."[11] To take a later example, in eighteenth-century Egypt, a collection of blessings and prayers for the Prophet by a fifteenth-century Moroccan Sufi "was the most commonly owned book after the Quran."[12] European scholars were largely uninterested in these sorts of texts; they wanted to know the facts of Muhammad's life, as closely as they could.

When Gustav Weil published his biography *Muhammad the Prophet, His Life and His Book* (1843) in German using Arabic manuscript sources, it ushered in "an entirely new era in Islamic studies in Europe."[13] It was the first major advance in about a century. (Weil, who was among a number of important Jewish Islamicists working in Germany, would go on to publish a two-volume German edition of Ibn Ishaq/Ibn Hisham, a history of the early caliphate, and a German translation of the *Arabian Nights*, which ended up being excerpted for American student use because it was, the editor said, "good modern German of an easy kind.")[14]

In the next two decades, the number of sources at the disposal of Europeans increased rapidly. Scholars working in India, where in some regions a Muslim minority constituted a ruling elite, were largely responsible for these developments. Europeans were instrumental in editing and publishing manuscripts of early texts, sometimes with accompanying translations.[15] Additionally, their own biographical writings drew on early sources, a fact advertised in their titles. Aloys Sprenger, an Austrian medical doctor who joined the British East India Company and became principal of Delhi College, wrote *The Life of Mohammad from Original Sources*, which the Presbyterian Mission Press published in Allahabad in 1851.[16] A longer German version, with extensive source material, appeared later but garnered substantially less attention from Muslim readers. Indeed, scholarly work in German—which had recently replaced Latin publications for university careers in Germany—was mostly read by other Europeans.[17] Despite their pioneering role in research on Muhammad's life, scholars like Weil were neglected by Indian and Egyptian authors, who were far more likely to read works in French or English. Sprenger was widely read in India in part because his *Life* appeared in English.

Anglo-Muhammadan *Lives*

Tarif Khalidi argues that two British *Lives* of the nineteenth century "haunt" modern Muslim biographers.[18] The first is Thomas Carlyle's 1840 lecture "The Hero as Prophet." Carlyle began by explaining, "We have chosen Mahomet not as the most eminent Prophet; but as the one we are freest to speak of."[19] He addressed an audience likely to be amenable to his claim that they were free to discuss Muhammad because "there is no danger of our becoming, any of us, Mahometans."[20] His presumption that there was no danger of conversion was not entirely accurate—there were communities of Muslims in Britain, and a handful of Europeans did convert over the course of the nineteenth century—but unlike medieval Christians who had sought to reinforce boundaries, Carlyle considered a defensive stance unnecessary.[21] His view was not universally shared; less generous appraisals of Muhammad's life directed to Protestant missionaries in India or Sunday school children in America circulated widely. Carlyle, though, presumed a secure identity that would be neither offended nor threatened by any perceived slight to or glorification of Muhammad.

Carlyle delivered his lecture, in which he pronounced Muhammad "a true prophet"—if not the truest—in the heyday of British imperialism. The French invasion and occupation of Egypt in 1798 had marked a decisive shift in British and French colonial patterns. Western European provincial power struggles, such as the Napoleonic wars, played out on the world stage. French control spread in Africa and receded in India; the British expanded their control throughout India while maintaining African and Asian colonies. Eventually, the British came to dominate in Egypt as well, invading in 1882 and establishing a protectorate that, as the Ottoman Empire declined and eventually collapsed, took increasingly stringent measures to secure British commercial, diplomatic, and military interests. As later chapters will show, this interlude was decisive for the establishment of a colonialist party line on women and Islam, which is still broadly influential, and came to affect how people thought about Muhammad's marriages.

Biographical writing on Muhammad was also deeply shaped by the increasing popularity of the biographical genre in western Europe, particularly England, as well as by European scholarly interest in the historical Jesus. The former, related to the country's national-heroic story line, concerned military figures of various sorts. The latter, part of a new biblical studies agenda, sought to integrate archaeology and critical textual methods with historical scholarship. Interwoven with these developments was a romantic sensibility.

Carlyle, deeply influenced by the German writer Goethe, linked ideas of genius with notions of greatness. Muhammad's unspoiled natural genius allows him to do things that will affect the world. Carlyle emphasized the primitive, the lack of artifice and artificiality, in his thinking about Muhammad's relation to environment as well as to his inner self. Muslims were not his target audience, though he became "the favorite author of all Islamic modernists in India."[22] Muslim authors appropriated his praise for apologetic purposes, a trend that only increased after the 1911 translation of his lecture into Arabic. An early twentieth-century Muslim author writes that "Carlyle unveiled, as it were, the beauty of the Holy Prophet to the Western eye."[23] Conventional wisdom deems his lecture, which includes its share of negative remarks, "a vehement and unusual rehabilitation of Muhammad."[24] It was not entirely unprecedented in its generally positive view of Muhammad; in addition to French works like that of Boulainvilliers, *An Apology for the Life and Character of the Celebrated Prophet of Arabia, Called Mohammed, or the Illustrious* by Godfrey Higgins predated it by more than a decade.[25] Yet is has become a touchstone for Muslims seeking Western support for their claims about Muhammad's greatness.

Carlyle was less interested in Muhammad himself than in what the Prophet allowed Carlyle to say about humanity as a whole. As he wrote to American essayist Ralph Waldo Emerson, describing his lecture: "Beautiful people listened with boundless tolerance, eager attention" to his telling them that "man was still alive, Nature not dead or like to die; that all true men continued true to this hour." Muhammad—like Odin, "the Lama of Thibet," and others—was a "true" man. Truth was neither bound to Europe nor exclusive to Christianity. He was aware that in this latter claim, he was not merely stating an agreed-upon truth: "The Lecture on Mahomet . . . astonished my worthy friends beyond measure. It seems then that this Mahomet was not a quack? Not a bit of him! That he is a better Christian, with his "bastard Christianity," than the most of us shovel-hatted? I guess than almost any of you!"[26] Still, though Christianity might not have a monopoly on truth, it remained the byword for human morality: to say that Muhammad is "a better Christian" here means not that he accepted specific dogmas but that he embodied praiseworthy qualities.

If Carlyle synthesized the Romantic genius and the great man, William Muir represented the "Missionary-Orientalist complex."[27] It is widely recognized now that there was no one Orientalism.[28] Missionary, scholarly, and imperial aims were in tension and sometimes in conflict, both writ large and in individual lives. Muir's career intertwined evangelism, Orientalist scholarship, and service to the empire. He was a committed Christian, a serious Arabist, and a member of the Bengal Civil Service, serving nearly four decades in India (1837–1876) in former Mughal territory in the northwest, rising to the position of provincial lieutenant governor. He was good at his job, networking with other colonial officials— particularly those who shared his evangelical bent—and with "natives," including members of the Muslim scholarly class known as ulama. He skirted the formal policy requiring colonial officials' religious neutrality by supporting missionary activities in regions where he was posted with both his money and, more importantly, his pen. An early article on "The Mahommedan Controversy," published in the *Calcutta Review* (1845) less than a decade into his stay in India, argued that the time was ripe for evangelism, since "at every point of contact with Islam, Christianity has the temporal ascendancy." His rousing challenge was aimed at conversion of Hindus and Muslims alike: "Britain must not faint until her millions in the East abandon both the false Prophet and the Idol shrines, and rally around that eternal truth which has been brought to light in the Gospel."[29]

The evangelizing intent behind Muir's *Life* was no secret. Muir tells how the Reverend Karl Pfander, stymied in his efforts to convert Muslims, implored him to write a biography suitable for evangelism. Muir reviewed extant missionary *Lives* and found them sorely wanting: error riddled and off-putting in tone.[30] Their outmoded or offensive ways of presenting Muhammad hampered conversion efforts. Pfander originally desired, and Muir set out to write, a synthetic, sensitive, Christianizing life in the vernacular. The project took on a life of its own, though, expanding and shifting in intent and audience as well as language.

The collision of Muir's evangelical aims and scholarly approach resulted in the magisterial four-volume *The Life of Mahomet from Original Sources*. Published between 1858 and 1861, and in abridged form in 1878, Muir's *Life* has been a major resource and reference for scholars and lay readers. Though ultimately unsuited for use as an evangelical tract, it was widely read by missionaries and by Indian Muslims with sufficient English competence. In 1905, nearly a half century after its publication, Muir's obituary called it "the standard presentment, in English, of the Prophet of Islam."[31] At the same time, it has come to symbolize what is bad about Orientalist views of Muhammad.[32] Muir's biography was based on meticulous primary-source research as well as engagement with extant scholarship, but though he was faithful to his sources, he presented information gleaned from them in unflattering ways: "It is precisely because of its deadly accuracy," Khalidi writes, "that Muir's *Life* was found so distasteful by Muslim readership."[33]

Though Muslim writers have explicitly criticized Muir's approach and conclusions, the publication of his *Life* forever altered the enterprise of pious biography. It wove a handful of topics—authenticity of revelation, character, behavior with women—into a source-critical narrative history, fusing polemic and scholarship. What Muir ultimately accomplished was a grand restatement of Muhammad's life in his Arabian setting, grounding his study as firmly as possible in historical materials. Though far from aiming at any sort of apology, he rejected "the medieval polemic based on limited sources and an irrational bias against Islam and its prophet."[34] He sought to overcome both obstacles, though he was more successful at mining new sources than eliminating "irrational bias," at least in the views of his Muslim critics.

Muhammadan Controversies

The evangelical movement of which Muir formed part was far from the only religious contestation occurring in India. The nineteenth century was fertile ground for religious controversies and new identitarian movements both within and between religious communities. In keeping with broader currents of reform in the Arabian Peninsula and Arab world, Indian Muslims were engaged in debates over authority, tradition, and the proper approach to matters of worship. Broader revivalist currents, including move-ments originating in the Arabian Peninsula, reverberated among Muslims in India.[35] The formation of the scholarly community at Deoband, as well as the Barelvi movement, resulted in internecine struggles and a flowering of scholarly and popular output. The proper way to celebrate Muhammad's life was one crucial node in those discussions.

The Ahmadiyya have their origin in the same period in the work and life of Mirza Ghulam Ahmad (1836–1908). Ahmad, from Qadian in India, came to prominence in the 1870s as a scholar and controversialist, who "attained wide fame in the subcontinent as one of Islam's foremost champions against the inroads of colonial missionaries and similar groups critical of Islam or committed to the conversion of Muslims."[36] He debated other Muslims, Hindu reformers, and Christians. Eventually, his claims to be the prom-ised messiah alienated many of his supporters, but he continued to have active followers in colonial India. After his death, the move-ment split over whether he also fulfilled a prophetic role; both groups have proselytized actively, especially in the United States and Europe.

To discuss these as intra-Muslim shifts, as I have just done, already misrepresents the situation because it presumes that Mus-lim and Hindu were neatly distinguished at the outset and then fractured further. In fact, the development of these religious iden-tities was less the precondition for than the outcome of nineteenth-century developments.[37] Some medieval Bengali tales of Muham-mad's birth "placed the event within the all-embracing Indian religious scene by having Brahma, Vishnu, and others foretell the Prophet's coming."[38] In a Gujarati poem from the turn of the sev-enteenth century, a Brahmin gives the newly born Muhammad his sacred thread.[39] Ronit Ricci finds similar congruences in seventeenth-century Tamil texts.[40] To call this "boundary blurring" implies that there were boundaries to be blurred rather than a complex topology of the sacred. Beginning in the eighteenth century, exclusivity and purity as religious values came to be increasingly celebrated by at least some elite thinkers, resulting in less crossover.[41]

New mechanisms for print interchange were intertwined with, and facilitated, these developments. A swifter process of polemical exchange in periodicals, pamphlets, and other print media characterized the middle decades of the nineteenth century. Hindus had vigorous interchanges concerning widow remarriage and other topics.[42] Intra-Muslim debates took place through the press, too. Print media facilitated the regular exchange between Indian Muslims and Europeans, as in the published fallout from and followup to the 1854 debates between missionaries and Muslim scholars.

In these writings, all parties presumed shared norms about evidence, facts, and proof, and appealed—intermittently—to ideals of objectivity, tolerance, and universalism. Though the transition was not without its rough moments, there came to be a shared notion that accuracy and insult were relevant categories for assessing portraits of Muhammad. One consistent key in modern Muslim treatments of Muhammad is the perceived need to combat negative portrayals—or, as one author puts it, "the misleading teaching and willful misrepresentations which are so common."[43]

The theme of rebutting (Western) misconceptions has become ubiquitous in studies of Islam, even those aimed primarily at Muslims.[44] This stated aim is such a predictable feature of writing about Islam in the twenty-first century, by both Muslims and sympathetic non-Muslims, that it is difficult to imagine that it once was not so. Yet for centuries, people engaged in polemics felt free to point out the "errors" or "lies" of their opponents. Some Muslim writings still take this tone and refer to "refuting Orientalist calumnies"—often those by Muir. But the dominant approach, which has its origins in the nineteenth century, suggests that one's opponents are not so much in outright error as merely and sadly mistaken, and that if the facts can be clearly illustrated, they will abandon their "preconceptions" and recognize the legitimacy of Muslim assertions. As reformer Syed Ameer Ali puts it, the aim is "to disabuse the minds of many readers of false impressions and false prejudices."[45] Such claims may be partly rhetorical flourish, but they also indicate a (perceived) agreement on standards of proof to which one can appeal, and an ongoing dialogue—or the pretense of it—between Muslim and non-Muslim authors.[46]

Attempts by Muslims to correct Western "misunderstandings" also provided a means by which other objectives, including scoring points in internal Muslim debates and power struggles, could be pursued. Two of the authors whose engagement with Muir was most important were also deeply involved with projects for Muslim reform. The first, Syed Ahmad Khan (1817–1898), was a traditionally educated civil servant with whom Muir had a "close, complicated, fraught yet finally symbiotic relationship."[47] Ahmad Khan—who eventually became "Sir Sayyid"—was by birth a member of the Muslim scholarly class and by profession a member of the colonial service. Although he eventually became known as a modernist and an advocate of European-style education, founding the Mohammedan Anglo-Oriental College (now Aligarh Muslim University), Ahmad Khan had a fairly typical inculcation into the tradition, even penning a devotional text celebrating the Prophet's birthday. The second, Ameer Ali (1849–1928), was among the most prominent Indian Muslims who sought to talk back to their British colonizers—to rebut their claims about Islam in general and Muhammad in particular. Both men's English-language writings merged biography and polemic and, especially in Ameer Ali's case, became important resources for Muslims in India and elsewhere, including Egypt. British authors also read these works, though European authors did not engage with Muslim authors in nearly the proportions that the reverse happened. As Susan Buck-Morss has noted, "colonized people," including "Muslim intellectuals," have been "routinely required" "to argue for [their] beliefs on truly foreign, and in many ways unpalatable, discursive terrains" since Napoleon's invasion of Egypt in 1798.[48]

Tales of the Prophet

Three main things were at stake in nineteenth-century biographies. One was a matter of theology: Where (if anywhere) did Muhammad fit in a history of prophets sent by God to guide humanity? The second, without necessary confessional commitments, was where Muhammad fit in the history of human reformers or leaders. The third crucial issue, on which answers to the others depended, was epistemological: How do we know? What sources are available? Are they trustworthy? How should they be used, and by whom? As one might expect, European authors, most of whom were Christian, and Indian Muslim authors had varying views on the theological issues. Debates tended to hinge on the second and third points, with Muslim critics of scholars like Muir often arguing that their religious commitments biased them so strongly that they could not use the sources properly, leading them to an unjust verdict on Muhammad's merits. Muslim authors also disagreed with one another about these questions.

The major problem for Muir and other British thinkers was how to understand Muhammad's claims to have received revelation from God. Ideas about demon possession were no longer in vogue, and claims of deliberate and total fraud were less easily accepted than they had been when Prideaux was writing a hundred and fifty years earlier. Few were, like Carlyle, willing to accept Muhammad's complete sincerity and attribute his revelations to a welling up within him from deep in nature. George Lathom Browne's question in his 1856 *The Æra of Mahomet,* is more typical: "Was this madness or imposture?"[49] Others refused these dichotomous positions and saw Muhammad as confused or conflicted. John Davenport, who collaborated with Ahmad Khan and whose 1869 *An Apology for Mohammed and the Koran* has been cited by Muslim authors, declares it "more than probable that he really and conscientiously believed himself to be the divinely inspired Apostle of God."[50]

Muir, on the other hand, believed that whatever legitimate stirrings of a prophetic impulse Muhammad may have once had, he made a fateful choice to present his proclamations as God's speech. Thus, a salutary reform effort became twisted by his ambition for worldly success. Muir connects Muhammad's "temptation" and slippage into believing himself a prophet of God with the temptation of Jesus by Satan: Jesus "rejected the suggestion, and throughout his life on earth refrained from bringing the divine power which he possessed to the relief of his personal wants." Muhammad, by contrast, "arrogated a spiritual power which the records of his life too plainly prove that he misused to subserve his personal

necessities and even his erring desires."[51] Here, though, Muir hes-
itates: Muhammad was "not, indeed, possessed of any supernatural energy," but perhaps his "early doubts . . . and his suspicion of
being under the influence of genii or evil spirits, suggest the en-
quiry whether that suspicion rested on any real ground, or was the
mere creation of a nervous and excited fancy."[52] The comparison
with Jesus allows Muir to note that Muhammad claims to continue the legacy of the biblical prophets, among whom he numbers Jesus, but in fact clearly diverges.

Muhammad's mission is intimately connected with the Qur'an,
about which nineteenth-century writers were not particularly
complimentary. In this, they followed in the footsteps of their Enlightenment predecessors. As Swedish scholar Tor Andrae notes,
"Voltaire called it 'an incomprehensible book which violates our
common sense upon every page,' and since Voltaire most European readers have found that the Koran is the most boresome
reading that can be imagined."[53] This notion that non-Muslims are
likely to be left cold by the Qur'an has wide currency, perhaps
owing to historian Edward Gibbon's influential formulation: "The
harmony and copiousness of style will not reach, in a version, the
European infidel; he will peruse, with impatience, the endless incoherent rhapsody of fable, and precept, and declamation, which
seldom excites a sentiment or an idea, which sometimes crawls in
the dust and is sometimes lost in the clouds."[54] Gibbon's words
are self-fulfilling: others have called it "inexpressibly tedious" and
"a mostly impossible book."[55]

Even Carlyle, convinced of the Qur'an's merits, denigrated its
style, calling it "[a] wearisome confused jumble." This is fitting,
though, since it is not really a book but "a bewildered rhapsody"
whose "primary character" is "genuineness."[56] The unpolished

nature of the text corresponds to the unrefined messenger who brought it: "The rude message he delivered was a real one withal; an earnest confused voice from the enthusiastical unknown Deep."[57] In this view, Carlyle was influenced by Goethe, for whom "untamed, spontaneous authenticity was everything," and who declared, "The only true art is characteristic art. If its influence arises from deep, harmonious, independent feeling, from feeling peculiar to the self, oblivious, yes, ignorant of everything foreign, then it is whole and living, whether it be born from crude savagery or cultured sentiment."[58] Carlyle valued Muhammad's authentic barbarian originality.

Carlyle's view of the Qur'an as "a fiery mass of Life cast up from the great bosom of Nature herself" was not widely shared.[59] Most held more prosaic accounts of the Qur'an's origins. Muslim dogma, disdained only by some philosophers, held that the Qur'an was God's verbatim divine speech, delivered to Muhammad through the agency of the angel Gabriel.[60] Needless to say, non-Muslims rejected this characterization, though some accepted the Muslim belief that Muhammad was illiterate.[61] They were left with two options: either it came from inside Muhammad or outside. Medieval scholars who depicted Muhammad as a heresiarch favored a demonic origin. Muir entertains this option from time to time, but does not insist on it; some parts of the Qur'an may be explained by "the natural workings of the Prophet's mind,"[62] and others clearly derive in some part from biblical sources or monotheist communities.

Jewish scholars mostly assumed that Muhammad took a significant portion of the Qur'anic text as well as his religious ideas broadly from Jews, either those living on the Arabian Peninsula or those he encountered on his journeys. German Jewish Orientalist

Abraham Geiger even titled a study *What Did Muhammad Take from the Jews?* Susannah Heschel observes that like many of his colleagues, "Geiger was remarkably sympathetic to Islam: Muhammad was a genuine religious enthusiast, not a seducer or fraud or epileptic."[63] German Jewish scholars tended to view Islam positively—in part because, she argues, "imagin[ing] an Enlightened Islam" became a means "to insist on a 'purified,' rational Judaism."[64] For these scholars, Islam's Jewish origins were to be celebrated.

In strong contrast, Christian scholars typically thought Muhammad had help from errant Christians—like the Syrian monk and Khadija's cousin Waraqa—and believed his religion a perversion of Christianity, not a demonstration of its vitality and adaptability.[65]

Sometimes what was problematic about Muhammad's use of Christianity was not just his rejection of its main doctrine, the divinity of Christ, but also its confusion of Christianity with other sources: the admixture itself was impure and dangerous. Echoing medieval condemnations of Muslim monstrosity, which insisted on Islam's "unnatural hybridity," Browne refers to "the plausible creed which the fanatic concocted out of the idolatry of his native tribes, and the vagaries of the numerous Christian heretics with whom he met in his commercial journeys."[66] American Baptist John Walton thought Islam "was partly borrowed out of the Christian Bible, and partly hatched out of the enthusiastical Brain of Mahomet."[67] Tom Stecker, in his 1900 drama, puts his own view in the mouth of a merchant speaking to camel drivers. He describes "a curious mongrel creed / Concocted from the morsels he hath stolen / From Christian, Jew, and Gentile."[68] In *The False Prophet*, prepared for the Massachusetts Sabbath School Society, Harvey Newcomb listed perverted Christian dogma, Jewish scripture, and

Arabian superstition as Muhammad's sources.[69] Longtime missionary S. W. Koelle viewed Islam as "a compound of Jewish fanaticism and Roman despotism."[70]

Whatever its origins, few doubted that the Qur'an could be attributed to Muhammad himself. Stanley Lane-Poole, writing for a popular audience, was categorical: "The Korān is known beyond any doubt to be at this moment, in all practical respects, identical with the prophet's words as collected immediately after his death. . . . Its genuineness is above suspicion."[71] By "genuine," he means that it records Muhammad's own words, not that it is revelation. Lane-Poole saw the Qur'an as the product of "a simple enthusiast confronted with many and varied difficulties and trying to meet them as best he could by the inward light that guided him."[72] Browne, also writing for generalists, was in the dubious minority: "Of the Koran as given out by Mahomet, we have no means of judging. That Qur'an from which alone we have to decide, what is or is not the Islam faith, was the work of another generation, and no doubt grossly interpolated and corrupted."[73]

Muir's assessment falls in the middle. Though noting the careless way early Muslims collected and preserved written copies of its verses, he believes it was effectively safeguarded in the tenacious memory of early Muslims, whose culture cultivated memorization. He is confident of its essential reliability: "I have examined the Corân and admitted its authority as an authentic and contemporary record."[74] Though the Qur'an went through a complex and uneven process of compilation, it was reliable as a record not only of Muhammad's words but also of his life. Prophetic traditions were to be less easily trusted, but unlike Lane-Poole's judgment that Muslim methods were worthless ("a totally useless and preposterous criticism"),[75] Muir endorses them up to a point; tradition, properly scrutinized, can provide important facts about Muhammad's life and career. Still, he subordinates them to the Qur'an: "The sure light of the Corân will be the pole-star of the historian; and by it he will judge tradition."[76]

That these accounts for scholars and the general public explicitly discussed source reliability is striking. Even if Lane-Poole was ultimately casual in how he chose *hadith* ("those which strike the attention and do not seem peculiarly improbable"), he nonetheless described the process for his readers.[77] Books about Islam, Muslims, and Muhammad targeted to lay audiences ran the gamut from novelistic renderings—such as that by Washington Irving (1783–1859), which also included occasional footnotes—to toned-down scholarly offerings. The abridged version of Muir's opus (1878) ran to 613 pages, not counting the index; more than a tenth was devoted to "Sources for the Biography of Mahomet." This essay had come at the beginning of the original edition, indicating its primacy; its inclusion in the abridgment, even relegated to an appendix, shows that lay readers could be expected to take an interest. When the third edition appeared in 1894, Muir put it back at the beginning. In his preface, he reasons that it should come first, "as the value of a history depends entirely on the credibility of the evidence on which it is based."[78]

Historian of colonial South Asia Avril Powell suggests that the removal of some of the technical source apparatus from "later editions reflects the *Life*'s transition from a serious scholarly challenge to Muslim readers into a popular reference book for readers in Britain."[79] The book was indeed popular, but it is precisely its "challenge to Muslim readers" wherein Muir made his most enduring impact, occasioning rejoinders.

The Muslim reaction of "amazed horror" to biographies by Muir and Sprenger spurred responses.[80] Ahmad Khan's came in the form of *A Series of Essays on the Life of Muhammad and Subjects Subsidiary Thereto.* Composed in Urdu while Ahmad Khan was in England in 1869, it was published in 1870 in English; an expanded Urdu version appeared later.[81] A lengthy essay on Arabian geography and topology kicks off the compendium, followed by an essay on Muhammad's ancestry. Later essays discuss Muslim "tradition": mostly *hadith* books and methods, Muslim "theological literature," the Prophet's birth, and the impact of Islam on humanity. Ahmad Khan's *Series of Essays* is not "a fully-fledged counter-biography."[82] Instead, the topics align with those Muir addressed. Ahmad Khan asks the same sorts of questions that European scholars were asking: Was Islam on balance beneficial to humanity? How does Islam compare to other religions? (This assumes, already, that there are discrete entities called "religions" that can be compared on their merits, whether doctrinal or historical.) And, most importantly, how does Muhammad compare to other prophets?

No incident better encapsulates the disagreement between Muir and his critics than the so-called Satanic verses controversy. During a period in Mecca when he was under pressure from elites, Muhammad reportedly pronounced a passage from the Qur'an that attributed intercessory powers to three Meccan goddesses who were known as "daughters of Allah"—Allah being, in pre-Islamic Arabia, the name of a major deity. According to Muslims who believe this incident happened, Satan cast these verses into the Prophet's mind; God, however, could not allow such corruption to stand, and revealed new verses that reject the very idea of God having daughters or other subordinate deities.

Such are the main features of the story as found in early and classical sources. Muslim tradition wavered as to whether to accept it as true. The problem of the Satanic verses is bound up with the question of the integrity of the Qur'anic text, the reliability of the *hadith* literature, and the deep theological issue raised by the Prophet's seeming fallibility.[83] Some, such as the fourteenth-century Syrian Ibn Taymiyya, saw in the ultimate resolution of this incident the proof of God's guarantee of safeguarding the Qur'an from corruption.[84] Modern Muslims, too, disagree about what really happened. Their debates take into consideration Western interlocutors and the fact that their writings might provide fodder for criticism of Muhammad and Islam.

For Muir, the story's inclusion in early books serves as guarantor of its truth—up to a point. Rather than seeing any Satanic intervention, he attributes these verses instead to Muhammad's attempt to placate the Meccans. However, when Muhammad eventually realizes that their content will compromise his core mission and message, he repudiates the verses and replaces them with the current set.[85] Referring to "the narratives of Wackidi and Tabari," Muir writes: "Pious Mussulmans of after days, scandalized at the lapse of their Prophet into so flagrant a concession, would reject the whole story. But the authorities are too strong to be impugned. It is hardly possible to conceive how the tale, if not in some shape or other founded in truth, could ever have been invented."[86] Unlike Sprenger, who believes that the biographical texts sometimes include wholesale fabrications about miracles and other unlikely goings-on, Muir sees a "kernel" of historical truth in all such stories, no matter how fantastical.[87] Ahmad Khan, on the other hand, rejects it wholesale, despite its presence in early biographies. He reasons that accounts of the supposed event contradict each other.

64 THE LIVES OF MUHAMMAD

Their irreconcilability points to their untrustworthiness; they are not to be taken as authoritative.[88] In these debates, then, the question of source methodology is paramount.

At the opposite pole from the anxiety-provoking Satanic verses incident, the night journey and ascension are for Muslims a uniformly positive moment in Muhammad's life, perhaps the pinnacle of his prophetic experience.[89] Stories and images of the ascension were a central—perhaps *the* central—element of Muhammad's life story over the centuries. One night, not long before his migration to Medina, Muhammad lay down to sleep in his cousin Umm Hani's home; during the night he was transported to "the farthest mosque," traditionally situated in Jerusalem, and from there to the heavens, where he encountered past prophets, conversed with angels, and negotiated with God over the daily prayer obligations of Muslims—bargaining God down from fifty to five. Unlike the Satanic verses incident, which according to him has no *reliable* support in traditional texts, Ahmad Khan sees Qur'anic grounding for the ascension.[90] Was the ascension "a mere vision" or a "bodily" journey? Muslims have long debated this question.[91] Sprenger overstates the case when he declares, "All historical records are for the latter opinion; the former is upheld by some skeptics only."[92] Sprenger paints Muslims as credulous and the tradition as unreliable. But it is true that those who claim the journey was a vision were a minority.

Whether agreeing that it "really" happened or not, to focus on this point obscures earlier ways of treating the ascension. Muslims were attentive to the beauty and sublimity of the story itself and the spiritual truths it conveyed. Authors fleshed out the narrative in myriad ways. It figured prominently in preaching and proselytizing as well as sectarian conflict among Muslims.[93] It told about the relation of Muhammad to other prophets, particularly Abraham and Moses. Its affirmation of Muslim ritual worked also to establish the superiority of Muhammad to other prophets, in part through narrating, though circumspectly, his vision of God. Mystics adopted the model of the ascension to describe spiritual progress. In a twist, the story of the ladder by which Muhammad ascended to heaven was known to medieval Europeans, including the author of the Divine Comedy.[94] "How ironic," renowned Islamic studies scholar Annemarie Schimmel observes, "that the hero of the true [ascension], the Prophet Muhammad, should have been placed by Dante among the schismatics in the lowest part of Hell!"[95]

The same dynamics at play in the story of the ascension also apply to the lesser-known story in which the boy Muhammad was playing near his foster mother's home when two angels approached him, held him down, opened his chest, and removed a miniscule black speck. This purified him and made him fit to receive the Qur'anic message. Non-Muslim scholars have sometimes seen this legend as an example of how Muslim tradition has sought to fill narrative gaps in the Qur'an, which alludes to having "opened [his] breast," by inventing stories to explain its obscure passages. Muslim tradition treats the Qur'anic statement as a reference to a real event, though Muslims again disagree over whether to understand it literally.[96] Muir, too, views the Qur'an and other early accounts as generally reflecting actual events of the Prophet's life: though his miracles are "puerile fabrications . . . we can generally trace in tradition some real incident on which they were engrafted, which prompted the idea, and gave to fancy a starting-point for its fairy creations and illusive colouring."[97]

The opening of the breast, which Ahmad Khan discusses in conjunction with the ascension, provides a useful counterpoint to the story of the seal of prophecy: in one account, something extraneous is removed from Muhammad's body; while in the other, something extra on his body is recognized not as superfluous or dangerous but as meaningful. The seal of prophecy—a bodily mark, mole, patch of hair, or "fleshy excrescence" the size of a pigeon egg—was between his shoulder blades. Ahmad Khan, like other modern Muslim scholars, downplays the role of this mark, but like the encounter with Bahira, it confirms objectively Muhammad's status as prophesied messenger.

As he interprets various facts about Muhammad's life, Ahmad Khan repeatedly attacks Muir's methods—from which sources he uses to how he interprets the materials he finds there. According to Ahmad Khan, Muir uses unreliable sources when it suits his purposes and repeats stories of miraculous occurrences or qualities credulously, when the right kind of Muslim would not accept them; he fails to grasp the more relaxed standards for biographical reports than for prophetic traditions with legal implications.[98] Just because accounts are *included* in the biographies does not mean that a good scholar will depend on them; the compilers' job was to collect, not to sort or discard them.[99] Sprenger, like Muir, depends on untrustworthy sources: "two Moslem authors (Wâkidi and his Kâtib [i.e., Ibn Sa'd]), regarded in the Mohammedan world as the least trustworthy and most careless biographers of Mohammed."[100] By contrast, he himself relies "on the writings of Ibn-Hishâm and Ibn-al-Athîr. The former, in spite of the animadversions of Muir, will always continue to occupy the position of the most careful and trustworthy biographer of the Prophet. The latter," Abu'l-Fida's main source, as noted earlier, "for his critical acumen, the simple and chaste elegance of his style, and the extensive erudition displayed throughout his splendid history, might justly claim a place in the rank of the greatest historians of Europe."[101] How quickly Ahmad Khan moves from condemning Muir's misapprehension of the Muslim biographical tradition to holding up European scholars as the standard to which Muslim authors must be compared!

In Ahmad Khan's view, by accepting the wrong sorts of Muslim sources—out of ignorance, incompetence, or malice—Muir, Sprenger, and others come to erroneous and unwarranted conclusions about Islam.[102] Take a banal example, which Ahmad Khan approaches with absolute seriousness: Did the Prophet dye his hair? Muir sees contradictions within the tradition literature on this point. Ahmad Khan instead reconciles the various accounts, some of which suggest henna use and others that reject it. Muir's inability to reconcile the texts shows that he is unqualified to use them.[103]

Ahmad Khan may not consciously have been aware of the underlying problem. He was from a scholarly family, trained in traditional ways of reading texts. Although he makes unorthodox arguments in the course of his *Series of Essays* and other writings, his criticisms assume that Muir is hampered by not having a teacher to walk him through the texts, to point out what is to be trusted and what is not, to explain that mere inclusion does not guarantee reliability. As Timothy Mitchell puts it, discussing medieval historian Ibn Khaldun, "The entire practice of Arab scholarship revolved around the problem over overcoming the absence in writing of the author's unequivocal meaning."[104] The same is the case—indeed, is perhaps even more the case—for texts that are compilations, such as traditional biographies and *hadith* collections. Reading them involves more than an ability to decode the words.

Ahmad Khan does not articulate this point explicitly, instead appealing to methodological principles that he presumes Muir shares, including objectivity. Neatly reversing Muir's practice of taking unflattering or critical things from the Muslim tradition as unwilling witnesses, for Ahmad Khan, if antagonistic Christian scholars say something flattering about Muhammad, they are to be taken at face value.[105] Since they would not acknowledge it were it not indisputable, it can thus be taken as a given.[106] In incorporating European sources into his book, Ahmad Khan simultaneously bolsters his own authority by arrogating theirs and undermines (other) Indian and Muslim authors by favoring Western statements as authoritative. Use of non-Muslim sources by Muslim authors is, of course, an old tactic. Early Muslim authors used not only biblical models but also biblical passages as "sources of attestation."[107] Ahmad Khan follows in their footsteps, citing Western praise and also arguing for Muhammad's prophethood based on biblical scripture.[108]

His attempt to generate evidence for Muhammad's prophetic role on the basis of biblical texts was largely disregarded by Christian controversialists, who preferred to argue on other grounds, especially the Muslim biographical tradition. Where Ahmad Khan might claim that a particular fact about Muhammad's life, attested in the Qur'an or authentic traditions, illustrated his fulfillment of biblical prophecy, Muir read the same sources differently: either the event was not credible or it did not mean what Muslims wanted it to mean.[109] In particular, Muir dismissed arguments that presumed any supernatural influence on Muhammad (though he did not entirely rule out the possibility of demonic interference). Ahmad Khan insisted that Muir unfairly rejected stories about Muhammad similar to those that he accepted in the life stories of

Jesus and Moses. (This was the obverse of the argument found in *The Three Impostors:* "Whenever there is the same reason as in the case of Mahomet for charging any person with imposture . . . they should be placed in the same category. And, for example, in the case of Moses, there is the same reason.")[110]

Muir errs, in this view, by not approaching Moses and Jesus with the same skepticism that he brings to stories of Muhammad. Rather than undertaking "an unprejudiced and candid investigation [using] fair, just, and legitimate reasoning," Muir approaches the tradition literature prepared to find it affected by (in Muir's terms) "superstitious reverence" and "fond devotion," which distorted stories and inaccurately invested Muhammad "with supernatural attributes."[111] Ahmad Khan asks, with a great deal of vim, "May not all the miraculous deeds of Moses"—he lists quite a few—"be considered as only so many amusing tales, invented and fabricated by that prophet's ardent and zealous followers"? Or, for that matter, "What would become of Jesus and his devout and zealous followers were everyone to discard, as merely so many fabrications and idle inventions, the traditions which represent Christ as rising from the dead" and so forth?[112] Muhammad must be treated with the same impartiality. *The Three Impostors* argues for the men's equal fraudulence; Ahmad Khan argues for their equal validity.

Ameer Ali takes Ahmad Khan's work in a slightly different direction. Comfortable in English—he studied law in England, spent time there off and on for more than three decades, and then lived in England after his retirement from his position as a judge in India—Ali wrote several books, among them a popular *History of the Saracens* and works on Islamic law, including one about women. His two studies of Muhammad's life garnered him worldwide notice among Muslims. *A Critical Examination of the Life and*

Teachings of Mohammed first appeared in 1873.[113] A revised and edited version appeared in 1891 as *The Life and Teachings of Mohammed, or the Spirit of Islam;* it is by *The Spirit of Islam* that the book is commonly known.[114] Orientalist David Margoliouth thought it "probably the best achievement in the way of an apology for Mohammed that is ever likely to be composed in a European language."[115]

Ameer Ali situates Islam on the world stage and in an interreligious framework that is more cosmopolitan than that of Ahmad Khan. Where the latter argues that one must treat Muhammad in the same fashion that one treats Jesus or Moses—that is to say, within an Abrahamic, biblical paradigm—Ameer Ali's broader canvas includes Buddhists and Hindus in the religious history of the world. He focuses on human progress and universal norms. Some of Muhammad's seemingly questionable actions are perfectly understandable in context. Given the circumstances of time and place, he had to make certain compromises in order to accomplish what he did. His accomplishments are proof not only of his prophetic mission but of his superiority to other prophets in that he brought to fruition his vision. Muhammad was the last prophet, and there is no need for further prophecy, but there *is* a need for additional reform. Humanity's trajectory is toward enhanced freedom and vitality. Ameer Ali was among the first generations of people to be seduced by the idea of history as progress, laid out in the closing years of the eighteenth century by the Marquis de Condorcet. This view of history as forward movement merged with ideas about Muhammad as the "seal of the prophets," the last divinely sent messenger.

Muhammad's Muslim biographers would have experienced a tension between this model of Muhammad as a figure from the past and that of Muhammad as someone to whom Muslims should relate in an eternal present. What was the relationship between the Muhammad of history, increasingly at the center of interreligious debates, and the Muhammad of devotion? Ahmad Khan's own life illustrates a shift in emphasis if not a change of heart: in his early twenties, he wrote a devotional text for the Prophet's birthday celebration with the evocative (and, in the original language, rhyming) title "The Polishing of Hearts through Remembrance of the Beloved One."[116] Although this text may have had a reformist bent, the commemoration of Muhammad as God's beloved is a strategy for individual spiritual progress; Ahmad Khan's later work reflects a concern with Muhammad as someone whose "benefit to humanity" can be determined once one sorts out questions of evidence and bias.[117] Thinking of Islam as a religion benefiting humanity in the sense of measurable human progress, stacking civilizations up next to one another and comparing the reforms they wrought is a very different sort of strategy for human betterment than is meditation on prophetic virtues as a tool for spiritual self-improvement.

Through the decades chronicled here, devotional texts, the sort that Muir dismissed as "the veriest inanities which, by any possibility, could be imagined," continued to be written and to circulate.[118] At the same time, the language of humanity and progress was widely adopted. Writing in India, probably in the 1930s, Mohammad Ali Salmin writes that "the Great Holy Prophet . . . worked for the benefit of humanity. . . . He identified himself entirely with his work for Humanity."[119] Such concepts did not entirely displace effusive content; rather, "devotional" and "modernist" approaches came to coexist.[120] Salmin's biography, mostly apologetic and engaged in contesting negative portrayals of Muhammad, opens with a set of Arabic and English blessings on the Prophet, which evoke a believer's longing for closeness to him: "On account of the exceeding desire of seeing you, we have almost reached the point of death. . . . My poor heart . . . is now a martyr of love for the Prophet."[121]

"Competitive Hagiography"

Hybrid biography flourished with the ongoing proximity of Christians and Muslims in India and elsewhere.[122] The nineteenth and twentieth centuries may have their only parallel in the first two centuries of Islam, in terms of the speed and scope of transformation. The exchanges were not a one-sided imposition but a mutual if lopsided process.[123] And, indeed, it was not merely a two-player game: Hindu polemicists participated as well, as in the famous debates held, as public spectacles, in Shahjahanpur in northern India in 1875 and 1876. Sponsored by the British authorities, three men took the stage to argue for the truth of their religions—a Protestant scholar and school administrator; a Hindu reformer whose Arya Samaj movement played a crucial role in the transformation of Indian religion in the nineteenth century; and Qasim Nanautvi, a founder of the famous college at Deoband and "a towering figure in the intellectual history of Islam in South Asia."[124] (On other occasions, Arya Samaj representatives debated with Ahmadi controversialists; as noted previously, India's religious landscape was complicated with numerous lines of fracture within as well as between "religions.")[125]

Although the point of the Shahjahanpur convocation was to decide "the true God"—which, as SherAli Tareen points out, assumes that the way one defines religion has to do with a set of dogmas and doctrines that can be logically argued, and moreover to which a public audience is crucial—participants debated the merits of their respective revered figures. When Muhammad's miracles came up for discussion, Nanautvi affirmed not only that Muhammad performed miracles well beyond bringing the Qur'an but that his miracles were superior to those performed by Jesus.

Nanautvi's emphatic praise for Muhammad's miracles was part of a long tradition. Comparisons between Jesus and Muhammad were not new, nor was the central place of miracles in those comparisons.[126] Byzantine Greek polemics against Muhammad had insisted that "Mahomet performed no miracles; his supposed miracles are the fruit of the imagination of his crude and barbaric adepts; the Qur'an, far from being one [that is, a miracle], is an incoherent and contradictory assemblage of doctrines borrowed from here and there; as to Mahomet's moral conduct, it is a tissue of debauchery, of carnal pleasures, of lies and of blood"; such accusations constitute "the ideological infrastructure under which concrete biographical elements are grafted."[127] Medieval European comparisons were likewise unflattering to Muhammad and agreed that he did not perform legitimate miracles.[128] One early Eastern polemic insisted that "of the three founders of religion, Moses, Jesus, and Muhammad, only this last did not perform miracles which have confirmed his status as God's envoy."[129] Both the growth of miracles in the Muslim biographical tradition and the denial of those miracles by Christians were spurred by the desire to enhance or detract from Muhammad's stature vis-à-vis other biblical figures and Christ himself.[130] (For Muslims, Christ fit into the category of biblical prophet, not more special than others; for Christians, obviously, the case was different.)[131]

Ahmad Khan had objected to the unequal treatment of Muhammad and these other foundational figures in his *Series of Essays*. Yet he emphasized the natural nature of prophecy and Muhammad's humanity, seeing miracles as "unnecessary" and irrelevant to Muhammad's mission as God's messenger.[132] In this, he followed other Indian thinkers, such as the eighteenth-century figure Shah Wali Allah, who had begun to shy away from the miraculous elements of Muhammad's life. Muslim critique of the "extravaganzas" and "fables" found in traditional accounts of the Prophet's life gained steam in the late nineteenth and twentieth centuries.[133] Numerous Egyptian modernists would reject miracle stories as colorful additions to the biographical tradition. They had precedents among earlier Muslims, a minority of whom have always held that Muhammad's only miracle was the Qur'an, although various special signs and portents attached themselves to him.

By the mid-nineteenth century, many European authors looked on claims of miraculous deeds dismissively—not just by Muhammad but by anyone. They used Muhammad's reported insistence that he did not work miracles to critique their own traditions. Although Muhammad's (supposed) lack of miracles figured prominently in evangelical anti-Muslim tracts, other European thinkers treated Islam as a more rational religion precisely because it (supposedly) minimized miracles. Higgins did not deny that many Muslims attributed miracles to Muhammad, but he absolved the Prophet himself for any such claim: "some of his followers, long after his death, believing that he performed miracles, declared that he professed to have that power: a thing he certainly never pretended to."[134] In fact, he "totally denied from the beginning any supernatural endowment of this kind . . . , and in the Koran the working of miracles is repeatedly disclaimed."[135]

The (minority) denial of miracles by Muslims was used by polemicists, who always exploit divergence within a tradition to their advantage, as evidence that Muhammad was not a legitimate prophet. Though popular Muslim belief clung to the notion of prophetic miracles, learned Muslims rejected them, and Muhammad himself had equivocated or temporized or denied them altogether.[136] Another strand of argument was that Muhammad's miracles were only trickery. Christian evangelists in nineteenth-century India continued to cite Muhammad's lack of miracles as proof that he was not a prophet.[137] (When the miraculous status of the Qur'an was raised, non-Muslims, not particularly complimentary about it, scoffed.)

Koelle compares Muhammad and Jesus in his 1889 *Mohammed and Mohammedanism Critically Considered*.[138] He declares that only from the viewpoint of the superior religion—that is, Christianity—can one truly judge Islam, since "only by the light of the higher religion can the lower be rightly estimated."[139] The missionary's task of conversion is made more difficult by "the transcendent halo of the mythical Mohammed."[140] Muslims must be brought to realize "that all the boasted equality or superiority of Mohammed to Christ rests on mere fiction, devoid of all foundation in fact."[141] Like recent historians who attend to the early Muslim biographical literature, Koelle focuses on the ways in which Muhammad is modeled after Jesus and, more broadly, on using Muslim sources "to illustrate how the glowing imagination and devout admiration of the Moslem believers have metamorphosed him, and enveloped the genuine natural original in the fictitious halo of a dazzling radiance and a supernatural glory."[142] Koelle laments not merely the invention of miracle tales by credulous followers (encouraged, in his lifetime, by Muhammad himself) but their fantastical excesses in comparison to biblical miracles.[143] The bible's "wonders resemble beautiful flowers of Paradise, springing up from a purely ethical ground," while "Mohammedan marvels look like unreal phantoms of the air, produced for the purpose of ostentatious display, and result from an unethical trifling with the supernatural."[144] Thus, these exaggerated accounts of Muhammad's miracles prevent Muslims from recognizing the true glory of Jesus.[145]

Muhammad's miracles also had staunch defenders, and the arrival of the East India Company and missionaries at the turn of the nineteenth century prompted some to highlight them.[146] Nanautvi, the Deobandi representative at the Shahjahanpur festival, waxed eloquent about Muhammad's miracles. Not only did he perform miracles like Moses and Jesus, as Ahmad Khan had suggested, but his miracles were superior to theirs. What Koelle had seen as exaggeration in this case indicated the superiority not only of Muhammad but of Islam.

Evolution of Religion

The Shahjahanpur festival, juxtaposing Christian, Hindu, and Muslim arguments for the superiority of each faith, took place in a context in which new ideas about hierarchies of religious life framed debates. The Bombay Tract and Book Society's *Life of Mahomet*, a work Muir panned for its scholarly inadequacies, placed Islam on a spectrum of non-Christian religions arrayed by relative sophistication.[147] Instead of understanding Islam as being worse than paganism because its manner of being false allows it to be mistaken for truth, here Islam is perceived as better because it is closer to Christianity (and Judaism, having drawn from both of them), while both Hinduism and Greek mythology are further from the truth. American Baptist missionary Frances Mason held a similar attitude: Islam was superior to idolatrous Hinduism.[148]

This view of Islam as better than pagan religions because it is a step on the path toward Christianity stands opposed to earlier centuries' view of Muhammad as an antichrist. The Antichrist is dangerous precisely because his seeming closeness to the true faith allows him to lead believers astray. An evolutionist logic, elaborated further over the course of the nineteenth century, helped portray Islam as an improvement, but a partial and incomplete one, over non-monotheistic faiths.[149] As Irvin Schick points out, "Europe's exploration of the world during the colonial age was always productive of power asymmetries" that functioned "within an evolutionist hierarchy."[150] Even if the Bombay Society missionaries would have rejected Darwin's hypothesis, they were shaped by many of its constituent ideas.[151]

In contrast to Christian views that positioned Islam as having begun to ascend the ladder of monotheism toward Christianity, some Muslim authors predictably situated Islam at monotheism's apex. Ameer Ali, for instance, concludes that Islam represents monotheism's fullest flowering. "Neither Christianity nor Judaism had succeeded in raising" the debased "moral and religious condition of the Arabs."[152] (He quotes Muir at some length to support this claim.) Both idolatry and human sacrifices were practiced by pre-Islamic Arabs.[153] Muhammad used the folklore and legends "floating among his people" and "adopted them as the lever for raising the Arabs as well as the surrounding nations from the depth of social and moral degradation into which they had fallen."[154] Yet Ameer Ali does not proclaim that Islam supersedes Judaism and Christianity doctrinally. Such a tactic would ill suit his audience and betray the universal creed he rhetorically espouses. Instead, as Chapter 3 will explore further, Ameer Ali is among those using Muhammad's success in social transformation to elevate Islam over other religions.

Chapter 3

Eminent Muslims

Five years after the emigration, Muslims in Medina faced ongoing hostilities with Meccan opponents. When the Meccans threatened to attack, the Medinan community was struggling with hypocrites—untrustworthy nominal Muslims—and fickle Jewish allies, whose support could not be ensured. The Muslims were grossly outnumbered and outmatched in horses and weapons. How could they hold off the Meccans? A Persian convert suggested a strategy new to the region: dig a trench to supplement Medina's natural fortifications. It was backbreaking work, in which the Prophet assisted, but it paid off when the ditch stymied the attacking cavalry. The Meccans tried to persuade an allied Jewish tribe, the Banu Qurayza, to attack on another front, but Muhammad thwarted that plan. The Meccans eventually lifted their siege, and the Banu Qurayza were punished for their treachery: an arbiter they chose ordered the women and children enslaved and the men executed.

In Medina, Muhammad was not only a prophet but also—and in some contexts, primarily—a community leader and military commander. These latter elements of his role were long taken for granted by Muslims. His military expeditions were among the earliest stories recorded; Waqidi's *Book of Campaigns* was devoted to them. In thirteenth-century Egyptian Sufi Muhammad al-Busiri's famous *Burda* ("Cloak Ode"), an edition of which was printed in Leiden in 1761, the Prophet's "military achievements are elaborated in gruesome detail." He leads "an ocean of an army on floating steeds / That threw up clashing waves of heroes / Each of them entrusted to God and expecting heavenly reward / Assailing, and completely devoted to the extirpation of idolatry."[1] Although al-Busiri spends far more time enumerating Muhammad's matchless excellence ("ascribe to his person whatever you want in terms of nobility / And ascribe to his power every greatness you want") than his battle prowess, it was Muhammad leading warriors that permeated anti-Muslim writing; the claim that Islam was spread by the sword recurred in Christian polemics throughout the centuries.[2]

In the nineteenth and twentieth centuries, however, a few essential things changed.

First, *Lives* of military heroes and other "great men" came to form a regular part of British biography. Second, and in tension with the first development, the use of violence came to be seen by large sections of the educated public and scholars as illegitimate unless justified by a compelling interest, such as self-defense (a notoriously elastic concept). The first meant that Muhammad's military exploits and, far more importantly, his and his followers' success in conquering and ruling large swathes of territory made him a figure of interest. The second meant that Muslim accounts of his military endeavors sought to justify his use of force in terms that would resonate with European Christian and other critics who charged that he was too wrapped up in worldly ambition and plans for military domination. In tension with this attempt to downplay Muhammad's military victories and to play up his defensive use of force, Muslims subject to foreign occupation treated Muhammad as a successful general partly as a way to envision alternative realities for subject peoples.

It was not just Muhammad. Early Islamic figures, including his successors, were relevant to problems of leadership that bedeviled modern Muslim societies chafing under colonial rule. Heroic figures—for Sunnis, Abu Bakr, Umar, Uthman, and Ali, the four so-called "rightly guided" successors to Muhammad who ruled from 632 to 661—were models for action. These men's success in the politico-military sphere made them tempting subjects, and their religious credentials mattered as well. Just as Europeans of earlier centuries had struggled to comprehend how Muslims, so clearly in the wrong religiously, could have managed to wrest away the Holy Land and, from the city formerly known as Constantinople, threaten the heart of Europe, Muslims in northern Africa and South Asia were confronted with the loss of sovereignty to powers they had, not long before, seen as barbaric and inferior. Some Muslim thinkers responded, just as medieval Christians had, by criticizing their own societies for moral and other failures that had led to foreign domination. In a new twist on old patterns of reformist thought, some Sunni thinkers turned to ideas of a pristine early tradition, before it was corrupted by improper innovations and the accretions of a scholarly tradition that, they thought, was collapsing under its own weight. Salafism, which prioritized the purported conduct of the first Muslim community, was a broad trend that developed into both Islamic modernism and puritanical Wahhabism. Both reform movements owe a profound debt to Protestantism, including its assumptions about authority and texts. These movements and tendencies predated and coexisted with colonialism, and developed alongside Orientalist scholarship and in engagement with it. Its assumptions affected those modern accounts of Muhammad and his Companions. Alternately sectarian and ecumenical tendencies among Muslims led to the glorification of early figures in ways that consolidated and affirmed preferred versions of early Muslim history, including the roles of Muhammad's wives and kin, which resonated with the new emphasis on Muhammad the man as well as Muhammad the prophet.

Success and Succession

Perhaps paradoxically, given that Christian Europeans were now in power over vast tracts of Muslim-inhabited land, Islam's worldly success was a major preoccupation for Muhammad's biographers from the mid-nineteenth century to the mid-twentieth century. William Muir repeatedly warns his readers not to adopt the commonsensical view that Muhammad's success validates his religion. Although Muhammad's teachings had obvious and immediate impact on the world, whereas Jesus's career did not lead swiftly to perceptible external change, one should not take this for an indication of the relative importance of the two figures. Jesus "ministered . . . among the Jews, whose law he came not to destroy but to fulfill, and in whose *outer* life, therefore, there was no marked change to be affected." In other words, the lack of *visible* social change actually attests to Jesus's success. By contrast, Muhammad's success in winning adherents and dramatically reshaping the practices of "a nation of idolaters sunk in darkness and vice" is to be taken for granted, since "converts to exhibit any consistency whatever must go forth with a bold and distinctive separation."[3] Muir dismisses or highlights Muhammad's real-world legacies where it suits him, downplaying the end of idolatry but lambasting the interconnected evils of polygamy and slavery, which he attributes to Muhammad.

Aloys Sprenger approaches the spread of Islam differently, granting the premise that the faith's success has some bearing on the merit of those responsible for it. If Muhammad himself had led a revolution, he would have had an "irrefutable" case for his religion: "we should be obliged to acknowledge his doctrine as absolute truth because it was victorious." But the "false religion" had other historical causes for its success,[4] most notably in the role of a group of advisors, foremost among whom was Abu Bakr. As he describes it, "after his death they founded an empire which surpassed that of the Romans." Rather than being "hot headed fanatics," these men used "wisdom and perseverance" and "were guided by the most consunmate [sic] prudence and by cool reflection; and their objects were in most cases noble, and the means which they employed were rarely objectionable."[5] Broadly, where Muir is suspicious of worldly success—an odd position for one in the employ of the British Empire—Sprenger connects it to virtue.

Unlike Sprenger, Ameer Ali attributes Muslim successes to Muhammad himself rather than to his successors. Like Muir, success for Ameer Ali is manifested in Muhammad more than in Jesus, but this is a good thing rather than a sign of corruption. In an extended passage, Ameer Ali quotes Muir regarding the "spiritual torpor" of Arabia at the time of Muhammad. Previous monotheistic revelations had worked but "slight and transient influences . . . upon the Arab mind" and "people were sunk in superstition, cruelty, and vice." (The words are Muir's.) Muir notes the "arousing of spiritual life" reawakened for the first time "since the days when primitive Christianity startled the world from its sleep and waged a mortal conflict with Heathenism." Muhammad, according to Ameer Ali, completed his "Mission," and in this fact—the fact of the whole work being achieved in his life-time—lies his distinctive superiority over the prophets, sages, and philosophers of other times and countries;—Jesus, Moses, Zoroaster, Sakya-Muni [i.e., Buddha], Plato, all had their notions of Realms of God, their Republics, their Ideas— through which degraded humanity was to be elevated into a new moral life. All had departed from this world with their as- pirations unfulfilled, their bright visions unrealized; or had be- queathed the task of elevating their fellow-men to sanguinary disciples or monarch-pupils. It was reserved for Mohammed to fulfil his mission and that of his predecessors. It was reserved for him alone to see accomplished the work of amelioration.[6]

In praising Muhammad's elevation of "degraded humanity . . . into a new moral life," he ignores Muir's arguments in favor of Jesus's goodness and Muhammad's rank ambition and instead uses Muir's dismal portrait of pre-Islamic Arabia to highlight the immensity of Muhammad's task and, therefore, the glory of his accomplishments. He goes further, however. Muhammad is more impressive than Jesus not only because he manages to fulfill his mission during his own lifetime but also because he finishes the job that earlier messengers, including Jesus, had left incomplete.[7] In emphasizing Muhammad's accomplishments, Ameer Ali also tries to refute criticism of his methods in accomplishing them, explaining Muhammad's use of force through the measures of man in wide circulation at the time: He acted in self-defense. Had he not, he could have held lofty principles but not made a dramatic change in the world, bringing his vision to fruition. Muhammad was justified in using force not because he had God on his side (though he did), but because his movement required lifting a people out of ignorance. To do this in the face of Meccan opposition necessitated defensive military action. He undertook social reform and betterment, using force in legitimate ways, and was ultimately successful. He was, in other words, a great man of history by the categories of the British overlords. Indeed, accepting the use of force for social amelioration, and viewing its success as proof of the greatness of those who wield it, might seem to tacitly justify British rule over India. In his assessment of Muhammad's goals and means, Ameer Ali may have had in mind John Davenport's summary: "Mohammed, a simple Arab, united the distracted, scanty, naked, and hungry tribes of his country into one compact and obedient body, and presented them with new attributes and a new character among the people of the earth."[8] But Davenport sees Muhammad as a happy medium between the excessively spiritual (and therefore impractical) Christianity and the example of Moses, who not only had a more limited mission but also employed rough means to achieve it.[9]

Davenport's *Apology* fits within a spectrum of diverse publications on Islam appearing in Britain; in the United States, Christian tracts dominated. In the newly independent United States—in the early nineteenth century the country was but a few decades old—few Americans had met Muslims. American authors of evangelical works on Muhammad and Islam were not bound by the same imperative as British missionaries in India not to offend lest they lose out on converts. Most American books about Islam and Muhammad were addressed to other Christians, and Islam was often a foil for promoting the superiority of Protestantism—or one branch of it—over other traditions, particularly Catholicism within the United States and other forms of Christianity outside of it.

As the nineteenth century progressed, American missionizing in the Middle East increased dramatically. The official stance of the American Board of Commissioners for Foreign Missions was not unlike that of many other American Protestants concerned with proper doctrine: "the great pillars of the Papal and Mahometan impostures are now tottering to their fall."[10] When they did go on missions to convert those whom Palestine-bound Boston missionary Pliny Fisk called "the followers of that artful impostor, who arose in Arabia," they were often equally concerned with making converts from local forms of Orthodox Christianity.[11] Very few Muslims converted, and in one estimate, "probably only a few hundred eastern Christians became Protestants."[12]

Even once Americans became concerned with real-world Muslims, they lagged far behind Europe in the production of scholarship on Islam and Muhammad. Instead, publishers in New York and Boston churned out popular accounts, the best known of which was probably George Bush's *Life of Mohammed*. Bush, a Methodist preacher and a distant relation of the presidents Bush, followed Humphrey Prideaux closely in much of his content, but his framing was very different. Prideaux, whose work had appeared in several American editions, had been concerned with heretical Christians; Bush, like early modern English authors, saw in Muhammad and Islam the fulfillment of biblical prophecies about the end times.

Take his explanation of Islam's success, for example. Rather than attributing it to either the sincerity of its founder (Carlyle) or the virtues of his successors (Sprenger), or deeming it unimportant when compared to Christ's purity of motives (Muir), for Bush, how "an obscure individual, sprung from the roving tribes of Arabia, following no higher occupation than that of a caravan-trader, possessing no peculiar advantages of mental culture, nor distinguished in the outset by any pre-eminence of power or authority" came to found a religion and empire that swayed millions and has persisted for more than a millennium "presents a phenomenon which increases our wonder the more steadily it is contemplated." It can only be explained, in Bush's estimate, by "the intended providential bearings of the entire fabric of Mohammedan delusion upon the church of Christ."[13] That Muhammad's success must be understood as part of a divine plan that will ultimately result in the triumph of Christianity is echoed by Murray in his translation of Abu'l-Fida.[14]

The Man Mahomet

Though Bush is strongly negative toward Islam—at least as much as anyone can be when convinced it is part of a divine plan—he, like Muir, allows Muhammad some virtues. Bush views him as "by nature a man of a superior cast of character," but according to a relative rather than an absolute measure: "the age and the country in which he arose and shone were rude and barbarous; and the standard which would determine him great among the roving tribes of Arabia might have left him little more than a common man in the cultivated climes of Europe. Men's characters are moulded as much by their circumstances and fortunes as by their native genius and bias."[15]

In addition to basic virtues of honesty, chastity, truthfulness, and resolve, there was the more complicated question of manliness. Stanley Lane-Poole saw Muhammad as effective in his exercise of power, displaying "manly bearing under obloquy and reproach," but also as effeminate and having a "nervous and excitable" disposition.[16] This combination of "weakness and strength" was, for him, one of "the inevitable inconsistencies of a great man."[17] Sprenger believed Muhammad "unmanly" and even prone to hysterical oversensitivity.[18] According to Sprenger, he was very sensitive to bad smells, having a surprisingly "delicate constitution" for one of "semi-barbarous habits."[19] Muir objected to Sprenger's characterization of the prophet as "of weak and cunning mind," since that sort of man "could never have accomplished the mighty mission which Mahomet wrought."[20] Yet he alternated between terming him womanish and linking him with the masculine virtues of the Arab wilderness.[21] Such vacillation carried over from early modern European thinking about "Turks" (largely "synonymous with Muslim and Islamic"): indeed, one scholar suggests it was the "principle of inner-contradiction, of inconstancy," that defined views of the Turkish character.[22] This allowed "Turks"— and by extension, Muhammad—"to represent for European men both a self-denying virility that was appealing, and yet also everything they imagined themselves not to be."[23]

For these nineteenth-century thinkers, his status as "The Arabian Prophet"[24] helps to account for Muhammad's genius: his authentic, pure, uncosseted character developed in and was suited to the austere and wild Arabian desert. Yet barbarity (or "rudeness") only tells part of the story. Contradictory visions of Muhammad coexisted. Just as he could be weak and hysterical while also being strong and virile, simplicity could coexist with luxury.[25] With "Muhammad" as a metonym for Muslims in general and Muslim leaders in particular, Arabian harshness and defiant Bedouin independence morph into decadent palaces and harems and silks and tyrannical sultans. Muhammad and the Abbasid caliphs and the Ottoman sultans blended into one another, the decadence and corruption and lust of one explaining, justifying, and exemplifying the same qualities in the other. In the East, sexuality was tied to power, and power to (potential) immorality. Passion improperly channeled was kin to, or perhaps even led to, power improperly wielded. Yet passion, simplicity, and even a measure of savagery informed what spiritual merit Muhammad possessed. These two models—austerity versus extravagance, wilderness versus urbanity—clashed, but the power of the model was not in its coherence but in the authority of the author to impose (his) authority over it, to define people and places authoritatively for his audience.[26]

Muir vacillates in his presentation of Muhammad, cataloging Muhammad's virtues but only to make the reader accept more readily his ultimate conclusions about his lapses. For Muir, Muhammad—perhaps led by a good impulse early on—comes to believe in his divine commission and thus is led to commit various acts out of "the grand conception that he was destined to be the Reformer of his people and of the whole world."[27] Praiseworthy descriptions occupy several sections: He displays "unwavering stedfastness [sic]" at both Mecca and Medina, where he offers a "denunciation of polytheism and idolatry." But despite the "earnestness and honesty of Mahomet at Mecca," "at Medina, worldly motives mingle with his spiritual objects," with "rapid moral declension: the natural consequences."[28] Following Edward Gibbon, Muir links the gradual decline of Muhammad's character and morality to the shift from Mecca to Medina. As Peirce Johnstone remarks, "as his power grew, his character suffered."[29] Muir ultimately renders the sweeping verdict, moving from Muhammad's (inconsistent) character and actions to Islam as a whole. By acknowledging Muhammad's "moral courage" and personal qualities, he aims to lead the reader to trust his judgment, so the reader will accept his verdict that Muhammad's vices outweigh his virtues and that the "benefits of Mahometanism" are "outweighed by its evils."[30]

Like Napoleon, but Better

Although these biographers aimed at a comprehensive assessment of Muhammad's character, they were preoccupied by his achievements. British biographers had come to measure a life largely by impact: territory conquered or governed, making one's mark on the map. No longer did goodness or sanctity or proximity to the divine merit attention. *Lives* of military heroes such as Nelson or Wellington were largely concerned with their subjects' accomplishments, including the world-changing reverberations of their deeds; character was important but primarily in relation to actions.[31] Even antiheroes such as Napoleon were vital for people to understand. British authors may have deplored Old Boney, but he also inspired a certain awe.

By the twentieth century, time and distance had dimmed Napoleon's association with evil, leaving untarnished his reputation for military and political brilliance. This reputation spread beyond Europe. During his student years, the Pakistani scholar Fakir Syed Waheed-Ud-Din was assigned a brief biography of Napoleon, which led him to a long-standing fascination with and admiration for the general. Many years later, Waheed-Ud-Din read a biography of Muhammad, which led him to a similar fascination. Describing these encounters with books in the preface to *The Benefactor*—his Urdu biography of Muhammad and the first four caliphs—Waheed-Ud-Din affirms that he came to judge the Prophet superior to Napoleon, since the former combined achievement with religious merit.[32] Works such as *The Benefactor* reflect a century's accumulated shifts in view of Muhammad's significance—and, indeed, the significance of any prominent figure. Though Muhammad's political and military deeds, as well as his acts in community, had been the subject of a great deal of reflection and retelling, especially by Muslims, they were not why he mattered for most of Muslim history.

In his study, translated into English in 1964 and published by the Nation of Islam, a Black Muslim religious movement, Waheed-Ud-Din emphasizes social rather than spiritual achievements. *The Benefactor* was among a number of Pakistani-produced Islamic books that were sold and circulated by members of the Nation of Islam in the 1960s.[33] Aiming at "the lay reader, both Muslim and non-Muslim," Waheed-Ud-Din avoids, according to the translator's foreword, "apocryphal and theological controversies," focusing "instead on those progressive and social values which motivated the early Muslim community and its outstanding leaders"—most centrally, Muhammad, but also his rightly-guided successors.[34]

Though obscure in comparison to some other twentieth-century biographies of Muhammad, Waheed-Ud-Din's book showcases some key features of hybrid *Lives*, including the increasingly global nature of intra-Muslim conversations, in which English-language publications, such as those by South Asians, played a growing role. *The Benefactor* targets a mixed audience, stakes a position on when a life is of merit, and illustrates the interplay of reading and writing in the formation and transmission of ideas. We may well begin with the book's explicit address to both Muslim and non-Muslims. Pious biographies of the Prophet were clearly written for Muslims. Medieval tracts against Muhammad were read primarily by non-Muslims looking for useful arguments and strategies, even if those arguments were theoretically aimed at Muslims.[35] Like the Bombay Tract and Book Society's anonymously authored and generally unremarkable *Life*—by 1856 in its third edition—*The Benefactor*'s claim to a mixed audience is unlikely, certainly before it was translated into English but even after that; still, we should note its assumption that the same work *could* be meaningful to and appreciated by Muslims and non-Muslims.

Waheed-Ud-Din's address to both groups is plausible only because there has come to be common ground about what makes a life significant. He sets the religious dimensions of Muhammad's mission aside and focuses on social values. This goes beyond the idea that Muhammad was historically significant, which Carlyle and others had agreed about. Waheed-Ud-Din contends that Muhammad's program of social reform and betterment ought to elicit approval from non-Muslims. It is not (only) as prophet that he can be evaluated but also as statesman.[36] In a similar vein, Ghulam Malik titles the final chapter of his late twentieth-century biography "Greatness," meaning both prominence and social improvement. He writes, "Muhammad's mission was not confined to religion alone, but included other germane roles he played as a soldier, statesman, teacher, reformer, and prayer leader. He established social justice by introducing socio-economic reforms. He banned alcohol, gambling, prostitution, and usury; also he did away with the abominable female infanticide." Moreover, Muhammad anticipated abolition, human rights ("the Universal Declaration of Human Rights, proclaimed by the United Nations in 1948, echoes the Quran about the inalienable rights of human beings"), and women's rights: "The Prophet Muhammad pioneered and recognized women's rights in the Islamic society."[37]

Concern with improvements wrought in society has always been present in the *sira* literature to some degree, and these merits are inextricably bound up with Muhammad's personal acts. It finds anchor in the Qur'anic statement that Muslims have in God's messenger "a beautiful example."[38] In the last two centuries, this notion of ethical exemplarity has become bound up with the notion of historical importance. Muhammad *acted* in ways that one can use as a template for one's own behavior, as Muslims have always held, but he also *did* great things that are out of reach for ordinary people. Yet Waheed-Ud-Din is not just writing about Muhammad the great man; he is writing about Muhammad the *reformer*. He was a man with a plan, and that plan will reshape society in positive ways.

Omid Safi observes that modern biographers have focused on "Muhammad as a community leader and social engineer," whose role as "nation-builder" has overshadowed the "cosmic and mystical" role that he played in previous centuries. Rather than a "cosmic being whose intercession is to be hoped for, a channel of mercy and grace to this world," Muhammad is a "great man," a "genius," and a different sort of model.[39]

The most important modern biography of Muhammad reflects this transformation. Like *The Benefactor*, Muhammad Husayn Haykal's *Life of Muhammad* stands at the intersection of two bodies of literature and is deeply influenced by ideas about "greatness." Unlike *The Benefactor*, it has itself become a classic text. It draws on early Arabic sources, but the textual underpinnings of Haykal's *Life* are modern and Western, in details like the choice of topics and phrases and more fundamentally in assumptions about what makes men great. Haykal's *Life of Muhammad* marks a watershed moment, the point at which Western and Muslim writings have become so intertwined that one can no longer speak of influence or reaction but interaction and fusion.

India, Egypt, and British Rule

There were key linkages between the Indian subcontinent, where Waheed-Ud-Din wrote, and Egypt, where Haykal did. British rule in India shaped the occupation and governance of Egypt, both because many officers had experience in India and because "the Indian experience provided the only real model for ruling people understood as having an ancient civilisation and deeply entrenched, stable forms of self government."[40] Although French became and remained the language of elite Egyptian social discourse until sometime in the twentieth century, English was increasingly important in intellectual life from the late nineteenth century on, providing a vehicle for Indian Muslim texts to have an impact beyond the circles of Urdu readers.

Building on the engagement with prophetic biography of figures like Ahmad Khan, Ameer Ali, Qasim Nanautvi, and Ahmadi leader Muhammad Ali, Indian Muslim writers expressed themselves in both languages from the late nineteenth century through the interwar period: "Between the two World Wars, in the subcontinent the market was flooded with biographies of Muhammad written in both Urdū and English. The Sīrat movement, which started in the Panjab in the 1920s, made a deep impression throughout all of India. The movement was designed to glorify the civilizing mission of Muhammad."[41] Scholars marshalled traditional learning for new pedagogical purposes. Urdu was taking on a religious cast, used increasingly as a vernacular language for Muslims rather than only for Persian-speaking literati.[42] Among the most influential works for later generations of Muslims in the Indian subcontinent was the multivolume biography by Shibli Numani (d. 1914), completed and published posthumously by Suleman Nadvi (d. 1953). It was eventually translated into both Arabic and English, but the immediate influence of Urdu publications on Egyptian intellectuals was negligible. South Asian Muslim scholars often read Arabic because of its centrality to religious scholarship, but the reverse seldom occurred. Haykal and his cohort continued to read Ameer Ali and other Indian works composed or published in English. They also read the European interlocutors—mostly French and English—with which their Indian Muslim counterparts engaged, particularly Carlyle, Muir, and Washington Irving.[43] Gustav Weil was occasionally cited but rarely read.

English and, to a lesser extent, French were used to communicate not only between Europeans and colonial subjects but also between and among colonized peoples who did not otherwise share a language. Arabic had long served this purpose for Muslim scholars, much as Latin had for medieval Christian scholars. The shift owed in part to the rise of a new class of Muslim intellectuals, some of whom had no formal religious scholarly training. Their approaches to prophetic biography challenged the monopoly of the traditional scholarly classes, and experimented with new forms. These authors, some of whom had studied in Europe, were extensively engaged with European writers in European languages.[44] Well into the twentieth century, female writers, even those whose primary spoken language was Arabic, sometimes bypassed literary Arabic in favor of French. Another factor was the rise of new reading publics: even if important Indian *sira* authors could read and write in Arabic, their non-clerical audiences could not.

A handful of books influenced Egyptian and South Asian writers disproportionately. When it came to books about Islam in general and Muhammad in particular, Muslim intellectuals "preferred and neglected books quite out of proportion to what was available."[45] In the first decade of the twentieth century, Haykal was part of a circle of intellectuals reading works by such British thinkers as John Stuart Mill (*On Liberty*), Herbert Spencer (*Justice*), and Thomas Carlyle (*Heroes and Hero Worship*), all of whom shared "the assumption of the unique role of the individual or great man in social development. This man was not only able to embrace the dictates of reason set against the ingrained conservatism of his society which was often founded on religious belief; he was destined to do so as part of a sociohistorical law of evolution. Conversely, the people should follow obediently."[46] Haykal was interested in French thinkers, too, and wrote a lengthy study of Jean Jacques Rousseau in the 1920s, valuing the philosopher not for his ideals about equality but because his ideas could help quell social unrest.[47] But it was exceptional individuals that preoccupied Haykal. In 1929, he published *Egyptian and Western Biographies*, a series of profiles of Egyptians and Europeans. His selections included Khedive Ismail (he, like seven others among the ten Egyptian figures, bears the title "Pasha"); Cleopatra, the first person and only woman profiled; and Qasim Amin, whose entry mentions the "liberation of women in Egypt."[48] Western figures were "giants of literature and the arts," including Beethoven, Shakespeare, and Percy Bysshe Shelley, to whom he devotes the book's longest entry.[49]

As this list of political and artistic figures demonstrates, Haykal's preoccupation with extraordinary individuals only later manifested in focus on early Islamic figures. *An Essay on Eight*

Words—an 1881 book by a scholar at Cairo's teacher training college—considered key terms "'current on the tongues of the younger generation today,' nation, homeland, government, justice, oppression, politics, liberty and education."[50] Conspicuously absent are *religion, faith, shariah,* and *Islam.* By the 1920s and 1930s, however, biographies of the early caliphs were part of a broader trend of "popular Islamic literature about early Islamic society and the exploits of Islamic founding fathers."[51] A few works came to focus on founding mothers—the Prophet's wives—as well.

What was the connection between Islam, Muhammad, and topics such as liberty and nation? Haykal's preface makes clear that success is the linchpin: "Muḥammad did not have to wait long for his religion to become known, or for his dominion to spread. God has seen fit to complete the religion of Islam even before his death."[52] Haykal merges Ameer Ali's argument that Muhammad brought his assignment to fruition during his lifetime with Carlyle's rousing conclusion about the spread of Islam in the century after Muhammad's death. He frames his argument about Muslims under domination: "no religion has ever conquered Islam despite the fact that its people have fallen under all kinds of tyrannies and unjust governments. Indeed, reduction of their worldly power has made the Muslims more strongly attached to their faith, to their Islamic way of life, and to their Islamic hope."[53] To escape from the current unjust tyranny of diminished power, Islam provides the path, and Muhammad, the example. Again, Muhammad emerges from and is surrounded by other heroic figures. Though he is certainly different from them, his role depends on them. The tension in Haykal's oeuvre, and that of his contemporaries, is between Muhammad's peerless genius and the greatness of his close companions.

The Hero and His Sidekicks

Before the last few decades, it was common for European books about Muhammad to contain chapters recounting the stories of his successors, at least through the first four caliphs. Thus, Irving wrote *Mahomet and His Successors*. Other authors joined the story of his life to the story of his religion (*Mohammed and Mohammedanism*). Centuries earlier, authors like Ibn Ishaq had situated Muhammad in a lineage of biblical prophets tracing back to Adam, and of Muslim leaders stretching to their present. Ibn Hisham emphasized the Abrahamic and Arabian genealogies. Ibn Sa'd placed Muhammad in the midst of followers and opponents, telling us a great deal about them.[54] Shi'i authors included his biography in works devoted to the Imams.[55] Other influential biographies of Muhammad, like that of Tabari, were embedded in larger universal histories. Today, some have been extracted from those larger works to circulate in discrete editions, such as that by the fourteenth-century scholar Ibn Kathir.[56] In Haykal's work, the Prophet, though interacting with others, stood alone—as did, in his subsequent books, early Muslim heroes: Abu Bakr (*Abu Bakr the Righteous*), Umar (*Umar the Just*), and Uthman (*Uthman ibn 'Affan: Between Caliphate and Kingship*).[57] Haykal died before getting to Ali.

Haykal was not the only Egyptian thinker of his era to write about these early figures. 'Abbas Mahmud al-'Aqqad, author of the 1942 book *The Genius of Muhammad*, also wrote *The Genius of the Righteous One* (referring to Abu Bakr), *The Genius of Umar*, and *The Genius of the Imam* (Ali), as well as volumes on Amr ibn al-'As, the conqueror of Egypt; legendary swordsman and prophetic Companion Khalid ibn al-Walid; and Aisha (*The Righteous Woman,*

Daughter of the Righteous One).[58] (Despite the fact that he published biographies of Aisha and Muhammad's daughter Fatima, al-'Aqqad was widely perceived as a misogynist and known as the "enemy of woman."[59]) His series concluded with a 1954 biography of Uthman, perhaps left for last because he did not present as dynamic a figure of leadership.[60] Although Muhammad's successors were figures of interest, and had been so to Western authors since the nineteenth century, it was the Prophet's life above all that preoccupied Egyptian intellectuals and resonated with their audiences. No longer could one observe, as Muir had, that Muslims were not particularly concerned with the Prophet's biography.[61] Yet it was not primarily the traditional scholars who were rewriting that biography. Rather, in Egypt at least, a new intellectual class engaged with European writings was spurred to take up the topic. Al-'Aqqad reports that his interest in the idea of genius was sparked by a conversation he had about Carlyle's lecture—at a celebration of the Prophet's birthday.

The juxtaposition of a popular devotional gathering with a clearly politically inspired and oriented biography, derived from a British author's lecture to a British audience, suggests that in the era of printed books, the proper celebration of Muhammad was to be textual, not ritual. There is no necessary separation of the two; devotional texts associated with the *mawlid* had been written for centuries and printed as technology allowed. Devotional biographies continued to be written, telling miracle stories and lavishing prayerful praise on the Prophet. Still, there was a demonstrable shift in emphasis to biographies that focused on Muhammad's stellar qualities as a political leader, as a husband, and as a military figure.

The turn to Islamic subjects, then, was not primarily about belief or doctrine, and it intersected with the trend toward publishing biographies of historical, political, and military figures. Some explorations of these figures took creative forms, including a drama not quite suitable for the stage, a historical novel, and eventually an allegorical novel. As Ruth Roded has noted, "From the 1930s, virtually every major literary figure in Egypt composed a modern biography of the Prophet."[62] In addition to Haykal and al-'Aqqad, Taha Husayn, Ahmad Amin, Tawfiq al-Hakim, and, somewhat later, Naguib Mahfouz are among those who wrote.

In a way, so did Aisha 'Abd al-Rahman (1913–1998), writing under the pen name Bint al-Shati' ("Daughter of the Shore"). A literary scholar within interests and training in the religious sciences—she memorized the Qur'an as a child—like most women who have written Muhammad's life, she did so obliquely, through portraits of the women surrounding him. In addition to her best-known work, *The Prophet's Wives* (1959), she published *The Prophet's Daughters* (1963) and *The Prophet's Mother* (1966).[63] Though accounts of the life of Muhammad and his inner circle went back more than a millennium, her books were not full biographies of the women in his life. Instead, she aimed to give another perspective on Muhammad through exploring his relationships with them. She was responding, too, to the work of her countrymen, staking a position on both Muhammad's nature and the appropriate way to engage with European literature about Muhammad.

Among male Egyptian intellectuals of the era, respect for and engagement with European—French, British, and occasionally German—ideas and thinkers competed, clashed, and became interwoven with concern for and interest in Islamic history and precedents. Also in the mix were ideas about Eastern spirituality in contrast to Western rationality. These tensions can be seen in the career of Ahmad Amin (1886–1954).[64] Amin, who exemplified "the tornness of the Arab conservative,"[65] did not write extensively about Muhammad, but his writings include some "'self-consciously Islamic'" work and others with "the 'East-is-spiritual' theme."[66] Among the latter was his *The East and the West,* published a year after his death, in which "he expresses the opinion that Eastern civilization is based on religion and is more durable, whereas Western civilization is based on material pleasure and results in wars."[67] Seven years earlier, in 1948—the same year he, al-'Aqqad, and Haykal shared the King Fu'ad Prize[68]—he published a collection of profiles of modern Muslim reformers that "expresses the hope that the awakening East will become strong again without experiencing the defects that have marred the civilization of the West."[69]

This emphasis on Eastern spirituality, which Haykal shared, stood in tension with the social, political, and military accomplishments for which authors celebrated Muhammad. Al-'Aqqad's idea that Muhammad was simply the best at everything he did echoes in later works. Muhammad's battles were one arena for this. In a 1980 biography published in London, Afazlur Rahman writes, "A cursory study of the three battles of Badr, Uhud, and Azab shows superiority of Muhammad's war strategy, military tactics and defence plans over that of his enemies. He was always ahead of his enemies in military tactics and strategical moves. He always managed to know the plans of his enemies, forced them to attack at [the] most unsuitable position and time, commit mistakes and show their weaknesses and vulnerable points. Then he attacked them with determination and full force and rendered all their plans in vain."[70] The language here sounds much like that used in the Qur'an to describe God's foreknowledge and victories; it echoes the triumphalist tone of most accounts of Badr (624), where Muslims won a decisive victory, but it is a bit surprising to have it applied to the Battle of Uhud (625), which was almost a rout. Salmin's *The Holy Prophet Mohammad,* whose subtitle emphasizes Muhammad's role as *The Commander of the Faithful,* likewise affirms Muhammad as "the best and the greatest General" but places less stress on Muhammad's superior military strategy and more on the nature of his fighting: "in self-defence, and self-protection."[71]

This insistence on the justifiable nature of his conduct is in large part a response to the sort of polemic that, for instance, George Lathom Browne offered. After the conquest of Mecca, "Mahomet was now virtually a king, at whose command an army of fanatical warriors . . . was ready to enforce at the point of a sword submission to the prophet, and adhesion to his creed."[72] Yet for all that they repeatedly insist on Islam's having been spread by the sword, hostile biographers devoted surprisingly little attention to the particulars of Muhammad's conduct in battle. When Browne does report the next battle, Muhammad is first overconfident, "march[ing] heedlessly" into an indefensible position, from which many of his troops "turned and fled with the utmost precipitancy." He then displays "commendable courage" and, following a tactical error on his enemy's part, is able to win "an easy victory."[73]

Twentieth-century Muslim authors contested these kinds of portraits. They largely bypassed supernatural explanations for Muslim victory, instead attributing Muslim victories to the justness of their cause and the brilliance of Muhammad's leadership. Salmin, for instance, presents his actions as "part of a religious programme," attested to not only in "religious books" but also in "the history of the world."[74] He insists, echoing Haykal's stress on scientific method, that "the events related here or those about his life are not imaginary or mythical, but are historical acts faithfully recorded by authentic, and reliable people."[75]

Clash of Civilization

This insistence on authentic and scientific history suffuses Haykal's *Life*, standing somewhat at odds with its combative tone. Frequently pausing in its narrative to take Western authors to task, it epitomizes the essentially reactive and defensive tone of modern Muslim prophetic biography. Western works had set the agenda, and though Muslim authors might oppose the valuations set, the areas of focus—women, war, revelation—were largely predetermined. In an even more fundamental way, Haykal's *Life* owes its existence to European writings about Muhammad: it originated in a series of review essays of Émile Dermenghem's *Vie de Mahomet* (1929), which Maxime Rodinson called "a well-informed work, though without the trappings of scholarship."[76] He moved beyond mere review partway through the series of over a dozen articles (1932–1934). They appeared in book form in 1935 and shortly thereafter with expanded prefatory essays, which added a great deal of heft; depending on the edition, it contains between five and six hundred pages.[77] Haykal's use of Dermenghem was, he recalls in his *Memoirs*, suggested during a conversation "at a party when he asked for a European account of Muhammad's life which he could use in defending the Prophet against missionary attacks."[78]

Haykal includes Dermenghem as one of thirteen "foreign"—that is, non-Arabic—entries in his bibliography. Eight are English—including Ameer Ali, Irving, Muir, David Margoliouth, and Carlyle, but excluding Ahmad Khan—and five are French. A more extensive list of Arabic authors—including Ibn Hisham; Ibn Saʿd,

Waqidi's scribe; Waqidi; and Tabari—also appear, though he sometimes seems to have started with the Western sources and had reference to the Arabic originals as a second step; notably, a few of the Arabic texts were printed in Europe.[79]

It was not only in this respect that Haykal's biography was unusual. Today, conventional wisdom treats Haykal "as a convinced believer and as a modern man" and grants his *Life* a cherished place in the Muslim canon.[80] Yet the original title directly translates the standard Western *Life of Muhammad*. When Haykal's work appeared in Urdu several decades later, it bore the title *Sirat-i Rasul* (Biography of the Messenger).[81] The Urdu version harks back to centuries of tradition, drawing on the "connotative nimbus" of the term *sira*, linking Haykal's work to its "literary antecedents."[82] However, historian and biographer Charles Smith has argued that to read Haykal as offering an Islamic vision fundamentally misunderstands him.[83] For Smith, Haykal continued to promote thoroughly Western ideas about progress, science, individuality, and intellectuals. His criticisms of Western Orientalists aim to make his arguments palatable to a mass audience, while "attack[ing] the ulama and their authority" and appealing instead to "the true Islamic society established by Muhammad and experienced" during the reign of his first four successors.[84]

Haykal and his contemporaries were drawing on Muslim reform movements that looked to an early Islamic past and sought to bypass the clerical elite and its traditional forms of knowledge at the same time they were engaged in "a search for philosophical and legal norms from the Muslim past thought to be more appropriate to Egypt's needs as it confronted European military and economic expansion." Situating Haykal in context, Smith argues that "the notion that Western ideas might be isolated from Muslim thought and considered valid in themselves appeared only in the last decade of the nineteenth century and the first decade of the twentieth, the transitional period in which Muhammad Husayn Haykal was reared."[85]

Haykal's unpublished diaries show that by 1910 he was already thinking of Muhammad as just a man and not divinely inspired. During his heady Paris years (1909–1912), he grappled with big ideas about religion and reform. "He concluded," writes Smith, "that religions were not inspired by a divine being. Rather they were social phenomena reflecting historical circumstances. Likewise, prophets such as Muhammad were products of their time, self-inspired men despite their sincere beliefs that they had been chosen by God."[86] Haykal saw "the prophet as representative of the superior individual in history." Haykal thought that a small number of "superior" people would be inspired.[87] Swedish scholar and Lutheran bishop Tor Andrae, writing at the same time in German, held a similar view of the process of prophetic inspiration.

Smith posits that Haykal smuggles in Western ideologies in the guise of anti-Orientalist scholarship, but Haykal's complicated relationship to the Western materials he uses finds its basis at least partially in his writing practices.[88] Haykal borrows structure, plot, and theme—and sometimes entire sentences—from his sources. Understanding Haykal's effect requires close exploration of what he keeps, what he jettisons, and what he modifies from the texts on which he relies.

The two *Lives* Khalidi mentions as crucial—those of Muir and Carlyle—were influential for Haykal and his peers. Muir's *Life* had "provoked a new Muslim orientation towards the study of the life of the Prophet,"[89] in large part through its choice of sources as well as subject matter. Meanwhile, Carlyle's "lasting effect on the imaginary horizons of modern Muslim *Sira*" owes in part to a 1911 Arabic translation of *The Hero as Prophet*.[90] Serious translation is "the result of a series of creative decisions and imaginative acts of criticism."[91] Muhammad al-Siba'i's Arabic Carlyle is more nationalist and less romantic.[92] Fittingly, al-'Aqqad was less concerned with inner sincerity than with Muhammad's function as a model for conduct in personal, spiritual, military, and political spheres.[93]

Al-Hakim, another literary figure, had studied law in Paris for three years in the 1920s.[94] When he drew censure for his fictionalizations of Qur'anic stories, he responded by writing a play, *Muhammad* (1936). As one commentator notes, "that was the period when the leading Western-educated Egyptian writers, formerly accused of heresy and of polluting Islamic culture, were vying with one another and with the fundamentalists in turning to the Islamic legacy for their literary material, as though to prove to public opinion that they were no less Muslim than their fundamentalist critics."[95] This "avalanche of religious writings" was responding to its own Egyptian context while engaging with Western precursors—Voltaire and Goethe had, after all, written dramas of the same name.[96] As for the play itself, though "orthodox enough . . . it raised the problem of the permissibility of adapting sacred Islamic figures and themes to artistic treatment. . . . The question still remains unsolved in Arabic letters and the arts, but al-Hakim's *Muhammad* stirred no [significant] storm in the thirties . . . for the simple reason that al-Hakim never sought to have it performed. Artistically, too, it has no special merit."[97]

Haykal thus wrote among peers who were reading French and English authors and working out new ways of thinking and writing about early Islamic figures. Haykal's engagement with Western authorities carries on an intra-Muslim conversation by proxy:

What will a modern Muslim society look like? What sort of model does Muhammad provide for a proud people in a bad situation? Yaseen Noorani's account of the rise of Arab nationalist sentiments argues that "what took place in the rise of these values was not a clash of two irreconcilable cultures—the onslaught of secular Western modernity against an Islamic patriarchal premodernity—but the transformation of traditional cultural ideals from within, a process whose central dynamic lay in the transformation of virtue into nationality."[98] He sees a shift in "the traditional model of the self and its relation to collective order," increasingly "arising from innate human dispositions rather than from the sovereign authority of virtuous figures."[99] Noorani's insight helps clarify the role Muhammad's domestic arrangements played in modern Egyptian biographies. If the nuclear family and a companionate couple were central to the social order, so Muhammad—*innately* the best model for humanity—must also exemplify the best relationships. And yet his comportment would seem, on the surface, to be incompatible with precisely the sorts of arrangements seen as desirable.

Domestic matters were the subject of a great deal of scrutiny in early twentieth-century Egypt. Rifaʻa al-Tahtawi had broached some of these topics in the 1870s, and Muhammad ʻAbduh, a key reformist scholar of the era, made them a centerpiece of his writing. ʻAbduh railed against arranged marriage as "utterly and completely incompatible with modern subjectivity" and insisted on love as the necessary basis for marriage, which should be monogamous and centered on a nuclear family household.[100] Although he was primarily concerned with the pernicious effects of polygamy, he also assumed the need for females to be old enough and involved in the process of choosing spouses: if marriage is for the establishment of families, which are necessary to the nation, then wives must be competent and loving partners, not subordinates. Not everyone held this view. Al-'Aqqad devoted part of his substantial chapter in *The Genius of Muhammad* on Muhammad as a husband to explaining how Muhammad maintained a salutary discipline in his household. Although he objects to Western perceptions of Muslim backwardness, al-'Aqqad by no means advocates egalitarian marriages.

Haykal's way of approaching questions about Muhammad's marriages as well as other issues often depended on what he read, and his decisions to focus on or ignore issues seems to emerge from his composition practices. To perhaps a greater extent than these other scholars, "Haykal read widely but not intensively."[101] He often marked up only the first two or three chapters of a book, and sometimes a lone paragraph. He does what all writers do to a greater or lesser degree: he presents his own versions of the books he reads, emphasizing and ignoring selectively, unable to ever account for all that they contain.[102] Throughout his book, even where he gives the impression of drawing on a broader source base, he relies "almost exclusively" on Ibn Ishaq/Ibn Hisham "as his classical source."[103] He "consults Ibn Hishām constantly . . . borrows much material from him, and cites him extensively, primarily in direct quotations, [and] also when he does not expressly acknowledge it."[104] Of course, the selections of particular texts from the Muslim tradition were a capitulation to the "scientific" sensibilities of the Orientalists: Haykal accepted the premise, articulated so clearly by Muir, that early texts mattered.

Indeed, Haykal at times takes his early Islamic texts through the mediation of Orientalist biographies, particularly that of Muir.[105] Of more recent Muslim texts, he draws on Ameer Ali's *The Spirit of Islam* and borrows its practice of including lengthy apologetic sections alongside and interwoven with biographical material. (Dermenghem had also read Ameer Ali, as well as 'Abduh.)[106] Haykal starts with a contentious introduction and closes with two polemical essays. If Ameer Ali's text was in conversation with European scholarship, Haykal's was a more direct engagement. One commentator says that Haykal was "deeply read in anti-Islamic literature."[107] Given Haykal's scattershot reading practices, it is probably more accurate to say that he was deeply preoccupied by it.

Though Dermenghem takes pride of place in the *Life*'s origin story, Prideaux's famous polemic bleeds through the background, and Muir's *Life* serves as both foil and resource for Haykal.[108] He engages with Muir and Carlyle in ways beyond what he indicates directly in the text.[109] Haykal's use of Irving perhaps provides the clearest glimpse of what he was attempting. Irving features prominently in Haykal's closing essay on "Islamic Civilization and the Western Orientalists." Haykal calls him "one of the greatest writers" of nineteenth-century America and alternately praises and criticizes Irving's *Life*. Irving's theological understanding "fell short of grasping the spirit of Islam and its civilization. Hence his false interpretation of the problem of divine providence and predestination. Perhaps Irving had some excuse in that some of the Islamic books which he may have read do in fact point in the direction of his interpretation."[110] This criticism is only superficially about Irving's failure to understand Islamic teachings. The real problem is that some Muslim scholars hold erroneous views; Irving picks the wrong side in an intra-Muslim controversy. To acknowledge this, though, Haykal would have to admit that there is a legitimate debate, not just the correct view and a few Muslim authors who got it wrong. Here again, Western scholars become a means to attack views held by Muslims: by associating the erring Muslims with Orientalists, the opprobrium can be shared.

Haykal used Muslim sources equally selectively, relying most heavily on Ameer Ali's *Spirit of Islam*.[111] His relationship to the classical sources is equivocal and he sometimes misrepresents them. For instance, regarding the Satanic verses incident, in which Muhammad was induced temporarily to allow the worship of three Meccan goddesses, Haykal writes, "These are the arguments on which stands the claim for veracity of the story of the goddesses. They are all false, incapable of standing any scrutiny or analysis. Let us begin with the argument of the Orientalist Muir."[112] The refutation that follows admits that the story appears in some early Muslim sources (Ibn Sa'd, Tabari) but places blame for repeating it on European scholars: it "arrested the attention of the western Orientalists who took it as true and repeated it ad nauseam."[113] Haykal rejects Muir's analysis on rational grounds and also asserts that the story is rejected by Ibn Ishaq, who, Haykal tells us, "did not hesitate at all to declare it a fabrication by the heretics."[114] Here, as with his criticism of Irving's view of free will, Haykal takes a Westerner to task for his reliance on the wrong Arab sources, a strategy that Ahmad Khan also employed to generally good effect. Haykal insists that his discernment among Muslim sources owes to a scientific approach to the tradition.

Ashis Nandy argues that "empire succeeded only when the colonized found—or were made to find—something to love in imperial culture."[115] In the case of biographers of Muhammad, it was often a critical, historical, or scientific method, for which European scholars stood as exemplars. The historian Abd al-Aziz Duri called for careful appraisal of early sources, such as Ibn Ishaq/Ibn

Hisham, to extract facts about "the Prophet's life" by means of "a sound evaluation of the sources" and "a critical historical approach to the accounts in which this material has been preserved."[116] Influenced by the work of Orientalists but also aiming to rebut some of their global criticisms, Duri attempts to salvage a core of historically accurate prophetic biography, as well as to rehabilitate the reputation of historians as a class. Much like Ahmad Khan praises a medieval Muslim historian by saying he ranks with the best European historians, "Haykal's exploitation of Islamic history in the 1930s, although including apologetic attacks on the West duly emphasized in Western studies of Egyptian modernism, was founded expressly on a glorification of the Western historical method and its concern for scientific accuracy."[117]

Character and Cohort

Premodern biographies had things to say about Muhammad the individual and his character. Haykal's title reflects and enacts a shift from the individual as model to the individual as personality. Muhammad becomes a man with temperament and traits that comprise a personality unique to him and capable of explaining in some vital way his "contribution" or "impact" or "genius." This is a dramatic departure from Ibn Ishaq's aim to model Muhammad after the biblical prophets who served as the touchstone for his notion of legitimacy, and led to the incorporation of such legends as that he spent time working as a shepherd in his youth.[118]

The interest in Muhammad's Companions, wives, and kin tended to reflect similar concerns with social and familial issues of the day. The Companions attest to his sterling qualities; their virtues, including trustworthiness, guarantee his, and vice-versa. (Aisha's summation: "His character was the Qur'an.")[119] This only works to the extent that the Companions are revered. Yet although figures such as Aisha and Umar—the latter the subject of a massive biography by Numani as well as al-'Aqqad and Haykal—are particularly disparaged by the Shia, their emergence as vital figures in the middle of the twentieth century seems less intended to kindle sectarian fires and more to appeal to a seemingly simple, straightforward, early past that can provide lessons for a Muslim society in a turbulent time.

These lessons are about the proper shape of the family and the proper shape of society. Although Haykal and his countrymen insist on the religious resonance or authenticity of Muhammad and his close associates as models, they simultaneously present a less religious Muhammad. Or, as in Waheed-Ud-Din's *The Benefactor*, one whose religious successes are at least as noteworthy for their worldly effects as for their spiritual merit. To what extent Haykal's aim was to arrive at "a more secular culture through the undermining of Islam,"[120] despite his use of Islam as a language through which he could communicate to the masses, is unclear. Smith's contrarian interpretation posits Haykal as an elitist figure, caught between nostalgia for a hierarchical village power structure of patronage on the one hand, and an allegiance to European rationalism on the other, with suspicion of the Egyptian masses and their increasing power to disrupt the existing social order.[121] However, he concludes, "Paradoxically, Haykal's search for progress with order and his attempt to use Islam for that purpose encouraged retention of the values he hoped to undermine."[122]

Whether this is so can be debated. What seems clear, however, is that in India and Egypt, and broadly throughout the Arab world, the terms in which success and truth are discussed are no longer primarily indigenous. As Shaden Tageldin puts it in discussing a different set of texts, "an Islam once taken for granted by its adherents as self-evident *sign* has become subject to external verification by European Orientalism: to the *proof* of the Orientalist's translated text."[123] Nowhere is this clearer than in the material on Muhammad's marriages, the subject of Chapters 4 and 5.

Chapter 4

The Wife of Muhammad

By the time Muhammad had grown to manhood, he had gained a reputation as trustworthy and judicious. A wealthy widow named Khadija hired him to accompany her caravan to Syria. His performance so impressed her that she proposed marriage to him. He accepted. She was forty and he was twenty-five. They were happily married for twenty-five years. While she lived, he took no other wife. Her wealth and companionship gave him the support he needed to undertake his spiritual reflection and, eventually, his prophetic mission. After her death, he married other women, but she retained a special place in his memories.

A version of this story, often in nearly these exact words, appears in a striking proportion of books about Muhammad written in the last century, whether aimed at pious Muslim readers, American middle schoolers, college students, or the general reading public.[1] Phrases like "wealthy older widow" and "remained faithful" recur. Whatever the exact words, the same points surface repeatedly: their respective ages, that she was a widow, her wealth, the Syrian caravan expedition, her positive impression, and that the marriage took place at her instigation. We learn that her wealth gave him the leisure for retreat and reflection.[2] We are told that he took no other wives while she lived, and sometimes how unusual this was in the Arabian context. Authors sometimes mention that she bore him two or three or, occasionally, four sons who died in infancy and four daughters.[3] After she died, her memory "cast a long shadow over" his later marriages.[4]

All of these bits of information about Khadija are gleaned from early Muslim biographies. Other things in those sources drop out, leaving a few overlapping facts.[5] The formulaic repetition of these facts paints Khadija as "the pattern of a Musalman matron," as one nineteenth-century scholar phrased it, and reinforces an image of Muhammad as a model husband.[6] A similarly coherent but substantively different portrait dominated early modern English accounts, which consistently portrayed Muhammad's "cynical wooing of, and marriage to, the widow Cadygan [Khadija], to gain earthly power."[7] Those accounts, though, did not dwell extensively on the marriage; it was one more bit of evidence for Muhammad's craftiness and ambition. For early Muslim biographers, the marriage was a narrative way station on Muhammad's journey to prophethood, recounted in terms that emphasized his prophetic role. For modern authors, the marriage to Khadija becomes a key to showing who Muhammad "really was." Her role in his character formation is increasingly important as people write about Muhammad the *man* rather than Muhammad the *prophet*.

The recognition that Muhammad was both man and messenger was not new, but a palpable shift in emphasis occurred in the nineteenth and especially the twentieth centuries. It can be seen clearly in the title of Muhammad Husayn Haykal's biography, discussed in Chapter 3. Narratives of Muhammad's life had customarily borne the title *Biography (sira) of the Prophet* or *Biography of the Messenger of God*.[8] Haykal's title directly translates to *The Life of Muhammad*, the usual title for European biographies and the one used by Dermenghem in the *Life* that Haykal was reviewing. That he retained it when he expanded his review articles into an independent book suggests that he intended a different sort of biography than usual. The shift from "biography" to "life," and from a religious title ("the prophet" "God's messenger") to a personal name, indicates that we are no longer dealing with an account of a course of action (*sira* in its early meaning of "practice, procedure") but a life story.[9] Moreover, its subject is not a prophet or, rather, *the* Prophet but a man: Muhammad. The shift is from exemplar to individual, from type to personality.

Muhammad's modern biographers saw his character manifested in his relationships with women—first and foremost Khadija, but also, and as a clear counterpoise, his other wives as a group. Their centrality can be appreciated if we note that 'Abbas Mahmud al-'Aqqad's *Genius of Muhammad,* written at a time when questions about sovereignty, politics, and power were roiling the Egyptian public, devotes five pages to Muhammad as leader and forty-eight to Muhammad as husband.[10]

A Much-Married Man

Over the course of his life, Muhammad had about a dozen wives, depending on how one counts.[11] This is a large number of wives but an infinitesimally small portion of the hundreds of millions of Muslim women who have lived throughout history. Yet the two topics have become inseparable. Discussion of his wives is fraught with the weight of expectations about "the woman question" in Islam; many conversations about this latter topic, in turn, hinge on Muhammad's own married life as well as the example of the women of his household.

For contemporary Westerners, the association between Islam and women's oppression is strongly ingrained.[12] This has not always been the case. Muhammad's wives become more important as the idea of Muslim women becomes more important to discussions about Islam. The oppressed but alluring Muslim woman is a creature of the last few centuries. So is her counterpart: the pious, active female role model, of whom Khadija is the ideal example. And if she is a new kind of woman, Muhammad, as her husband, must be a new kind of man.

Muhammad's *Lives* have come to dwell at some length on his marriage to Khadija and to grant it prominence as the prime example of his married life. This might seem like an obvious thing to do; after all, by the usual reckoning, she was married to him for more than twice as long as any other woman. Yet premodern accounts tend to say little about their conjugal life beyond the proposal and marriage, the comfort and reassurance she provided to him at the outset of his mission, and his reaction to her death—scant details compared to the wealth of information about his later marriages and domestic arrangements, which transpired during the course of his public prophetic mission and communal leadership.

Khadija the Grand

Khadija may have been merited relatively few pages in early Muslim accounts of Muhammad's life, but they were important ones. She was associated with several turning points in his life: his first marriage; becoming a father; his prophetic commission; and, in the wake of her death, his departure from Mecca to Medina. Biographers recognized her exceptional nature and distinguished between her and his other wives. Ibn Sa'd set her apart in his compendium of early Muslim women, putting her first and leaving the rest of Muhammad's wives until after chapters on his daughters and other female relatives.[13]

Traditionally, she bears epithets including "the Grand" and "the Pure." As the member of the Prophet's household least subject to partisan wrangling, she draws allegiance from Sunni and Shia alike. The same is true, in a limited way, for Fatima: daughter of Muhammad and Khadija, and the only one of his children to survive him, though only by a few months. Yet if Fatima is never precisely deprecated by Sunnis, her marriage to Ali and motherhood of Hasan and Husayn establish her as a potent symbol for the Shia, who hold that legitimate rulers come through Ali's line. Hence, Sunni tradition sometimes disregards or marginalizes her.[14] Khadija poses no sectarian threat and may be praised with impunity.

Her noble genealogy and stellar personal qualities reflect well on Muhammad. That a woman of her caliber, whom Ibn Ishaq calls the richest woman of the Quraysh of her time, would choose him proves that she recognized his impressive character.[15] This much, we get from the traditional texts. (It is no surprise that contemporary authors forgo her extensive genealogy; the prolonged recitation of anyone's ancestry is of little interest to modern readers.) They also say, though few modern authors repeat, that not everyone was impressed with the match; Khadija might have gotten her father drunk to gain his approval (a story frequently retold by pre-modern polemicists). In other versions, he was already deceased, and her uncle stood in for him.[16] Modern Muslim authors often skim over the father's or uncle's involvement in the marriage because it sits ill with the image of Khadija as a self-assured and independent woman. Moreover, the question of paternal involvement in any adult woman's marriage is jarring to some readers;

works for general readers published in America almost uniformly omit any discussion of her kin. Works aimed at Muslims may mention it, especially if they were published in South Asia.[17] It is an open question whether such authors note her father's or uncle's role because they are determined to rebut the slander that Khadija deceived her guardian, which some earlier hostile biographers highlight, or because custom still presumes a level of familial involvement in marriages that is alien to contemporary Westerners, including Muslims living in Europe or the Americas.

Contemporary biographers almost uniformly make Khadija forty and Muhammad twenty-five; some do the math for their readers and note the fifteen-year difference. Many use this "fact" to present interpretations about Muhammad's character: evidence that he was not consumed by lust and that he was comfortable with a powerful woman. Traditional accounts sometimes stick with the ages twenty-five and forty, as Tabari does, and sometimes register disagreement about Khadija's age at the time of her marriage; though the age forty is mentioned, another view is that she was twenty-eight. Ibn Ishaq gives Muhammad's age as twenty-five, but notes that he might have been twenty-one or thirty.[18] Ibn Sa'd reports that someone asked Khadija's nephew, "which of them was older, the Messenger of Allah or Khadija?" He said, "Khadija was fifteen years older than him. The prayer was unlawful for my aunt before the Messenger of Allah was born."[19] Ibn Sa'd explains the anachronistic response, "'The prayer was unlawful for her' means she menstruated, but he is speaking as the people of Islam speak." To understand this response, one must know that menstruants abstain from ritual worship; Khadija had reached menarche before Muhammad's birth.[20]

Why forty? As anyone familiar with the biblical tradition knows, forty is a potent number. In the Hebrew bible, the flood lasts forty days, and the Israelites wander in the wilderness for forty years. Jesus fasts forty days and forty nights, according to the Gospel of Matthew, before the devil tempts him. And in Muslim tradition, Muhammad is usually said to have been forty when he received the first revelation from Gabriel in the cave on Mount Hira (though a few versions put him at forty-three).[21] One scholar suggests that the Prophet's age at revelation relies on the symbolic significance of the number forty: "In matters involving measurement of time, this usage of 'forty' is clearly devoid of specific chronological content."[22] For Khadija, this seems likely as well; that she supposedly bore Muhammad six or seven children suggests that it should not be taken literally.[23] We cannot assume, of course, that earlier scholars were ignorant of this point, since the facts of reproductive biology were no doubt more or less the same.[24] Instead, we ought to assume that they were aware of the symbolic resonance of forty and, further, that they expected their readers to be aware of it as well.

The suggestion that the symbolism matters more than factual accuracy suggests a rationale, too, for the devoted attention to Aisha's age that one finds in the early sources; Muhammad's marriage to Aisha, however, must await the next chapter.

Khadija the Comforter

If one were to construct a short list of candidates for the most important moment of Muhammad's life, the encounter with Gabriel in the cave would head the list. (Other contenders would include the migration to Medina and the ascension, though his marriage to Khadija appears in some accounts, particularly the more recent ones, as a pivotal point.)[25] Though Khadija was not on Mount Hira, she became a key part of the story shortly afterward.

In Ibn Ishaq's account, Muhammad turns to Khadija after his encounter with the angel leaves him shaken and wondering whether he was "poet or possessed."[26] Khadija does three things to restore Muhammad's equanimity and faith.[27] First, she comforts him physically ("I came to Khadīja and sat by her thigh and drew close to her") and reassures him of his excellent character and her confidence that God would not allow such a thing to happen to him. Then, she goes to her cousin Waraqa ibn Nawfal, "who had become a Christian and read the scriptures and learned from those who follow the Torah and the Gospel." Waraqa affirms that if Khadija's tale is true, then Muhammad is a prophet like Moses, "the prophet of his people."[28] Khadija conveys this message to Muhammad, who then meets Waraqa himself and is both reassured of the legitimacy of his visitor and warned that people will oppose him. Third, Khadija devises a test to see if Muhammad's "visitant" is angelic or demonic. She asks Muhammad to move progressively closer to her, and he continues to see the angel until she begins to disrobe and make sexual advances toward him; the visitor departs, confirming that "he is an angel and not a satan."[29]

Khadija's role as comforter extends beyond this moment. When Ibn Ishaq tells of Khadija's accepting of Islam ("she was the first of those who believed in God and His Messenger and the truth of what he brought from Him"), he refers to both the opposition and insults Muhammad encountered and the ways in which she supported and comforted him "when he returned to her." Alfred Guillaume, translating this phrase, gives a domestic twist: "when he went home."[30] Modern authors build on these ancient descriptions of Khadija as comforter to depict the act of comforting as a wifely duty, and marriage as an institution designed to nurture emotional closeness. For instance, Pakistani author G. N. Jalbani, in his

English-language *Life of the Holy Prophet* (1988), treats the after-math of Muhammad's first revelation. He returned to Khadija, who wrapped him up and comforted him by expressing her confidence in his merits. Jalbani comments: "She no doubt knew him better, as no one can be better informed of the ways of a man than his own wife, who is in a position to have free access to his heart."[31] Similarly, British Muslim Ahmad Thompson: "No one—except Allah of course—knows more about a man than his wife, both his good and bad qualities, his strengths and his weaknesses."[32]

These descriptions of marital intimacy and wifely succor even take on religious overtones. Haykal calls Khadija an "angel of mercy," a coinage unusual enough that even though Arabic books typically omit vowel markers, the text includes them on the word angel to forestall confusion or misreading.[33] More frequent is the stock Victorian phrase "angel of hope and consolation" used by Stanley Lane-Poole in an introduction to selections from the Qur'an.[34] It passed into English-language South Asian Muslim works; Ameer Ali uses it.[35] More than a century later, Abdul Hameed Siddiqui writes, "for a quarter of a century *Khadijah* remained his angel of hope and consolation."[36] (Slightly later, Jalbani mangles the phrase: "He was much attached to Khadījah who was his angel of hope and consolidation [*sic*]."[37] The imagery of a wife as an "angel," however metaphorical, at least partially displaces the actual angel whose appearance led Muhammad to seek her comfort. As with Guillaume's translation, the emphasis has changed from the irruption of the divine into Muhammad's life to the importance of a domestic sanctuary, where an angel of the hearth awaits him. This imagery links the spiritual and the domestic—in John Davenport's *Apology*, "his soul and his hearth." These ways of speaking about Khadija draw on early texts that celebrate her pivotal role, yet they are decisively modern in their view of marriage as the center of one's emotional life, and the couple and nuclear household as the proper pattern for family living. Though he ultimately arrives at negative conclusions about Muhammad and Islam, a Christian author writing in 1895 had only praise for their union: "The home of Mahomet and Khadija was a bright and happy one, and their marriage fortunate and fruitful."[38] A recent self-published work on Muhammad and his family makes a similar point: "After his marriage with Khadijah, he had a happy family life."[39] Similarly, Driss Chraibi's 1995 French novella *Man of the Book* refers to Muhammad's "happy household" with Khadija, who provided both friendship and "a woman's love."[40] These authors envision households and families in familiar familial ways, which require forgetting the fostered cousin Ali, the presence of slave servants, and the adoptive adult son Zayd.

A rare objection to this view of conjugal life as the center of individual emotional life was raised by the Iraqi scholar and writer Amina bint Haydar al-Sadr, the sister of noted Shiʻi jurist Muhammad Baqir al-Sadr (both d. 1980). One of the relatively few Muslim women to write biographically about Muhammad, Bint al-Huda (Daughter of the Right Path), as she was widely known, wrote a lengthy essay, "Women and the Prophet." Though she generally avoided the topic of polygamy in her copious writings, she had to confront it in writing about Muhammad's life and wives. Like other authors, Sadr places Khadija in a central position: "It is only Muhammad's first, long-term, monogamous marriage with Khadija" that Sadr presents "in unambiguously positive terms. The polygamous marriages contracted after Khadija's death are represented as deficient in various [ways] and/or as examples of the Prophet's charity."[41] She, too, stresses "love and companionship" between the spouses. However, emphasizing that Muhammad did not forget about other important women in his life when he married Khadija, Sadr "challenge[s] marriage as a private institution between two people, founded on a rupture with their previous lives and relationships."

Love Marriage

When Haykal wrote his biography in the mid-1930s, he was directly engaging French and Anglo-Muhammadan *Lives*. At the same time, he was responding to the circumstances of early twentieth-century Egypt. In addition to the shift of emphasis to religious topics, active debates about marriage served as a backdrop to his writing. The climate of ideas about companionate marriage, marriage age, and the "marriage crisis" could not but affect his portrayal of the Prophet. Haykal focuses on the inward and emotional dimensions of Muhammad's personhood, his character as manifested in his relationships with women. To do so, he borrows from the attribution of motives and feelings to Muhammad that had begun to emerge in nineteenth-century Western lives. In other words, he talks about love.

Moderns posit a primary role for sexual acts and identities in the constitution and definition of a self.[42] Marriage is often viewed as the single most central adult relationship. Classical authors placed less stress on marital conduct as a laboratory for evaluating the self or on the emotional bond between spouses as the prime locus for strong ties of love and obligation. That is not to say that conjugal love was unimportant before the modern era. The question of what Muhammad felt for which wife appeared from time to time in accounts of his life.[43] Yet friendships and kin ties might be equally or more important. Where early biographies mention Muhammad's affection for this or that male figure— Zayd, Ali, or Abu Bakr, most often—there is an implicit contest about closeness and legitimacy in succession.[44] In modern biographies, Khadija has the greatest emotional and even spiritual resonance. In a passage that also shows Shi'i emphasis on Muhammad's descendants, Seyyed Hossein Nasr writes,

> The marriage with Khadījah was of very great significance in the life of the Prophet of Islam for it provided for him the companion on whom he could rely completely in the most difficult period of his life and who was endowed with the necessary moral and spiritual virtues to act as the perfect wife of God's most perfect creature and the mother of the prophetic family—the *Ahl al-bayt* [people of the household]—whose light was later to illuminate the world.[45]

Here, Khadija's virtues make her not only Muhammad's ideal partner but also a key player in the transmission of Muhammad's light.

Focusing on Khadija's politico-religious activities as well as her role as "partner" and "life companion," Pakistani lawyer Muhammad Anis-ur-Rahman goes so far as to make Khadija "the right hand of the Holy Prophet" in establishing Islam.[46] *The Historical Role of the Venerable Woman* describes her and Muhammad as "twin preachers."[47] Her courage and, not least, her wealth, "which financed the revolution," were vital for the spread of Islam.[48] The emphasis on Khadija's wealth is in keeping with focus on her business success—she was divinely chosen for marriage, he asserts, in order to show that Islam supports working women.[49] Nonetheless, her wifely virtues earn lavish praise: "The unique success of the mission of the Holy prophet was achieved on account of the woman who provided peace and tranquility, inspiration and encouragement, solace and comfort to the messenger of Allah."[50]

Joining the domestic and the religious, American writer-poet Tamam Kahn imagines Khadija as "the rock upon which Muhammad built his family and his religion" as well as his "closest confidant."[51]

Similar qualities surface in other accounts. Siddiqui writes of Khadija: "She gave *Muhammad* ease of circumstances, freedom from the cares of daily life, strength, and comfort of deep mutual love, factors which contributed to the furtherance of the mission of the Prophet." And he adds, "In spite of conspicuous difference in age, *Muhammad's* love for *Khadijah* never wavered."[52] Also mentioning the age difference, Malik calls it "a perfect match" and claims that "they were deeply devoted to each other and much in love."[53] This attention to the difference in their ages as a factor that *should* have led to Muhammad's disinterest or wandering eye is alien to the classical Muslim tradition—perhaps because no one actually thought of Khadija as being forty. Western authors who discuss this marriage linger on the question of her "youthful charm" or lack thereof. Davenport, for instance, calls her "his beloved partner" and notes, "Notwithstanding that at so advanced an age she must have lost every youthful charm, yet Mohammed had remained faithful to the last, and refrained, as already said, from taking other wives."[54] Thomas Carlyle, and others following him, notes not that she was beautiful but that despite her age she was "still beautiful."[55] Washington Irving describes her as "past the bloom of years when women are desirable in the East."[56] Émile Dermenghem, too, comments on her presumably faded attractiveness, which makes Muhammad's faithfulness and devotion all the more remarkable. Rodinson speculates that since her wealth put her "in a position to make demands," she might have insisted on a clause in their marriage contract preventing him from taking an additional wife.[57] Less cynically, Nasr attributes his abstention from taking other wives despite the fact that "she was fifteen years older than he and polygamy was a very common practice" to the marriage's perfection: "a marriage which was so complete and in a sense absolute that the Blessed Prophet did not marry another wife as long as Khadījah was alive."[58]

A Series of Unfortunate Events

Khadija's death provides biographers with another chance to emphasize her centrality in Muhammad's story. The narrative connection between her death and that of Muhammad's uncle, Abu Talib, who had raised him after his grandfather's death, provides an opportunity for authors to once again comment on the significance of their tie and the role Khadija played for him; to move the narrative of Muhammad's life forward with his move to Medina; and—not least important—to transition to the second stage of his life as a husband, beginning with his marriages to others.

The joining of Khadija and Abu Talib's deaths is at least as much literary artifact as historical fact: two events happen in temporal proximity and become, through their insistent juxtaposition in biographical writings, thematically conjoined as the Year of Sadness.[59] Elsa Marston's 2001 "book report biography" describes this as "a double blow—truly disastrous" under the subheading "Loss of Some Vital Support."[60] This link is ancient, going back at least to Ibn Ishaq/Ibn Hisham, which reads, in part: "Khadīja and Abū Ṭālib died in the same year, and with Khadīja's death troubles followed fast on each other's heels, for she had been a faithful support to him in Islam, and he used to tell her of his troubles. With the death of Abū Ṭālib he lost a strength and a stay in his personal life and a defence and protection against his tribe."[61] Tabari, though he draws on Ibn Ishaq, is less effusive about Khadija's role, noting, "After this, Abū Ṭālib and Khadījah died in a single year. . . . Their death was a great affliction to the messenger of God. This is because after the death of Abū Ṭālib, Quraysh went to greater lengths in molesting him then they had ever done during his lifetime."[62] He makes no mention of any particular loss occasioned by Khadija's death. George Sale, in the preliminary discourse that introduces his 1734 translation of the Qur'an, signals these deaths as unfortunate but does not wax lyrical about either loss.[63]

Martin Lings, a British convert to Islam, weighs the relative impact of the two deaths differently in *Muhammad: His Life Based on the Earliest Sources* (1983). One scholar calls this book, popular among English-reading Muslims, "an uncritical English conflation of the traditional Muslim accounts" and a "curious undertaking," while another, more diplomatic scholar deems it "a traditional history based on Muslim sources."[64] Referring to the Year of Sadness, Lings writes that "the Prophet suffered a great loss in the death of his wife Khadījah. She was about sixty-five years old and he was nearing fifty. They had lived together in profound harmony for twenty-five years, and she had been not only his wife but also his intimate friend, his wise counselor, and mother to his whole household including 'Alī and Zayd." Lings emphasizes the length of their marriage as well as the tenor of their relationship: intimate, friendly, harmonious. He presumes a patriarchal family unit—it is *his* household—and assigns her the maternal role. (Others play up Muhammad's role as paterfamilias: "Muhammad was a loving and affectionate husband, as well as a loving and deeply attached father.")[65] He then contrasts it with the next "loss [which] followed closely upon the death of Khadījah, a loss less great and penetrating in itself, but at the same time less consolable and more serious in its outward consequences. Abū Ṭālib fell ill, and it soon became clear that he was dying."[66] Similarly, Nasr acknowledges, with Tabari, the practical impact of the loss of Abu Talib, "his most powerful protector," but emphasizes the emotional impact of Khadija's death during "the bleakest period of his life": "The loss was almost unbearable at the beginning and practically nothing could console him."[67]

Though Muhammad's grief at Khadija's death has antecedents in the classical sources, the emotional tone for these twentieth-century Muslim writers was set by nineteenth-century British commentators. Davenport's *Apology*, for instance, says, "The death of this his beloved partner was indeed a heart-rending calamity for him. For twenty years she had been his counselor and supporter, and now his soul and his hearth had become desolate."[68]

Several life transitions happen in the wake of Khadija's and Abu Talib's deaths. Most significant for early biographers is the emigration from Mecca to Medina. Yet it is difficult to parse the relationship between narrative transitions and life transitions: the story has been told so often with these events connected that they seem causally linked, even though the emigration happened two or three years after these deaths. The other transition that concerns us here is Muhammad's remarriages, which happened more quickly.

The narrative link between Khadija's death and Muhammad's remarriages, specifically those to Aisha and Sawda, is also ancient. The story, based on a *hadith* account, appears in early works. This conjunction was used by hostile biographers—Humphrey Prideaux, for example, in a passage that many copied. Haykal's version owes at least as much to Prideaux's account, filtered through later authors, as it does to that of Ibn Hisham.

Prideaux frames the remarriages to make a moral point. He ignores the prophet's tender feelings and focuses instead on his calculations and plotting:

> And now *Cadigha*, his Wife, being dead, after she had lived Two and twenty Years with him; to strengthen himself the more, he took Two other Wives in her stead, *Ayesha*, the Daughter of *Abu Beker*; and *Sewda*, the Daughter of *Zama*; and a while after he added to them *Haphsa*, the Daughter of *Omar*; whereby making himself Son in law to Three of the Principal Men of his Party, he did by that Alliance the more firmly tie them to his Interest.[69]

In modern accounts, Muhammad's remarriages only reinforce Khadija's centrality. Traditional sources often mention the intervention of a matchmaker, who suggests Aisha if he wishes to marry a virgin and Sawda if he wishes a matron; Muhammad charges her to pursue both matches.[70] This focus on priority—most sources agree that the marriage to Aisha was first, though it was consummated only after a delay—and intervention tend to drop out of more recent accounts, which instead raise the question of motivations.[71] That polygamy itself needed justification never occurred to Muhammad's premodern Muslim biographers.

The Wives of Muhammad

Prideaux and earlier authors had seen improper motives for his marriage to Khadija. By the modern era, however, non-Muslim as well as Muslim authors had come to see that marriage as at least unobjectionable and, more often, admirable. As a result, those who would condemn Muhammad's marital conduct face a conundrum. Muhammad's conduct after Khadija's death gives a very different impression of Muhammad as a husband than does his conduct up to that point.[72] (As Carlyle put it, "He seems to have lived in a most affectionate, peaceable, wholesome way with his wedded benefactress; loving her truly, and her alone.")[73] How, then, to explain his behavior in taking many wives? Some Western authors have held, essentially, that power corrupts; Muhammad's changed marital conduct is of a piece with a larger change in his morals. He moves from ethical exemplar to bloodthirsty warrior. Among Muslim authors, the Iranian Ali Dashti, in his *Twenty-Three Years*, is an unusual example of this approach, though Dashti—who was part of a broader tradition of deliberately controversial writing—tempers his criticism by positing that Muhammad never really recovered from his grief at Khadija's death.[74] W. Montgomery Watt—whose *Muhammad at Mecca, Muhammad at Medina*, and abridged overview, *Muhammad: Prophet and Statesman*, are widely accepted as generally reliable accounts in the usual mode—hypothesizes that after the loss of "his faithful wife and helpmate Khadījah," Muhammad was compelled "to be more self-reliant, and that may have been necessary for the ultimate success of the religious movement." Watt speculates that even though he remarried, it was less for "spiritual companionship" than for political reasons; "there are signs that deepening religious experiences were taking the place of human companionship."[75] For Watt, just as it was for Siddiqui, Jalbani, and many others, the marriage to Khadija was exceptional, emotionally and spiritually supportive, and companionate. Would Khadija's faithful and devoted husband have taken a dozen wives in a decade? (An American doctor writing shortly before World War I opined, in his work on "the lives of three great epileptics," that Muhammad's "veering from the monogamous ideal" resulted from "the setting in . . . of premature mental decay.")[76]

The centrality of Muhammad's multiple marriages to critical biographies led to a reactive focus on refuting criticisms. Prideaux had used Muhammad's marriages as an illustration of the role of (blameworthy) ambition and political interest in his actions and, thus, as part of a broader condemnation of his imposture, fraud, and general degeneracy.[77] Muir's tone is different; he focuses on polygamy, divorce, and slavery as core problems with Islamic morality, judged not just as personal failings of the Prophet, who had fathered Ibrahim by the slave woman Mariya, but as characteristic ills of Muslim civilization, blame for which may be laid in part at Muhammad's door. As Arthur Wollaston, also a British colonial official, echoes, after Khadija's death and Muhammad's remarriages, "henceforward polygamy became an institution in the Muslim world, hallowed as the custom thus was by the example of their Prophet who, it should be kept in mind, up to this period had limited himself to a single wife."[78]

Muslim authors took up the pen in response. Although some, like Ameer Ali, chose to address slavery, most allowed that charge to pass largely in silence. Often there was a tacit shift in the way Muhammad's slaves were referred to—Mariya becomes a wife—or an occasional pugnacious remark. But what stood out for Muslim apologists was by and large polygamy, and they devoted themselves to explaining Muhammad's multiple marriages. (Only in the middle of the twentieth century did concern about polygamy begin to be overshadowed by concern about Aisha's age.)

It was not only the increased entanglement of pious biography with scholarly, popular, and polemical Western writing about Muhammad that led to an increased focus on polygamy. Questions about marriage were part of larger ongoing debates in societies such as India and Egypt, as well as in European nations. Religious thinkers, including Muhammad 'Abduh in Egypt, were formulating opposition to polygamy in religious terms at the same time legislatures were deciding about Muslim women's access to divorce and minimum marriage ages. Although legal reforms to limit polygamy were ultimately unsuccessful in most Muslim-majority societies during the first half of the twentieth century, there were vocal critics of the practice, both male and female. It is one thing, though, to suggest that a practice has no place in a modern Muslim society, that its costs outweigh its benefits; it is quite another to attach any opprobrium to deeds of the Prophet. Thus, whatever broader concerns about polygamy Muslim authors may have had, when they discussed it in the context of Muhammad's life, they defended his actions.

Often, the reactive framing is explicit. Hafiz Ghulam Sarwar's 1961 biography, published in Lahore, contains an appendix on Muhammad's marriages bearing the subtitle "A Refutation of the Lying Accusations of European Writers." Siddiqui's Indian biography from 1969 includes a section entitled "Fabrication of the Orientalists," concerned with Muhammad's marriage to Zaynab.[79] An early example, also from the Indian subcontinent, is Syed M. H. Zaidi's 1935 *Mothers of the Faithful*, subtitled: *Being a Discourse on Polygamy with a Biographical Sketch of the Wives of Muhammad refuting the allegations of the non-Muslims against them and the Prophet himself.* Published in Calcutta the same year as Haykal's *Life*, it shares its preoccupation with perceived Western attacks. Zaidi's preface details two intended audiences, the second of which is Muslim women, whom he hopes to inspire with the life stories of the prophet's wives. His first aim, however, is "to explain to the non-Muslims, especially the European Christians, the circumstances connected with Muhammad's numerous spousals [*sic*] after the death of his first wife, the noble Khadija."[80] It is not just Muhammad's polygamy that is of interest, but specifically his polygamy *after* Khadija's death. His monogamous marriage to her serves as Exhibit A for the defense.

Although formulated as a response to outside criticism, the "allegations of the non-Muslims" have become troubling to Muslims as well. Zaidi's "European Christians" allow him to address justifications for Muhammad's marriages to Muslim readers without acknowledging that Muslims may wonder about the prophet's actions. By positing the non-Muslim addressee when making apologetic arguments, authors like Zaidi externalize their own anxieties. These anxieties, whatever their origin, testify to new Muslim sensibilities.

In Zaidi's book, polygamy takes center stage. More than anything else about Muhammad's marriages, their sheer number requires explanation or refutation: "circumstances" serve to "explain" (and perhaps excuse) his conduct. The information Zaidi gives has long since become predictable: Western criticisms are unjust and unfounded; Muhammad married repeatedly to protect vulnerable widows and strengthen alliances. As S. M. Abbasi puts it, "The accusation that he was a licentious man because he married so many wives is absolutely false and mischievous. His marriages were all forced upon him, by circumstances. . . . In every case of such marriage . . . it was a personal sacrifice on the part of the Holy Prophet to have contracted the marriage, or the circumstances obliged him to do so."[81]

Zaidi's book straddles genres: it is a polemical engagement with Western literature and a collective biography of the Prophet's wives. It is this engagement with critics that compels extensive attention to Zaynab, ex-wife of Muhammad's (ex-)son Zayd.[82] This marriage has been the focus of a good deal of contention over the centuries; Watt, writing in 1961, could still call this "the most controversial of all Muḥammad's marriages."[83] Siddiqui makes the claim, "So far as the fanciful stories and calumnies of the Orientalists are concerned, we can only say that these are so absurd that any one having even a grain of sense in him would unhesitatingly reject them as mere fabrications." In particular, he singles out "Muir and so many others like him," who repeat the story of Muhammad beguiled by a glimpse of a disheveled Zaynab. There is, he writes, "absolutely no truth in these stories which have been fabricated in this connection."[84] Siddiqui seems to be unaware that these stories, rather than being invented by Orientalists, appear in Arab sources, where they are treated with varying degrees of acceptance and endorsement by compilers.[85] He proposes a somewhat novel rationale for Muhammad's marriage to Zaynab: "to give a fatal blow to the distinctions of high birth."[86] Zayd was a freed slave, and Zaynab, an aristocrat. On their divorce, Siddiqui writes, "Muhammad (peace be upon him) was generous enough to marry her himself and thus retrieved for her family lost prestige and also removed the false conception that the divorce of a woman at the hand of a freed slave ever degraded her position."[87] Most importantly, in a rationale also described by other authors, "the real objective behind this marriage was to bury forever the un-Islamic custom of adoptive kinship which had taken a deep root in the minds of the people. As the Holy Prophet was the last link in the golden chain of prophethood, he was required to purge human society of all those customs and superstitions which ran counter to the canons of *Islam*."[88] Aisha 'Abd al-Rahman, however, sees Muhammad's attraction to Zaynab as reliably reported by Tabari and considers it "proof of his humanity" that "his heart went out to Zaynab."[89]

Apologetics and Mainstream Writing

The more frequent arguments, however, were not specific to this marriage, nor did they revolve around the undoing of deleterious custom. Muhammad's multiple marriages were usually explained as creating alliances or caring for vulnerable widows. Custom, too, could also be an exculpating argument—Sale saw it as a good enough reason for Muhammad's entanglements. So did George Bush.

Of course, not everyone was content to skip lightly over his many marriages. Departing from the incident of Muhammad's marriages to Aisha and Sawda, American Harvey Newcomb's *The False Prophet* (1844)—written as a dialogue between a mother and her children, and drawing heavily from Bush—leads into a discussion of Christianity's superior sexual ethic: "Christianity," the mother tells her daughter, "is the only religion in the world, which does not allow men to have more than one wife." The daughter declares: "Oh how unnatural . . . I think it must destroy the peace and happiness of families." Through a rhetorical sleight, something defined as universal among non-Christians is nonetheless stigmatized as unnatural; it follows, then, that only Christianity accords with human nature. Polygamy's "effects upon society . . . have always been debasing. It has done more, perhaps than any other custom, to degrade the female character. . . . And whatever debases female character injures the whole face of society. Yet, this odious practice prevails throughout the whole heathen world."[90] After a pause, during which her daughter explains that she is weeping because "I was thinking what we owe to the Lord Jesus, and how ungrateful I have been to him for the benefits he has purchased for me with his own blood," the mother continues:

> Among the heathen, females are generally degraded almost
> to the condition of slaves. . . . In some places, their condition
> is so wretched that life is considered a burden; and parents
> often destroy their female children, to save them from the mis-
> eries of life. Among the Mohammedans, women are not al-
> lowed to appear in public. Some of their great men have many
> wives. They keep them shut up in a kind of prison, which they
> call *harems*. These women are subject to the will of their lordly
> master; and if he is displeased with them he has power to cut
> off their heads! In India, when a man died, they used to make
> a great pile of dry wood, and put his dead body upon it, and
> bind all his wives and lay them by his side, and then set the
> wood on fire and burn them all together.[91]

Newcomb's anti-Muslim tract wanders fairly far from the specific focus on Muhammad's biographical material; his polygamy is an entrée into the larger problem of polygamy, which segues into the degraded status of heathen women more generally. Bush, from whom Newcomb draws much of his narrative and some of his language, is more sanguine about one element of Muhammad's conduct, and does not blame him for "the mere circumstance of multiplying his wives," since "a heathen people cannot be fairly judged by the rules of Christian morality."[92] A universalist model, in which all are judged according to the same standard, exists in tension here with a relativist standard, which, though it may save heathens from particular sorts of blame, nonetheless does so by viewing them as insufficiently advanced morally. Both Bush and Newcomb, however, draw the line in religious terms: heathen versus Christian. Yet Bush's absolution lays the groundwork for a heavier charge of failing to *observe those rules of morality which he himself laid down, and which he enforced upon others by such terrible sanctions.*"[93] That is, "under the pretence of a special revelation, dispensing him from the laws imposed by his own religion, had the female sex abandoned without reserve to his desires."[94] He titillates but refuses to provide particulars of "how completely the prophet's imposture was made an engine for promoting the gratification of sensual passion," citing the requirements of "decorum."[95]

Monogamy and Polygamy

For most of the twentieth century, monogamy and polygamy were the poles that defined Muhammad's marital conduct and therefore character. His monogamous and happy companionate marriage to Khadija, now conventional wisdom, was to be understood as the norm for his conduct. His other marriages were attributed to pity, protection, or politics.

In traditional accounts, Muhammad's wives appear from time to time throughout the narrative. He gets married to one after a battle, or an interpersonal crisis prompted by illness, jealousy, or some external event occurs and is documented in its chronological place. Anecdotes likewise appear in other types of works. Stories about intra-household conflict illuminate the revelation of particular verses of the Qur'an, some of which might otherwise remain opaque. *Hadith* accounts detail mundane incidents with legal implications. Though quite a few works have a chapter or section that lists Muhammad's wives and provides some biographical detail, they are typically instead woven into the narrative fabric.

As Muslim biography became increasingly responsive to Western critique, Muhammad's marriages become a worthy topic of discussion in and of themselves. Muir talks about his marriages along the way, but Dermenghem includes a separate chapter on "The Harem." Haykal follows, with a chapter on "The Prophet's Wives" and another on "Ibrāhīm and the Wives of Muhammad." Ameer Ali devotes an extensive section to addressing criticisms of Muhammad's marriages, and Ahmad Khan talks about polygamy and divorce at length when weighing the impact of Islam on human society.

Prior to the last two centuries, biographers did not concern themselves with *justifying* Muhammad's marriages—why defend something no one found objectionable?—but they did sometimes report motivations, implicitly or explicitly. Sometimes, for instance, Muhammad was struck by a woman's beauty. At other times, there was speculation about practical motives: perhaps his marriage to Sawda made sense in part since he was a widower with four daughters and she was an older woman with experience,[96] or his marriage to Umm Habiba might have been to strengthen an alliance with her father, his Meccan antagonist Abu Sufyan.

The explanation that many marriages took place for the forging or strengthening of alliances with staunch supporters and former antagonists makes perfect sense. We can see the extent to which leadership was a family matter if we recall that among the first four men to lead the community after Muhammad's death—those the Sunnis retrospectively came to recognize as rightly guided caliphs—the first two, Abu Bakr and Umar, were Muhammad's fathers-in-law (he was married to their daughters, Aisha and Hafsa, respectively); the second two, Uthman and Ali, were his sons-in-law. Family ties matter even more for the Shi'a, who recognize Ali—also Muhammad's paternal cousin and, with Muhammad and Khadija's daughter Fatima, progenitor of Muhammad's only surviving descendants—as Muhammad's legitimate successor. When reading these accounts, it is vital to recall that the stories about Muhammad's wives reported by early biographers and *hadith* compilers were told by those who had a stake in enhancing or denigrating the reputations of the wives and their relatives—and the factions with which they were associated—in the aftermath of Muhammad's death and the ensuing contests over political leadership of the community. These reports were not transparent reflections of fact but narratives aimed at conveying particular notions about which women were trustworthy or favored. (As historian Chase Robinson observes, "Whereas late antique Christians quarreled about Christology, Muslims quarreled about the conduct of seventh-century Muslims as it was remembered and recorded in history.")[97]

These texts, however, have been plundered by modern biographers with different agendas. Ignoring the complex structures and motivations of those who wrote those early texts, modern writers treat them as straightforward storehouses of data that are either reliable or unreliable. Stories about the wives that may have been told for particular reasons now become understood in different ways.

Although lists of wives frequently appear as supplements to texts (as do lists of battles in which Muhammad participated, names of his horses, and the like), premodern authors did not concern themselves with how Muhammad treated women as a class, his wives as a group, or his female Companions. When they do play up one or another episode, or praise one wife over and against another, the point might be competition between factions (or a hermeneutical motive relating to explicating the Qur'anic text), not any kind of broader claim about gender or a desire to show anything particular about women's status. In fact, women as a collectivity, defined by their gender, seldom appears in the early biographies. Modern non-Muslim biographies often seek to derive something about Muhammad's character from how he related to women, as well as how his relations with his wives might have influenced his views on women more generally. Apologetic Muslim biographies illustrate the shift even more clearly, as they seek to define and defend his noble character by showing how he was enlightened in his relationships with his wives: he had impeccable motives for marrying them, he treated them with scrupulous fairness when allocating his time, he never hit them or spoke harshly, and he shared household chores. Again, apart from the concern with justifying his polygamy, the other elements are present in premodern biographies as well, but there they illustrate other things: his status as legal exemplar, his gentle manner, his humility, his concern for the vulnerable.

The defensive and reactive treatment of Muhammad's polygamy is typified in *The Holy Prophet Mohammad: The Commander of the Faithful* by Muhammad Ali-Al-Haj Salmin, written in the 1930s. In the section on "The Home Life of the Prophet," Salmin writes, "A charge, that he practiced polygamy and allowed his followers the same, is levelled against him; but it can easily be explained." Salmin, using the passive voice and legalistic phrasing, attributes to unnamed accusers the "charge . . . levelled against him."[98] Salmin mounts his defense: "This is a fact that he contracted these marriages due to political circumstances and with a higher humanitarian consideration in view to save the honour of the women of those followers who laid their lives in sacrifice in the cause of Islam. That the motive of sensuality had nothing to do with these marriages, will be clear enough to any one who studies his private life dispassionately."[99] These sentences mix appeals to rationality ("fact," "clear," "studies," "dispassionately") with references to sentiments both praiseworthy and not ("humanitarian," "honour," "sacrifice," "sensuality"). He goes on to describe the Prophet's character as it relates to his treatment of his wives: "the Prophet was the model of a husband and householder, being courteous, kind and just to all of them, often helping them in their household duties." Note that in Salmin's presentation, the household work properly belongs to the wives.[100]

Ghulam Malik (1996) sounds the same broadly apologetic note, although with somewhat less attention to lust and a slightly less defensive tone. He, too, appeals to the need to correct improper views: "One of the most misunderstood aspects of the Prophet Muhammad's life has been the plurality of his marriages. Before passing any superficial judgment, it is necessary to delve into the socio-economic condition and political situation of Arabia in general, and particularly of the Muslim community, for a careful study of his marriages."[101] In a move adopted by both European apologists and essayists like Ahmad Khan and Ameer Ali, Malik notes that Islam does not link celibacy and piety and, further, that Old Testament prophets "practice[ed] polygyny without the slightest detriment to their character or deviation from fulfilling their divinely ordained missions."[102] He then moves on to the defense of Muhammad's premarital chastity, as mentioned previously, and turns to his marriage to Khadija.

Though Khadija herself was wealthy, widows were typically destitute, making Muhammad's marriages charitable. (This desire to emphasize Muhammad's role in protecting the downtrodden leads some authors to a palpable contradiction, stressing Khadija's wealth and independence but in the next breath explaining how women were chattels before the coming of Islam.[103]) Vulnerable widows were simply an extreme instance of female need for protection. Malik writes: "Women had not rights or economic security" but depended on their husbands or fathers.[104] In the first Muslim community, "the widows and orphans of the small Muslim community posted serious problems." This made polygamy "a necessity in Muslim society at that time."

Protection was joined by political motives. Thus, Malik concludes, "Objectively speaking, the Prophet Muhammad's marriages were motivated mainly by economic and political factors to the benefit of his Call and the community."[105] He quotes Watt to support his claim: "Doubtless, Muhammad's own marriages and those of his close companions as well were contracted to improve relations with his opponents and consolidate his political power."[106] This explanation is typical of much twentieth-century biography: pragmatic political justifications for plural marriages are viewed as positive. British Muslim author Ziauddin Sardar's 2012 biography emphasizes the social function of Muhammad's marriages: "Marriage is the lubricant of a society based on kinship. . . . It should not surprise us, then, that most of Muhammad's marriages had a political context." This is the case both for marriages, such as those to Aisha and Hafsa, that "constituted the glue that bound his companions to Muhammad" and for marriages that "cemented tribal alliances or served as a rationale for reconciliation."[107] Indeed, the translators of the volume of Tabari's history that deals with the first years after the migration to Medina devote a portion of the foreword to "The Marriage with 'Ā'ishah," in which they declare, "All Muḥammad's marriages and those he arranged for his daughters were made for political reasons."[108]

Author after author, Muslim and non-Muslim, insists that Muhammad's motives were political and therefore salutary rather than lustful and therefore deplorable. For earlier critics, though, political motives for marriage proved despicable scheming. Marrying women to promote alliances revealed a calculating disposition: Muhammad crafted a fraudulent persona to bolster his fraudulent religion. Ambition might not be worse than lustfulness, but neither was it a vast improvement. In their haste to defend Muhammad from charges of debauchery, writers argue that he was not attracted to these women—or, if he was, it was a happy bonus to be passed over as swiftly as possible. Few acknowledge his genuine attraction to several women. If they do, it is typically to downplay it and to stress the other factors, political or charitable, promoting his marriages.[109] For example, of Juwayriyya, Jewish captive from the Banu Mustaliq, Thompson writes, "Although Juwayriyya was young and beautiful and of noble lineage, the Prophet Muhammad was thinking of how to save her and all her tribe from an ignoble fate."[110] It is striking how frequently Muslim authors and sympathetic non-Muslim authors writing since the middle of the twentieth century overlap on these points. Dashti is virtually alone, in his *Twenty-Three Years,* when he suggests that Muhammad's multiple marriages signal "human weakness."[111]

Chastity and Caretaking

Muhammad's marriage to Khadija has always been worthy of note, though not always for the same reasons. Ibn Ishaq saw the marriage as confirming Muhammad's noble qualities and implicitly honoring the mother of his children and the resulting progeny, all of whom descend through Khadija. For more recent authors, she represents a companionate and monogamous marriage. Muhammad's monogamy with Khadija was already noteworthy for Ibn Hisham, who declares, "She was the first woman the Messenger of God married and he did not take another wife until she died."[112] But in this view, it proved her specialness, not Muhammad's continence. In contrast, after centuries of European criticisms of Muhammad's lustfulness, in modern apologetic works Muhammad's premarital chastity and longtime marital fidelity to Khadija serve as proof that he was not, as one author puts it, "sex-minded."[113]

In works from the Indian subcontinent from the late nineteenth century into the twenty-first century, authors tend to accept the model of the world in which climactic conditions lead to early puberty and strong desire. Thus, Muhammad's chastity—he "spent his 25 years like an angel"—is especially notable, given both the loose morals of pagan Meccan society and the fact that he lived in "tropical Arabia where puberty comes early."[114] Similarly, Muhammad Ali's *Muhammad the Prophet*—first published in 1924, revised half a century later, and by 1993 in its seventh edition—invokes the climate of Arabia to emphasize Muhammad's restraint and chastity: "If he had not been a complete master of his passions, he could not have led, up to the age of twenty-five, the exceptionally chaste and pure life . . . in a hot country like Arabia where development must necessarily take place early and passions are generally stronger."[115] Ali—who led the Lahore branch of the Ahmadiyya—notes that "even according to Muir," Muslim sources agree that Muhammad displayed rare "'modesty of deportment and purity of manners.'"[116] Ali's views about Muhammad's marital and sexual life are echoed by those who disagreed with the Ahmadi viewpoint on other religious issues. For instance, Ghulam Malik similarly defends Muhammad's sexual honor: he "had no romance in his life" and "preserved his chastity at a time when the Arab society was enmeshed in immorality." In fact, he improbably asserts that "the first time Muhammad came into contact with a female outside his family was with Khadijah" when he was twenty-five: "And soon they got married."[117]

Ali is concerned generally with polygamy: he argues that Muhammad's heart was "free . . . of all base and sensual thoughts" and ascribes his multiple marriages after Khadija largely to a desire to protect widows.[118] This protection does not consist merely or even primarily in providing the women food and shelter but in ensuring their chastity through satisfaction of their sexual needs, since "the statesman who neglects sex requirements leads society to moral corruption, ending ultimately in the ruin of the whole nation."[119] Polygamy was necessary so that sexually deprived widows would not cause social chaos. (Siddiqui likewise attributes Muhammad's marriages to "the feeling of compassion for the widows of his faithful followers" but stresses not their sexual needs but that "they were bereft of the love and care of their husbands.")[120] Both the permission for polygamy in general and the Prophet's personal practice emerged from the need to keep widows chaste. Ali goes further to convince his readers that the Prophet's motives were pure: "Nearly all of his wives were widows. Where self-indulgence is the motive, the choice does not fall on widows." Muhammad could have had virgins had he wanted them; there was "no dearth of virgins," and it "would have been an enviable privilege for any Muslim to be father-in-law of the Holy Prophet."[121] Ali assumes that fathers would make decisions about marrying off their daughters, placing the honor not on the wives but on their fathers. A 1994 Pakistani biography echoes this argument: "All his companions, male and female, had been so devoted to him that if he wanted to marry only virgin girls he could have done it and if he wished to keep any girl with him for a couple months for enjoyment, there was none to object him, but he never did so."[122]

So, Muhammad's "object was a far nobler one" than self-indulgence: "the protection of the widows of his friends" and "the moral safety of the Muslim society situated as it then was."[123] Additionally, in the cases of Juwayriyya and Safiyya, "widow of a Jewish chieftain," Ali cites "certain political reasons" for the marriages: "The Holy Prophet wanted to conciliate both tribes and that was the only motive in these marriages."[124] Zaynab's marriage was a special case, since she was Muhammad's cousin, originally "offered in marriage to the Holy Prophet by her brother" when she arrived at majority.[125] Muhammad "wedded her to Zaid, a slave whom he himself had freed"—note that nothing is said of their filial/parental tie, only that Zaid was "deeply attached to him." The marriage ultimately failed, but Muhammad did not want the stigma of divorce to taint her, especially since she was superior in social status to her ex-husband. Again, he felt it necessary to act personally:

> By this act, to which he was morally bound because the lady had been at first offered in marriage to him, he elevated the

whole class of divorced women who would otherwise suffer life-long humiliation in society. If he had any desire of self-gratification or if he had any passion for the lady, he would not have refused her when she was offered to him as a virgin. Refusal of her hand in the first instance, and taking her in marriage when being divorced she was lowered in general estimation, shows conclusively that his motive in this marriage was anything but self-gratification.[126]

These authors assume that men make decisions and "offer" their virgin female kin—daughters or sisters—in marriage, as Zaynab's brother had done and as fathers of virgins would have done out of a desire to make the Prophet their son-in-law. Ali also presumes that female inexperience is crucial to male desire and satisfaction: "Lust must needs have virginity for its gratification."[127] Widows and divorcees, who have had husbands before, must be protected and given an outlet for their own sexual desires in order to prevent rampant immorality. However, Ali assumes that they are not desirable in and of themselves. Zaynab's marriage, which gets special attention because of the "calumny" attached to it, is explained as aiming at removing the stigma surrounding divorce; nothing is said about Zayd's ambiguous kinship, the issue that preoccupied others.

Ali sums up his defense of Muhammad thus: "By disposition he was not inclined to polygamy, living a celibate life of unexampled purity up to twenty-five years and a married life of a monogamous husband up to fifty-four, but when duty called him to take more women under his shelter, he answered the call of duty."[128] Nasr offers a similar litany in *Muhammad: Man of God*, insisting that "the multiple marriages of the Blessed Prophet . . . were certainly not for sensual pleasure. He did not marry until he was twenty-five and then during all the years when the sexual passions are strongest in the male, he lived with one wife who was fifteen years older than he."[129] Muhammad's "attitude toward sexuality," which he views as "the basis of the Islamic attitude in this domain," must be discussed because "so much criticism has been made of it by Western writers."[130] His marriages were for political and social reasons: "If the Blessed Prophet had contracted marriages just for sensual pleasure, as so many adverse Western biographers have written, surely he would have married many women when he himself was young and at the prime of manhood and also chosen all of his wives from among young women. But a study of his life reveals very different facts."[131] Khadija's age renders her less a proper object of "sensual pleasure": Nasr alludes twice to her age in this passage as evidence that Muhammad was not motivated by passion in his marriages.

These passages draw their structure and main points from Godfrey Higgins's 1829 *Apology*. Ameer Ali quoted him on a number of points, including the relative maturation rates of men and women in hot climes. Higgins seems to have originated the argument based on the fact that when Muhammad married Khadija, it was at "the very time of life when youthful passion may be supposed to be at its height; and though, by the laws of his country, he was entitled to have a plurality of wives, he neglected to avail himself of this permission, and continued faithful to her as long as she lived." He goes on to criticize those who see his behavior as resulting merely from "gratitude to his kindest friend, the maker of his fortune."[132]

Through quotation in Ameer Ali's influential work, arguments by a British non-Muslim survive to be used two centuries later by Muslim apologists in works read by Muslims, though ostensibly directed toward refuting Western critics. Repeatedly, in works written by Muslims for Muslims, authors declare their aim to "answer allegations" of misconduct. Abbasi's prefatory words describing his objectives are typical: "The first and the foremost is to present the account of the lives of the Holy family objectively and secondly to rebut the false and malicious but sustained propaganda of the Western writers against Islam, its Holy Prophet (S.A.W.) and his family members."[133]

These rebuttals devote disproportionate attention to Khadija, not just in number of pages but in terms of psychic centrality.[134] Malik says it "would not be incorrect" to call their union "a love marriage between a wealthy widow and a poor young man." Nasr refers to this marriage as "perfect": it was "a marriage which was so complete and in a sense absolute that the Blessed Prophet did not marry another wife as long as Khadījah was alive. This fact is particularly important since she was fifteen years older than he and polygamy was a very common practice in Arabian, as in most other parts of the world, at that time."[135] For Karen Armstrong, "She had been Muhammad's closest companion, and nobody— not even Abu Bakr or the fervent 'Umar—would ever be able to provide Muhammad with the same intimate support."[136] Here and elsewhere, biographers enumerate Khadija's virtues but discount her attractiveness. Both her age and her nonvirgin status diminish her appeal for these mostly South Asian authors. Abbasi writes, for instance, of him marrying "a woman who is 15 years senior to him and has been widowed twice before."[137] Muhammad's faithfulness despite Khadija's diminished attractiveness proves that he was not motivated by lust.

Motives, of course, are notoriously tricky things. In fictionalization common to recent biographies, some authors imagine Khadija's feelings too. American convert Yahiya Emerick attributes to her both love ("she was falling deeper and deeper in love with him") and self-doubt: Would Muhammad reject her overtures? New-age guru Deepak Chopra envisions her inner monologues, which reveal Khadija as insecure, including about her sexual appeal.[138] Yet her outstanding qualities cannot pass unremarked. Emerick shifts between emphasizing Khadija's nobility and wealth and por-traying Muhammad as having the upper hand: "Although Khadi-jah was neither young nor a virgin, which were essential traits in a wife in pre-Islamic Arabia, Muhammad treated her as his loving life-partner from the start."[139] Emerick makes the reader feel that Muhammad was quite forbearing in failing to exercise his privi-leges to marry again. In contrast, early biographies stress that Mu-hammad, despite his moral excellence, was lucky to make such an advantageous alliance: "Khadījah was then the most distinguished of the Quraysh women in lineage, the most highly honored, and the wealthiest," Tabari reports, "and all the men of her tribe would have been eager to accept this proposal had it been made to them."[140]

In something of a contrast to Khadija's exalted status, both Emerick and Nasr—like many other authors—portray women's existence in pre-Islamic Arabia as downtrodden.[141] In a similar vein, Ameer Ali paints a deplorable picture of the "condition" of women in ancient India; already bad "during that vague and mythic period which passes under the name of the Vedic age," it "arrived at the depth of degradation under Brahmanic domination."[142] Since the nineteenth century, Muslim apologists tout the improvement to women's status brought about by Islam: "All know that before his prophethood the condition of women was a very pitiable one. She was the most degraded of Allah's creations, but the Holy Prophet raised her high, and set her up on a pedestal of her own high and sweet queendom."[143] But also striking is the way in which Muslim apologists adopt the condescending attitude of Western scholars toward Khadija, insisting on their happy companionate marriage, or her status as a trusting and comforting helpmate, while simultaneously downplaying her attractiveness—something that the early sources do not do. Premodern Muslim sources admittedly sometimes celebrate the attractions of young and especially virginal females; one could cite numerous examples, including references to Aisha. What is new is the application of this valuation to Khadija and the implicit view that because she was older and a widow—here, the acceptance of her age as given in the early biographies as literal rather than symbolic bolsters the idea that she was old and had lost her charms—it would have been charitable for Muhammad to marry her.[144]

A Different Perspective

Aloys Sprenger noted that "the amorous disposition of the messenger of God is considered as a virtue by most of his followers."[145] This was much more the case in 1850, when he was writing, than in 1950, when the discourse of politics, pity, and protection had taken hold. Yet there were exceptions to the reach of this delibidinizing discourse, which, in any case, was more prevalent in South Asia than in Egypt.

Pulitzer Prize winner Naguib Mahfouz's allegorical novelization *Children of the Alley* retells Abrahamic history, concluding with a figure named Qassem, who represents Muhammad.[146] Like his modernist countrymen, Mahfouz immersed himself in early Muslim sources and transmuted them into something quite distinctive. As a novelist, Mahfouz was more interested in truth than in fact. But though his presentation of Qassem/ Muhammad is in keeping with the classical tradition's celebration of Muhammad's sexual prowess—in contrast to Haykal's ambivalence, wavering between defensiveness and denial—in other respects he is thoroughly modern. Some modern Egyptian authors including 'Abd al-Rahman had been matter-of-fact about the Prophet's (post-Khadija) penchant for women, but Mahfouz's reference to earlier "hot-blooded adventures in the desert with their blind, burning hunger and their sad, transient satisfaction" are explicitly denied by other authors, who emphasize Muhammad's premarital chastity. But if Mahfouz posits premarital "adventures," he also makes Khadija loom disproportionately large—first as presence, then as absence. This is manifestly not the case in *hadith* collections, works of exegesis, or premodern Muslim biographies, though it is typical for modern accounts of Muhammad's life.[147] Indeed, almost all modern accounts repeat an anecdote in which Aisha is jealous of Khadija's memory and Muhammad chastises her, enumerating Khadija's virtues.[148]

Mahfouz goes on to write erotically of the connection between Qassem and the Aisha figure, who becomes the first of his wives after Qamar, the Khadija figure. Most other Muslim authors downplay love and desire in Muhammad's later marriages, even as they emphasize his model behavior toward his wives. Highlighting his charitable and political motives for these marriages, authors depict Khadija as special. He was a good husband to his other wives, but those marriages were not the ideal "example of married life" that his monogamous marriage to Khadija was. Thus, Golam Choudhury's praise, written in the 1990s:

The Prophet was a model of good family life. As a husband, he had a unique relationship with his first wife, Khadijah, and his subsequent marriages after the death of his first wife were based on a number of considerations. As an ideal husband, Muhammad had set a good example of married life and showed how the relationship between a husband and wife should be based on the injunctions of the Qur'an: on the basis of tenderest devotion on both sides and on mutual love and attachment.[149]

Chapter 5

Mother of the Faithful

Muhammad grieved Khadija deeply, but he did not remain unmarried for long. A matchmaker approached him and offered to find him a new wife. Did he want a woman who had been previously married or one who never had? She had in mind Sawda, fairly recently widowed, or Aisha, daughter of his intimate friend and early convert Abu Bakr. He asked her to arrange matches with both of them. Sawda agreed, and that marriage took place immediately. Aisha's situation was more complicated. Securing her release from an earlier betrothal was easy; her intended's family had not become Muslim and was glad to back out. A contract was then made between Muhammad and Abu Bakr, but Aisha remained with her family. Two or three years later, after the migration to Medina, the marriage was consummated and Aisha moved into quarters attached to the mosque, next to Sawda's apartment. By most accounts, she was then nine years old.

If Khadija represents the positive role model and the linchpin of Muhammad's maturation as a man and a prophet in Mecca, Aisha is the wife whose presence most colors his Medinan years and whose story continues to unfold after Muhammad's death. She was a vital, if sometimes problematic, figure for the construction of Sunni orthodoxy, a major reporter of prophetic traditions, and a jurist of some note. Her chastity was impugned during her lifetime and her participation in an intra-Muslim civil war put her at the center of debates over women's public roles. Humphrey Prideaux sees the political motivations behind their marriage as evidence of Muhammad's warped morality. For many nineteenth-century Christian authors, Aisha's status as a polygamous wife illustrated Muslim depravity. Since the middle of the twentieth century, it is Aisha's age that demands explanation, justification, or refutation. Tracking the attention to her age over the course of the last two centuries reveals a tension between models that treat Muslims as irreducibly different and irredeemably evil or as simply backwards and capable of reform—properly guided, of course.

The Muslim Textual Tradition

The two most trusted Sunni *hadith* compilations, those of Bukhari and Muslim, say that Aisha was six or seven at the time her marriage was contracted, and nine at consummation, as do Ibn Saʻd's sources. Ibn Hisham says nine or ten: "The Messenger of God, may God's blessings and peace be upon him, married Aisha daughter of Abu Bakr the Righteous in Mecca when she was a girl of seven years and he consummated the marriage with her in Medina when she was a girl of nine or ten years. The Messenger of God, may God's blessings and peace be upon him, did not marry a virgin other than her."[1]

Tabari provides some information on the ages of Muhammad's wives, including Aisha, as part of the biographical supplement to his massive history, in which ages are sometimes relevant but rarely important.[2] He expends a good deal more energy clarifying the women's genealogies and other facts about their lives, as well as the circumstances of their alliances with the Prophet. Still, it can be helpful to see how unusual Aisha is in this context. Only four entries mention age explicitly. Aisha was nine at consummation, which took place three years after the marriage and less than a year after the emigration. Umm Habiba, the daughter of Muhammad's Meccan antagonist Abu Sufyan, was "thirty-odd years old";[3] and Juwayriyya declares, "I was twenty years old when the Prophet married me." Safiyya, the youngest of those whose age Tabari gives, was "not even seventeen" or "just seventeen," according to her reported words "the night [she] entered the Prophet's room."[4] She was by that time once divorced and once widowed, the latter at Muslim hands. One can calculate rough ages at marriage for five other women from their birth or death dates; all were in their twenties or thirties. Aisha and possibly Khadija are the only wives whose ages have been the focus of any real interest. In both cases, any attempt to corroborate or refute specific figures is doomed to failure. Better to ask why the sources care. Given the generalized indifference to birth dates—even for the Prophet, let alone other key figures—the mention of ages must be significant, aimed at something other than mere informing.[5]

Early Muslims intent on recording Muhammad's life story paid attention to Aisha's age because she was a controversial figure. If biographers settled fairly rapidly on Khadija as a positive force in Muhammad's life, Aisha's presence was substantially more contentious. In a rivalry that may have given rise to later infighting—or that may have been written into the sources in the wake of that fighting—the dyad Aisha/Abu Bakr competed with the dyad Fatima/Ali for prestige and authority. In her magisterial study of the shifting treatment of Aisha over the centuries, the historian Denise Spellberg suggests that competition over status may have generated a need to affirm Aisha's youth and purity:

"All of these specific references to the bride's age reinforce 'A'isha's pre-menarcheal status and, implicitly, her virginity."[6] Insistence on her chastity is likely to have been prompted by other accounts that embroil her in scandal, such as the "affair of the necklace," during which she fell behind on an expedition in looking for a misplaced necklace, was brought back to the group by a young man, and was the subject of ugly rumors before a revelation exonerated her (in the Sunni version). Aisha's association with contests over succession to the caliphate made arguments over her excellence inevitable. Pointing to another passage in Tabari's *History* in which Aisha is said to have been born before the coming of Islam, Spellberg says she might have been twelve or thirteen at the time of marriage (and older at its consummation).[7] One explanation as to why a younger age would be preferable: It would mean that she was born into a Muslim household. Thus, insisting on her youth might prove her *religious* purity over and above concern with her sexual purity.

Aisha's age preoccupied early Sunni scholars but generated no significant reflection by later Muslims. Nor did medieval or early modern Christian polemicists care; they were bothered instead by Muhammad's general debauchery, as manifested in his polygamy, his followers' practice of sodomy, and—if they had to single out any—his marriage to Zaynab, which raised the specter of incest.

Prideaux viewed the marriage to Aisha as part of Muhammad's massive fraud: marrying Aisha as well as Sawda and Hafsa was part of a strategy to shore up alliances with their fathers.[8] Prideaux's account describes Muhammad's remarriages after Khadija's death. The link between Khadija's death and his remarriage to Sawda and Aisha (typically listed in that order in recent works) is ubiquitous.[9] Hafsa, whose marriage came somewhat later, is not usually listed in this series. Prideaux includes it because it provides further evidence for his claim that Muhammad was marrying to cultivate powerful allies, the better to perpetrate his imposture. Aisha's youth causes him no qualms: "*Ayesha* was then but six Years old, and therefore he did not bed her till two Years after, when she was full eight Years old. For it is usual in those hot Countries, as it is all *India* over, which is in the same *Clime* with *Arabia*, for Women to be ripe for Marriage at that Age, and also bear Children the Year following."[10]

Two American authors writing a century and a half later draw from this passage extensively to quite different effect. George Bush's discussion of the marriages is separate from that of Aisha's age and disconnected from his discussion of Muhammad's marriage to Khadija.[11] He sums up the situation in language clearly adapted from Prideaux: "in order to strengthen his interest in Mecca, he married Ayesha, the daughter of Abubeker, and shortly after Sawda, the daughter of Zama. By thus becoming the son-in-law of two of the principal men of his party he secured their patronage to his person and his cause."[12] Bush highlights Muhammad's political aims; Aisha's age and personal qualities hold no interest for him. He also omits Hafsa. This passage neither connects Muhammad's remarriages to Khadija's death nor mentions Muhammad's emotions. Aisha's age merits a brief remark only in the final full chapter of the work, which treats Muhammad's wives and concubines. Bush accepts climate's effect on female maturation: "Ayesha was married—such is the surprising physical precocity peculiar to an eastern climate—at the early age of nine; and survived her husband forty-eight years."[13]

Washington Irving takes a similar view of Aisha's age, though he expresses a concern alien to Prideaux or Bush—that of Muhammad's emotional needs:

> The family with Mahomet in Medina consisted of his recently wedded wife Sawda, and Fatima and Um Colthum, daughters of his late wife Cadijah. He had a heart prone to affection, and subject to female influence, but he had never entertained much love for Sawda; and though he always treated her with kindness, he felt the want of some one to supply the place of his deceased wife Cadijah. . . . He now turned his eyes upon his betrothed spouse Ayesha, the beautiful daughter of Abu Beker. Two years had elapsed since they were betrothed, and she had now attained her ninth year; an infantine age it would seem, though the female form is wonderfully precocious in the quickening climates of the east.[14]

Irving adds exotic details of their simple "nuptials": a "wedding supper" of milk and "twelve okk of silver" for the bride's dowry. He acknowledges possible political motivations ("Perhaps he sought, by this alliance, to grapple Abu Beker still more strongly to his side") but notes Aisha's beauty (which Prideaux had said nothing about), calling her "a beautiful child" and noting that she was "chosen in the very blossom of her years."[15] John Davenport's *An Apology for Mohammed and the Koran* (1869) likewise highlights her appearance: "About two months after the death of Khadijah, Mohammed married Sawda, a widow, and nearly at the same time Ayesha, the young and beautiful daughter of his bosom friend Abu-Bekr, the principal object of this last union being to cement still more strongly their mutual attachment."[16] Although he structures his account of the marriages like Prideaux, where Prideaux sees a power play ("he did by that Alliance the more firmly tie them to his Interest"), Davenport adapts Muir's language about Abu Bakr ("an alliance mainly designed to cement the attachment of his bosom friend") to highlight the reciprocal nature of their friendship.[17]

Other authors were both more critical of Muhammad's marital conduct and less interested in titillating accounts of the precocious development of young girls in the *"Torrid Zone."*[18] But these authors still did not object to Aisha's age. Muir, not one to miss an opportunity to criticize Muhammad for any perceived moral lapses, notes the standard ages of six or seven in discussing what he calls a betrothal.[19] He refers to her as a "precocious bride" or a "precocious maiden."[20] What bothers him about the consummation of the marriage when she was ten or eleven is not her age but the polygamous nature of the union; since Sawda had been for three or four years Muhammad's only wife, his consummation of the marriage with Aisha moves him decisively away from Christianity: "The unity of his family was now broken, and never again restored."[21]

Arthur Wollaston—like Muir, engaged in British imperial work in India—objects to polygamy and laments Muhammad's departure from monogamous precepts but nonetheless gives a romanticized description of the marriage, which began with a betrothal when "Ayisha [was] a child of about six or seven years of age."[22] After the immigration to Medina, Muhammad "celebrated his nuptials with Ayisha, to whom, as before stated, he had now been affianced upwards of three years." Aisha is a somewhat troubling figure—she "had from the first possessed an inscrutable hold over the affections of her husband"—but their devotion was mutual: "Faithful to her charge, the youthful wife—she was at this time but twenty years of age—watched and tended the bedside of her aged lord and master; the affection of so young and beautiful a damsel for the aged and infirm Prophet was touching and pathetic. It was," he says, "the *romance* of Islam."[23] (In striking contrast, thirteenth-century Dominican friar Ramón Martí cites this "touching" scene of Muhammad dying with his head on Aisha's breast as further proof of his lack of holiness: "the death or end of Muḥammad was vile, unclean, and abominable. And such a death is in no way appropriate for a prophet or a messenger of God.")[24]

David Margoliouth, whose biography is strongly negative in tone about all aspects of Muhammad's life—in one commentator's words, "no other work in the world was such a compendium of lies and calumny"[25]—plays up the negative traits to which Wollaston alludes, describing Aisha pejoratively as a "blooming girl who claimed premiership in the harem" and a "pert minx."[26] Her scheming overshadows her youth: "from the time of her emergence from childhood till her death at the age of sixty-six, she exhibited a degree of ability and unscrupulousness which should earn her a place beside Agrippinas and Elizabeths of history."[27] Margoliouth's Aisha is no victimized child. When Margoliouth refers to the marriage as an "ill-assorted union" because it joined "a man of fifty-three to a child of nine," he dramatically declares that she was "dragged from her swing and her toys."[28] Still, it is likely that he was primarily objecting to the disparity itself. In his catechistic *The False Prophet,* Harvey Newcomb has his mouthpiece condemn the age difference between Muhammad and Khadija in similar terms: a marriage with such a significant age gap "is transgressing a law of propriety which is found in the nature of things."[29]

Other twentieth-century authors describe her childishness without becoming overwrought. Gladys Draycott's 1916 biography is unperturbed by Aisha's youth, referring elliptically to her age on three occasions: "Abu Bekr's small daughter," "a merry child," and "his girl-bride."[30] She mentions her vitality, her beauty, and Muhammad's preference for her over his other wives (apart, of course, from Khadija, whom he mourns). Even as late as the 1970s and 1980s, biographers mentioned Aisha's childish habits without extensive condemnation. Martin Lings is matter-of-fact about the spouses' discrepant ages. He uses the age of nine without hesitation, and mentions her dolls and playmates.[31] John Glubb, whose main claim to expertise was having lived among the Bedouin for decades, wrote a popular biography (*The Life and Times of Muhammad*) in 1970, and he includes a reference to the marriage to Aisha in discussing the migration and the construction of the mosque and housing for Muhammad's family: "She was nine years old, while the Apostle was fifty-three. When she was married she brought her toys with her to her room in the Apostle's house, where she used to sit playing with them on the floor. Until the end of his life, Aisha was to be the dearest of his wives."[32] Glubb attributes the marriage to customary practice, noting that girls were often given for first marriages between eight and ten. He also suggests that Muhammad "enjoyed the company of mature, sensible women rather than that of young girls."[33] He does not say how this relates to Muhammad's favoritism of Aisha. Glubb's mention of "the Apostle's house" is notable for its unusual presentation of Muhammad as householder, given others' insistence that Muhammad had no rooms of his own but took turns among his wives.[34]

Muir and others took note of Aisha's youth in part because youthful female sexuality was on many people's minds. European and American attitudes were undoubtedly conditioned by broader portrayals of exotic sexualities and customs. In the late nineteenth and early twentieth centuries, some travelers and military officials posted in Egypt, for instance, partook of sex with young females: "a British officer on the Nile in 1884 'bought a very lady like little girl for £16' for the duration of his voyage."[35] Among the slaves Englishman James Burton had bought a few decades earlier were girls of about ten and twelve, whom he used for sex.[36] Other Europeans, however, were appalled: another mid-nineteenth-century traveler, Bayle St. John, observing "two ten year old apprentice dancers" being ogled lustfully by Egyptian Arabs "'could not help feeling saddened by beholding childhood thus profaned.'"[37]

For authors of this era, Muslims represent only one instance of a category of backward or primitive Others who diverge from Western Christian norms. Both titillated and condemnatory accounts appeal to the idea of an erotic East. Irvin Schick points out that "Western attitudes" about Islam have "been shaped by a combination of moral outrage and irrepressible concupiscence focused on the trope of 'oriental sexuality.'"[38] The idea goes back at least to Hippocrates that climate has an effect on sexuality, with heat linked to excessive and potentially deviant sensuality. The "orient" is hot, which affects its inhabitants.[39] Irving refers to "the quickening climates of the east," Bush calls them "eastern climates," and Prideaux, referring to "those hot Countries," affirms that India is "in the same *Clime* with *Arabia*." Prideaux shows most clearly "a trademark of xenological writing, where the similarity of the fundamentally dissimilar is taken for granted so long as each is different from 'us.'"[40] Sexuality was an essential element of what made these Others different, whether it was idyllic and sensuous, or depraved and decadent. Females in this imagined Orient are "wonderfully precocious" and are "ripe for *Marriage*" and childbearing when their Western counterparts would not be. Not scandalous, not repellent, but intriguing.

Both Irving and Prideaux think that there are two kinds of people: us, and those who live in hot places and mature rapidly. As Sprenger put it: "The Arabs, like all southern nations, marry early."[41] No universal morality or set of uniform standards applies. Gender and power play out in concrete places and in *ideas* about places, which slip into ideas about people. "East" and "savage" and "hot" describe the Other. If two groups are both "hot" and "savage," then, in a colonial equivalent of Euclid's first Common Notion ("Things which equal the same thing also equal one another"), they are alike, perhaps interchangeable.

Polygamy, too, can be linked to climactic effects on female development. Higgins, in a passage recycled by Ameer Ali to interesting effect, quotes from a book by W. Ouseley:

> "The warm regions of Asia make a difference between the sexes not known to the climates of Europe, where the decay of each is mutual and gradual; whereas in Asia it is given to man alone to arrive at a green old age." If this be true, it goes far to excuse Mohamed in allowing a plurality of wives, and it sufficiently accounts for the fact that Jesus never expressly declared himself on this subject, but left it to the regulation of the governments of countries; as it is evident that what would be proper for Asia would be improper for Europe.[42]

Similarly, Ahmad Khan quotes a British apologist who cites Montesquieu to the effect that polygamy owes to women's aging more rapidly than men: "women, in hot countries, are marriageable at eight, nine, or ten years of age;—thus, in those countries, infancy and marriage almost always go together. They are old at twenty. . . . It is, therefore, extremely natural that in these places a man, when no law opposes it, should leave one wife to take another, and that polygamy should be introduced."[43]

All of these thinkers assume that different places have different behavioral rules. They also share a broader presumption about men's sexual appetites: women age more rapidly, and so men take younger wives to satisfy themselves when they are not prevented from doing so by stringent rules of morality or religion.

Unlike some thinkers who view Muslim practice as a concession to the natural order of things, Newcomb foregrounds the lack of appropriate religious restrictions in *The False Prophet*. Muhammad's example provides a jumping-off point to blame heathens not only for sexual immorality but also for want of maternal feeling: in discussing the allegiance oath taken by pagan converts, in which they forswore idolatry, fornication, and infanticide, "as the Pagan Arabs used to do,"[44] the mother responds to her daughter's horrified questioning by connecting all heathen peoples. Just as her last discussion on the subject of morality joined "Mohammedans" and Indians, here she links the pagan Arabs to Polynesians and Chinese: "Yes, my dear; it is a common thing for heathen women to kill their children. Before the missionaries went to the South Sea Islands, there were scarcely any mothers, who were not guilty of this horrible crime; and now, in China, and many other parts of the world, multitudes of children are destroyed as soon as they are born."[45] Rather than discuss the improvement purportedly wrought by Muhammad in Arabia with the Qur'anic prohibition of female infanticide, which she had just mentioned, she sweepingly condemns heathen savagery. Like Oriental sexuality, Eastern women's sufferings were fungible, one gliding into the other, so long as all of them were different from "us."

These discussions reflect a never-resolved tension between a universal standard, against which all can be judged, and a particularist ethnic ideal, where some groups are simply insufficiently advanced to be held to the same standard. It has been argued that the development of a historical consciousness arose in the late eighteenth century in Europe and that "paradoxically, one of the consequences of this new historical consciousness in Europe was an *ahistorical* perspective on non-European societies."[46] I would suggest instead that over the course of the nineteenth and early twentieth centuries, the notion that non-European societies are backward reflects the view that they are capable of change. Rather than being incommensurable, they are laggards on a universal trajectory of progress.

Or, they are simply and irreparably different: condemnations of Muhammad's debauchery had long included the claim that he had tolerated homosexuality—specifically, sodomy.[47] In the early modern era, accusations of Turkish sodomitical practices were widespread. (Protestants also accused Catholics and American Indians of sodomy: all who were not them.)[48] In the late eighteenth century, fears of sodomy were displaced by obsession with female slavery and the harem. This shift from concern with the potential violation of male seamen to the plight of captured women and girls reflects changes in the region's power balance: "with Ottoman decline and British ascendancy, and the presumed safety of the latter's soldiers and sailors, came a new interest in the harem and stories highlighting not male but female vulnerability."[49]

Something else happened, as well, with the shift to women's plight: a connection between concern with "the woman question" in Islam and the rise of a humanitarian consciousness. In previous centuries, condemnation of Others' immoral practices did not require any concern for reforming them. But alongside nineteenth-century fascination with the effects of "sultry climates" on female sexuality, there was a developing interest in protecting young womanhood. A series of campaigns arose against child marriage—first in India, where reformers tried to raise the age of consent from ten to twelve in 1891, and later in Egypt and elsewhere.[50]

These campaigns owed in part to sometimes ill-conceived and badly implemented European intervention. Alongside the much-noted hypocrisy of some Victorians, who publicly espoused prudish morals while embracing libertinism behind closed doors, there arose a notion of social improvement, the necessity for certain members of the elite to actively work for the amelioration of social conditions: "a widening of sympathies . . . the birth of a modern social conscience. Among other things, this involves an imaginative awareness of what it means to be at the bottom of the heap . . . and this in turn imposes new responsibilities toward such people."[51] Previously, one could condemn immorality without seeking to reform the society that tolerated it. This shift to fix the root problems decisively shaped European intervention into Muslim societies, both directly, in colonial policies and interventions, and indirectly, in the intellectual arena—including in discussions of Muhammad's life.

If the diminished power of the Ottoman Empire allowed Muslims to be "transformed from demons to curiosities"[52] during the early modern era, European domination was an inescapable backdrop for nineteenth-century portraits of Muhammad and—inevitably—of Muslim women.[53] Mohja Kahf has argued that contrary to modern emphasis on the pitiful plight of Muslim women, medieval and early modern writings often depicted them as termagants: warlike, powerful, a little scary, and sometimes wanton, certainly not demure or ladylike. (Prideaux, for instance, called Aisha "a very wanton woman."[54]) Although Muhammad's pre-nineteenth-century critics denigrated his sensualism, his lustfulness, and his polygamy, they did not condemn the oppression of Muslim women in general or his wives in particular. Sexual immorality was a major concern for medieval and early modern thinkers, but women's sexual (or for that matter, social) oppression was not. "By the nineteenth century," however, "descriptions of the sufferings of women in the East had become a commonplace of xenological discourse."[55] Newcomb linked polygamy to female slavery, infanticide, and the immurement of women in harems.[56] Child marriage was primarily identified as a "Hindoo" practice and criticized as such in both Britain and the United States.

Coomar Roy's 1888 defense of the practice resonates with more recent Muslim apologetic literature on women's status.[57] He refers extensively to female seclusion, modesty, chastity, and so forth. His rhetoric departs from that of more recent writings when he asserts the goodness and propriety of wifely subordination; he assumes, probably correctly, that his audience shares his view, since he appeals to it as an obvious advantage of child marriage: being married early inculcates proper reverence for the husband in the child-wife. Mrs. Marcus B. Fuller's blistering polemic *The Wrongs of Indian Womanhood* (1900) presents the opposite view in its chapter "Child Marriage."[58] Belief in the superiority of the nuclear family unit over the joint family undergirds Fuller's argument; she defends personal, individual, companionate, love-based marriage.[59] Fuller argues against what she views as Hindu religious doctrine. Although Indian women were among the important activists for legal reform—including as advocates for the 1929

Child-Marriage Restraint Act—their writings on the subject did not make it into wide circulation in the West.[60]

At the close of the nineteenth century, India was generally perceived as the prime offender in child marriage, but it was frequently enough associated with Muslims that Fuller, in her screed about Indian women's oppression, denies that child marriage came from "the Mohammedan invasion." Muslims brought "the Zenana system," she says, but child marriage is woven into Hindu religion.[61] A slightly later document does make a specific reference to Islam: the 1909 U.S. Census Bureau's entry on Algeria affirms that "Mohammedan laws and customs respecting marriage are essentially different from any that obtain in Christian countries, and serve to emphasize the vast difference between Mohammedan and Christian civilization. . . . Polygamy is allowed, child marriage is common, and marriage has the character of a sale, in which the woman either sells herself to her husband or is sold to him by her father." It not only makes a broad statement about child marriage but connects it to prophetic precedent: "As a result of the efforts of the French Government to suppress the evil, child marriage is probably less frequent than it was formerly, but it has not been entirely stamped out; it has the sanction of Mohammedan law and the Koran, for the prophet Mohammed himself married his favorite wife when she was only 7 years of age."[62]

In the case of both India and "Mohammedan civilization," scholars make a concerted effort to insist that reform is generally impossible; here, the Census Bureau weighs in on the "sanction" of "the evil" of child marriage by scripture, law, and prophetic practice. This conceptual move to insist that religious texts be read literally, without interpretive gloss, and applied directly is not limited to Islamic texts. Some Indian reformers had insisted that "'child marriage is not a religious ordinance, but an irreligious enactment, and an inhuman innovation upon ancient customs.'"[63] However, C. N. Barham insists that this is not the case. Rather, one must confront such "lying sophists" and "those who take their opinion from the transient colouring of the daily press" with the facts. One should appeal to texts ("the laws, prophets, and Scriptures of the East") to prove that child marriage *is* a Hindu practice.[64] Part of what is at stake here is the acceptability of Hindu scripture (as canonized by European scholars): if to be a Hindu *means* to follow the Laws of Manu, then one cannot be both Hindu and modern.[65] A well-meaning falsehood that treats child marriage as mere custom is unacceptable, even if this allows one to oppose it. The author insists on recognizing and rejecting the irremediable barbarism (the "diabolical evil") of child marriage, which taints Hindu religion and Indian culture.[66] (Of course, the notion that one can discard custom is itself an artifact of modern approaches to scripture, which give texts sanctioning power greater than the weight of practice. Indeed, to view custom and scripture as separate and separable in the first place is innovative.) Similar arguments are put forth today by critics of Islam and Muhammad who argue that since Muhammad is known to have behaved in particular ways, or since the Qur'an or early jurists say particular things, Muslims must obey them and are not allowed to rethink their tradition. Of course, in Barham's view, if Hinduism cannot be reformed, then to reform, Indians must cease being Hindu.

Child Marriage and Modern Society

Marriage of minors in both India and Egypt served as an entry point into larger questions of worldview. In Egypt, a 1914 proposal to set a minimum age for marriage was, after much hue and cry about the intolerability of interfering with religious law and, notably, parental privilege, rejected. One opponent of the reform brought up Muhammad's marriage to Aisha.[67] A 1923 law set an age of sixteen for females and eighteen for males, below which no marriage could be registered or judicial relief obtained.[68] The Egyptian case illustrates a vision in which a national, modern Egypt is compatible with the notion of adult marriage and liberal subjects, with little attention to religion. A religious objection to establishing a minimum marriage age was enough to derail the 1914 legislative reform, but by 1923, it no longer was.

As the historian Hanan Kholoussy points out, this was less about protecting the interests of vulnerable girls than about "the role of the state in the production and promotion of modern nuclear families"—families that would be the "foundation stone of the emerging nation."[69] The three areas in which states attempted reform—polygamy, divorce, and marriage of minors—were of varying relevance.[70] Kholoussy points out: "That members of the state felt compelled to regulate the marriage of minors at this time is particularly significant because such unions appear to have been in decline by the early twentieth century.[71] "This suggests," she writes, "that some Egyptians wanted the government to establish a new means of monitoring the marital habits of the population to ensure that only adult Egyptians would marry and reproduce."[72] I would argue for an additional variable: the symbolic value of such reforms, regardless of their real or perceived practical impact. In India, marriage-age reform became a central project of the nation-state, which established a minimum age for marriage and required registration.[73] Marriage is a way of making proper citizens, proper national subjects, proper modern people—and, as a collectivity, a proper nation. And in the case of Egypt, it required a proper religious precedent, or the incorporation into religious rhetoric of new ideas about family and marriage.

Chapter 4 illustrated that companionate marriage and Muhammad as Khadija's husband—and her as his beloved partner, mother to his children, and domestic comforter—became central to his life story. The same narrative was not readily available for Aisha, who had co-wives and no children and was not, because of her youth, a suitable "partner." How, then, could this marriage be discussed in terms compatible with the new ideals about marriage and family that were circulating? As decades passed, Muslim thinkers came increasingly to rely on engagement with, and definition against, the works of Western thinkers.

Vituperative criticisms similar to those directed at barbarous Hindu practices have more recently been aimed at Islam and Muslims. These have emerged against a backdrop of paranoia about Muslim fanaticism and legitimate concerns about Muslim extremism. In the late twentieth century, in a renewed climate of criticism of Islam, divergent tendencies emerge in Muslim and non-Muslim sources. Muslim scholars engage in apologetics to justify Aisha's marriage. The dominant strategy is to contextualize it as historically appropriate to its time and place and to play up, as with the multiple marriages, the political motivations behind it. A less common strategy recalculates Aisha's age at marriage based on other indicators in the sources.[74] Only a few authors, mostly traditionalist South Asian biographers, celebrate her youthful purity, sometimes also making practical arguments about what her youth made possible. Enhancing and upholding her reputation is undoubtedly part of the late South Asian scholar Syed Suleman Nadvi's objective when he connects Aisha's age with her virginal status, mentioning "wedlock" at the "tender" age of six and consummation when Aisha was "only nine years of age."[75]

These few writers aside, most accounts of Aisha's marriage historicize assiduously. Purportedly objective American and European accounts may wax somewhat less rhapsodic about Muhammad's sterling virtues as a husband, but like apologetic biographers, they still emphasize both the connection with Abu Bakr forged by the marriage and the context of early Arabia, in which, as one Western survey puts it, the marriage was "not in the least improper."[76] Ziauddin Sardar frames the marriage with Aisha as being controversial now, but not at the time: "She was said to be 9 or 10 and he was 53. Conventions about the age of marriage are culturally determined and have changed radically over time."[77] His "was said to be" distances him from treating it as fact, while the mention of changing cultural standards suggests that even if it is true one should withhold judgment.

This fixation on changing standards of human conduct, on contextual explanation, has become commonsensical. We hear it so frequently we no longer really *hear* it. Certainly it is the case that people in the past recognized that different places/customs might call for different rules or conduct (when in Rome . . .). But the notion that social arrangements would change over time and, furthermore, that this change might be in the direction of progress rather than a decline from a pristine early stage is a recent development. It emerges in Muslim thinking in the nineteenth century and can be seen particularly in Ameer Ali's rebuttals to Muir and others' criticisms of Muhammad. This tendency is especially pertinent with regard to Muhammad's marital practices.

Modern texts, regardless of author, seldom bother with the anecdote according to which Gabriel came to the Prophet with a depiction of Aisha and told Muhammad that she was to be his wife. Ibn Sa'd includes the following report in his compendium: "The Messenger of Allah was so grieved about Khadija that people feared for him, until he married 'A'isha."[78] Another account concerns not his followers' worries but God's concern: "When Khadija died, the Prophet was terribly grieved over her, and Allah sent Jibril who brought him the picture of 'A'isha. He said, 'Messenger of Allah, this one will remove some of your sorrow. This one has some of the qualities of Khadija.'"[79] The comparison between the qualities of Aisha and Khadija is unusual, clearly meant to shore up Aisha's reputation; nonetheless, the link between Muhammad's fragile state ("people feared for him") and his remarriage to Aisha, who "remove[d] some of [his] sorrow," is significant. Recent authors tend to omit these plaudits and rationales, either because religious arguments are irrelevant to their audiences or because they are concerned with the practical dimension of the marriage.[80] Even in books ostensibly directed to Muslim audiences, arguments are framed in ways that respond at least implicitly to Western criticism; thinking about Muhammad's life is directly shaped by Western polemic and critique.

Western scholarship appears in apologetics around Aisha's age, in sometimes surprising ways. For instance, Syed M. H. Zaidi writes, in *Mothers of the Faithful*: "Ayesha was the young daughter of Muhammad's bosom friend Abu Bakr. . . . Her father was one of the most powerful, popular and well-to-do citizens. By this alliance, Muhammad's principal object was to cement Abu Bakr more strongly to his side." (He cites Davenport and Irving as authorities and follows the former almost verbatim in places.)[81] Note that Zaidi views Muhammad having his "principal object" be a political "alliance" as a *good* thing, precisely the opposite of Prideaux's view. He continues: "In response to his politic dictate and in acceptance of the earnest solicitations of his noble disciple [i.e., Abu Bakr], the betrothal was announced when Ayesha was 7 years of age; and she was married over 2 years later when about 10 as such is the ripeness of the climate and such too is the custom of the country."[82] He cites, for this information, Edward Gibbon, whose work he mistitles *Downfall of the Roman Empire,* and recommends to his readers also Ameer Ali and Prideaux. Astonishingly, then, a work explicitly framed as a refutation of non-Muslim criticisms of Muhammad's marriages draws on Prideaux's polemic. Though he replaces Prideaux's ages of betrothal and consummation (six and eight) with his own (seven and ten), Zaidi agrees with Prideaux about climate's impact on "ripeness" for marriage and the connection between the marriage to Aisha and the alliance with Abu Bakr. "Custom" is a more recent addition.

Zaidi's use of Prideaux might seem preposterous, but it highlights the wide variety of ways Muslim scholars read, cite, and repurpose Western works. A more recent biography takes from a different sort of Western authority. A 1969 work published in India, reprinted as recently as 2002 and distributed in the United States, devotes a section to Aisha's youth at marriage. The "new bride," Abdul Hameed Siddiqui writes, "was just attaining her puberty and was still in the house of her father. She was a precocious girl" (here, he references Nadvi's biography of Aisha; the term precocious was a favorite of Muir's) "and was developing both in mind and body with rapidity peculiar to such rare personalities." Muhammad "decided to consummate the marriage" after it was suggested by Aisha's parents.[83] The marriage strengthened the ties of friendship between Muhammad and Abu Bakr and abolished the idea "that it was contrary to religious ethics to marry the daughter of a man whom one declared to be one's brother."[84] Aisha's youth was particularly important: she entered "the *haram* of the Prophet at an impressionable age" and was thus guided appropriately in her development. Marriage at this "highly formative age" (Siddiqui avoids specific numbers) is good for the bride herself and the marital union. Siddiqui cites a Dutch doctor, to the effect that "the marriage of an elderly (senescent)—not, of course an old (senile)—man to a quite young girl, is often very successful and harmonious. The bride is immediately introduced and accustomed to moderate sexual intercourse."[85] Following this medical wisdom about sexuality, Siddiqui proceeds to lambaste "those Western critics of *Islam* who have criticized this marriage" for "los[ing] sight of the fact that this marriage did not involve sexual considerations alone." A crucial consideration was that Muhammad's other wives "were all of advanced age, and thus could neither share the feelings of the younger generation nor could they properly appreciate their point of view." They could not communicate with "the ladies of younger ages." Aisha's marriage "when she was at the threshold of puberty was a great necessity, as it was through her that instructions could successfully be imparted to the young ladies who had newly entered the fold of Islam."[86]

Siddiqui here combines tones, strategies, and sources of authority. Aisha's exceptional qualities led her to develop rapidly. Her youth enabled her to be of service to a broader Muslim population. Early consummation aided her moral development as well as her sexual initiation—a claim for which he cites a European figure. Like earlier authors, Siddiqui selectively incorporates Western authorities even as his justification shifts from climactic to medical. (Climate-based explanations persist in Muslim apologetics; S. M. Abbasi explains: "the climactic conditions in a tropical country like

Arabia, were conducive to the early development of human beings and the females in particular were precocious toward the growth of their body and faculties.")[87] Apparently without any sense of dissonance, Siddiqui moves swiftly from presenting the Dutch doctor's wisdom to railing against the ignorant pronouncements of "Western critics of Islam."[88]

Ghulam Malik's biography contains a chapter on "His Wives," which uses different but similarly overlapping strategies to discuss Aisha. He writes, "Aisha bint Abu Bakr was betrothed in Makkah when she was seven or eight years old. After nine months of the Hijrah, in 623, Muhammad married her, the only virgin among his wives, when she was only nine or ten." His use of "seven or eight" and "nine or ten" is slightly unusual. More typical is his claim that "at that time, such wide gaps in the ages of couples were not unusual or uncommon." His reference to a remote time period—"at that time"—suggests something archaic. Something else noteworthy becomes clear in Malik's biography: Muslim authors had adopted, even for works aimed at fellow believers, the terminology of betrothal or occasionally "engagement," which European authors from the nineteenth century forward used.[89]

By the standards of later Islamic jurisprudence—which had yet to develop during Muhammad's lifetime—the contract made between Muhammad and Abu Bakr was a binding marriage. Muslim biographers treated it as such for many centuries. Prideaux follows Muslim sources when he refers to it that way, as does Bush. But others, including Sprenger and particularly Irving, use the language of betrothal. Even if it was legally a marriage, it functioned like a betrothal: Western understandings become the crucial deciding factor rather than standard Muslim legal categories. Hence, the late-twentieth-century scholarly translators of a volume in Tabari's *History* in which Aisha's marriage is discussed explain that "what seems properly to be a betrothal was apparently called a marriage by the Arabs."[90]

Traduttore Tradittore

Similar issues of terminology crop up in Muhammad Husayn Haykal's discussion of Aisha's marriage, which reflects a complex engagement with Western writings. It avoids the sorts of apologetics used by twentieth-century authors, including those just discussed, but clearly reflects some level of unease about Aisha's youth; this is even more true for its English translation. Haykal mentions Aisha's age three times, once when he discusses Muhammad's marriages after Khadija's death, again when he discusses consummation of the marriage to Aisha, and a third time in his larger discussion of Muhammad's marriages, giving different ages each time.

Haykal depends on, and borrows heavily from, Prideaux, Irving, and Émile Dermenghem, but molds their material in keeping with his presumptions about sexuality, marriage, and the emotional life of the biographical subject. Prideaux sought to account for the influence of drives or motives (lust, ambition) on Muhammad's actions. Thomas Carlyle, nearly a century and a half later, had insisted, against Prideaux and his ilk, on Muhammad's sincerity but, like Prideaux, was not especially interested in Muhammad's feelings. In Irving's *Mahomet,* published not very long after Carlyle's lectures, the enduring preoccupation with the Prophet's sex life had become also concern with his feelings.

Irving brought his novelist's sensibility to his treatment of Muhammad's life.[91] Haykal, though primarily a journalist, had also written a novel, *Zaynab* (1913).[92] These writers' sensibilities—and perhaps the broader influence of novels on reader expectation—meant that in both works, life stories were premised on a coherent character revealed throughout and held a largely continuous rather than an episodic structure.

Haykal's *Life* retains some thematic sections—including one on Muhammad's wives, likely modeled on Dermenghem's chapter on "The Harem."[93] But two snippets on the marriages woven into the chronological narrative are especially revealing. He discusses Muhammad's marriages following Khadija's death in the context of Meccan tribes' rejection of Islam, which intensified his "pain and grief" at his loss:

> The mourning period for Khadija ended, and he thought of marrying, perhaps to find in his wife some of the solace he had when Khadija nursed his wounds. He thought he could strengthen the ties of kinship between himself and the early converts to Islam. He proposed to Abu Bakr for his daughter Aisha, but since she was still a child of seven years of age, he contracted marriage to her and did not consummate [the marriage] with her until two years later when she had turned nine. During these two [years] he married Sawda, widow of one of the Muslims who had emigrated to Abyssinia, returned to Mecca, and died there.[94]

Haykal revisits the marriage to Aisha three years later, again prefacing it with a summation of the religio-political situation and its effect on Muhammad's state. Whereas previously Muhammad was persecuted, insulted, and grieving, here he is "satisfied" and his community "tranquil in its religion":

> At this time, Muhammad consummated [the marriage] with Aisha, daughter of Abu Bakr, who was then age ten or eleven. She was a slender girl, sweet of feature, an agreeable companion, crossing from childhood into maidenhood. She craved play and merriment and was growing beautifully.[95]

In both passages, marriages fulfill emotional needs. In the first, Muhammad seeks the kind of companionship that Khadija had provided, yet neither a contract with Aisha nor marriage to Sawda suffices. In the second, Aisha becomes "a source of relaxation" from the burdens of government. Haykal conjures a domestic sphere, where Muhammad can shed his communal responsibilities and indulge his young wife's childish inclinations. She is described here in terms that most authors reserve for Khadija, as a domestic comfort to him. Interestingly, Haykal also attends to how Muhammad meets Aisha's need for shelter and "play and merriment," serving as "a sympathetic and loving husband but also a compassionate father" to her.[96]

In both what they say and what they omit, these excerpts from Haykal draw extensively on the facts and tone of the Western *Lives* Haykal has read. The range of "ten or eleven" set out in the second passage does not appear in any of these sources, so far as I can tell, but the ages of seven and nine, which he gives in the earlier passage, are attested by early Muslim authorities and, not coincidentally, mirror Dermenghem.[97] (In his later chapter "The Prophet's Wives," Haykal places the "proposal" at age nine and the consummation two years later.)[98] He takes nearly verbatim from Dermenghem Aisha's relationship to Abu Bakr, the two-year delay prior to consummation, and even the phrasing "thought of marrying," with which the text introduces his near-simultaneous arrangements with Sawda and Aisha.

Haykal plays up the emotional resonance of Muhammad's bond with Khadija, though he skims over Dermenghem's assertions that he lacked love and affection for most of his subsequent wives. Haykal omits Dermenghem's reference to Muhammad's "obstinate fidelity" to the aging Khadija, who had provided him comfort and tenderness.[99] Haykal generally treats Sawda in ways similar to Dermenghem, though he leaves out the name of Sawda's previous husband and the fact that, according to Dermenghem, Muhammad "seems to have had but little love for her."[100] He leaves out, too, the French scholar's titillating remark that "Aisha was the only one who went to his bed a virgin."[101] (Early Muslim sources remark on Aisha's virginity more circumspectly.)

Although Haykal downplays any criticism of Muhammad for withholding love from later wives, his emphasis on Muhammad's love for and bond with Khadija makes the contrast clear. Where love does emerge more explicitly, in the context of critiquing "Orientalists," he discounts its significance as a motivation: "If what is said about Aisha and his love for her is true, it was love that grew after marriage and not at the time of it. He proposed to her father for her when she was still nine years of age and waited two years before he consummated [the marriage] with her. It defies logic that he would have loved her when she was so young."[102] (Similarly, Muir had written: "The yet undeveloped charms of Ayesha could hardly have swayed the heart of Mahomet.")[103] Although Haykal here shifts the ages he provides, his main concern is not refuting Western critics who condemn Muhammad for Aisha's youth but insisting that this marriage, like that to Hafsa, daughter of Umar, was motivated by neither love nor desire; instead, Muhammad aimed to strengthen his "ties" to the fathers, his "two viziers."[104]

Haykal uses different language to describe Muhammad's connection to Sawda than he does when describing his connection to Aisha. The first passage is subtitled "Proposal to Aisha and marriage to Sawda." In the text, he uses the term "marrying" for Sawda, whereas for Aisha he uses "proposing," "contracting," and (not) "consummating."[105] He titles the second section "The marriage of the Prophet to Aisha." Haykal thus creates four possible ways of discussing a union: proposal, contract, consummation, and simply marriage. The classical Islamic texts Haykal cites distinguish between two events, marriage and consummation, and do not typically render the linkage with Aisha in three parts. Ibn Kathir, for instance, acknowledges that scholars debate which marriage occurred first but agree unanimously that the marriage with Sawda was consummated first.

There are two complementary explanations for Haykal's choice to treat Muhammad's connection to Aisha as a marriage only upon its consummation. We may speculate that as arranged marriages became somewhat less frequent in Egypt, more marriages took place when the spouses were mature, with little or no separation between the contract and the commencement of married life. Becoming legally married meant becoming socially married. To apply the legal term *marriage* to an arrangement that was not its social equivalent may have seemed confusing. Thus, writing of the proposal and contract and avoiding the term *marriage* gets around the legal category retrospectively applied to Muhammad's union with Aisha by earlier generations of Muslims. The second explanation is simpler: the word for "proposal" became associated with "betrothed" or "affianced" or "engaged" and was used in the English and French texts Haykal relied on (and, later, in their Arabic translations). It is likely that the accounts that used the term "betrothal," like Irving's and Muir's, affected his vocabulary.

If Haykal's departures from the classical Arabic tradition are relatively easily explained, Ismail Al Faruqi's English translation of Haykal's *Life*, which appeared four decades after its initial publication, takes substantially greater liberties, particularly with Aisha's age.[106] Al Faruqi places Aisha's age firmly in double digits; other changes make Aisha seem older and play down any sexual element of the relationship. Haykal had written, explaining the time elapsed between the contract and its consummation: "since she was still a child of seven years of age, he [Muhammad] contracted a marriage to her but did not consummate [the marriage] until two years later when she had turned nine."[107] Al Faruqi renders this as: "Since she was still too young to marry, the engagement was announced, but the marriage was postponed for three more years until 'Ā'ishah reached the age of eleven."[108] This "translation" omits the ages Haykal uses, giving no actual age for the "engagement" (a term not present in the original); adds in the number eleven; and says that "three more years" (rather than the original "two years") passed before "the marriage" (rather than *consummation*) took place. Al Faruqi's version sidelines sex entirely.

The less dramatic changes Al Faruqi makes to the second passage have similar effects. Both here and in the chapter "The Prophet's Wives," in which Haykal writes that Muhammad "consummated [the marriage] with Aisha," Al Faruqi states only that he "married" her. Although Al Faruqi refers to her youth when he calls her "a beautiful, delicate, and amiable young girl," Haykal's

Arabic, which I have rendered as "a slender girl, sweet of feature, an agreeable companion," alludes to physicality: the shape of her body, the lineaments of her face. The third element of the description, which might also be rendered "pleasant for companionship" or "desirable for intimacy," connotes specifically conjugal intimacy, a connection Al Faruqi's bland "amiable" forestalls. Haykal says she was "crossing from childhood into maidenhood," suggesting liminality.[109] Al Faruqi writes "emerging out of childhood and blossoming into full womanhood," going on to assert that she was "fully grown." His term "blossoming" suggests a process of transition, but "full womanhood" and "fully grown" evoke an adulthood at odds with other elements of the passage, which Al Faruqi renders more faithfully: Aisha's continued attachment to "play and amusement" and Muhammad's paternal affection.[110] His choice of modifiers is particularly surprising given that the phrase he translates as "full womanhood" denotes "youth, maidenhood." The phrase he renders as "fully grown" (in my version, "growing beautifully") contains no word for "full" or "complete" but hints at *incompleteness;* the word he translates "grown" can indicate growth or progress but is an active participle also used for "developing," as in the phrase "developing countries."

Of course, my renderings of these words are not the only possible ones, and with the exception of his alterations to the numbers given in the first passage, each of Al Faruqi's choices is individually defensible. One might even argue that given Haykal's self-contradiction as to Aisha's age at consummation, Al Faruqi is merely harmonizing the text to prevent reader confusion. Taken cumulatively, though, these choices result in a quite different overall effect. Presumably, Al Faruqi's aim was not to reproduce the text faithfully for scholarly readers but to translate an authoritative religious text for a community of believers for whom a more literal rendering of Haykal's text would cause consternation. On a spectrum of translations, from conservative (or mediatory) to additive (or creative), Al Faruqi's falls closer to the creative end.[111] Notably, however, rather than adding to the text, Al Faruqi often modifies by subtraction. About Muhammad's Coptic slave Mariya, reportedly the only woman to bear him a child apart from Khadija, Haykal had been equivocal, stating that she became a wife but also indicating that he visited her as men visit their slaves. Al Faruqi simply omits this line, while maintaining the surrounding text.[112] For Haykal's Egyptian audience in the 1930s, the practice of concubinage among the elite was a recent memory; Al Faruqi adapts the text for a 1970s American audience, for whom Muhammad's having a sexual relationship with a female he owned would have been deeply troubling.

As a counterpoint to this consideration of Haykal in English, let us take a brief look at the Arabic version of Irving's *Life of Mahomet*. It came out in 1960, with a second edition in 1966—three decades after Haykal consulted the original and around the same time Al Faruqi began his translation endeavor.[113] The Arabic translation of Irving's account of Muhammad's marriages to Sawda and Aisha makes two sorts of changes. The first concerns the emotional dimensions of Muhammad's relationship to Sawda. It omits the reference to Muhammad's "heart prone to affection, and subject to female influence" and merely says that he did not have a "strong love" for Sawda.[114] The second concerns Aisha's age. The translator keeps Irving's original numbers. However, he adds a footnote about the matter of Aisha's age at "betrothal" and marriage.[115] Aisha's youth, unproblematic for Irving's American readers in the mid-nineteenth century, posed difficulties for Egyptian readers a century later.

Panic and Polemic

More broadly, in speaking of Muhammad's marriage to Aisha, books published in the United States around the time Haykal's *Life* appeared in English and Irving's *Life* appeared in Arabic tended to adopt either condescending or condemnatory tones; the latter increased in frequency and stridency as the twentieth century wore to a close. Betty Kelen, in a popular biography (1975), wrote of a "betrothal" at age seven, placing the "marriage" shortly after the move to Medina, when Aisha was nine: "We need not dwell on the abuse to the child of such a marriage," since it was customary; further, "Ayesha was dear to Muhammad, and she loved the Prophet. We can conclude that the relationship between the two was free from outrage."[116] W. Montgomery Watt makes a similarly unperturbed assessment in *Muhammad: Prophet and Statesman*, though he allows that "This relationship between a man of fifty-three and a girl of ten must have been a strange one. . . . We must remember, of course, that girls matured much earlier in seventh-century Arabia."[117] These authors were writing before hysteria about child sexual abuse had taken hold in the American imagination. By the last decade of the twentieth century and especially the first decade of the twenty-first, Aisha's age had become a favorite argument of anti-Islam polemicists, especially but not exclusively online.[118]

In the wake of this public wrangling over Aisha's age, in which accusations of pedophilia have become part of a broader public discourse about Muhammad, those who wish to rescue Islam and Muhammad from blanket condemnation attempt to contextualize the marriage. Muslim apologists online and in print often repeat some variant of the physical-precocity argument, sometimes with a mention of climate; non-Muslim authors and those writing for mainstream general readers tend to stick with arguments from custom. Colin Turner's 2006 introduction *Islam: The Basics* mixes both. Fully aware of how such marriages are seen today, Turner mentions "paedophilia" and "child abuse" but hastens to reassure his readers that Muhammad's marriage to Aisha was common for the era and that "such marriages were almost certainly not consummated until both parties had entered adulthood, which seventh century Arabs tended to reach earlier than Westerners today."[119] (Turner says that Aisha was perhaps ten, though he also says, inaccurately, that the sources are not explicit about her age, then goes on to declare it "highly unlikely that Muhammad would have taken Aisha into his bed until she was at least in her early teens, which was wholly in keeping with the customs of the day, and in context not the least improper.")[120] This reference to Aisha as a teenager is, of course, highly anachronistic; Lesley Hazelton uses the term frequently in her recent biography *The First Muslim: The Story of Muhammad.* She suggests that in claiming that she was "six years old when she was betrothed and nine years old when the marriage was celebrated and consummated," Aisha may have played up her youth to appear extraordinary, since "to have been married at the customary age would make Aisha normal, and that was the one thing she was always determined not to be." Hazelton adds, without citing any specific sources, that "more restrained reports have her aged nine when she was betrothed and twelve when she was actually married."[121] Prolific religion writer Karen Armstrong's two biographies present similar accounts of Muhammad's remarriages. In the first, she denies a sexual motivation ("Aisha was only a little girl and at thirty Saw-

dah was past her first youth and was beginning to run to fat"—
pedophilia was not on anybody's radar, or she would have contested that claim) and plays up their "political dimension."[122] She
writes later that the wedding occurred when Aisha was nine but
"made little difference to Aisha's life. Tabari says that she was so
young that she stayed in her parents' home and the marriage was
consummated there later when she had reached puberty."[123]

Armstrong's later biography, like Al Faruqi's version of
Haykal, never mentions consummation, only a shift of residence.
Introducing Muhammad's marriages after Khadija's death, Armstrong writes that "Muhammad made some changes in his
household. He needed a wife." He married Sawda, and Abu
Bakr, "anxious to forge a closer link with the Prophet," took the
initiative "and proposed that he should marry his daughter 'A'isha
who was then six years old. 'A'isha was formally betrothed to
Muhammad in a ceremony at which the little girl was not present." She goes on to explain that "there was no impropriety in
Muhammad's betrothal to 'A'isha. Marriages conducted in ab-
sentia to seal an alliance were often conducted at this time between adults and minors who were even younger than 'A'isha."
Not only did they happen in Europe, too, "well into the early
modern period," but "there was no question of consummating
the marriage until 'A'isha reached puberty, when she would have
been married off like any other girl."[124] When it comes time for
the union to be sealed, however, Armstrong does not mention
consummation. Instead, among "changes in Muhammad's family life" that occurred in Medina was Aisha's (possible) reloca-
tion. Again, Armstrong invokes Tabari: she "may by this time
have moved into the apartment that had been prepared for her in

the mosque, though Tabari says that because of her youth she was allowed to remain for a while longer in her parents' house."[125] (Tabari includes several reports that that the marriage took place when she was six or seven.[126] He once notes that "when he married her she was young, unfit for intercourse."[127] However, he says nothing about puberty and consistently states that consummation occurred when she was nine.[128])

By the time of Armstrong's second biography, other writings had begun to accuse Muhammad of pedophilia and abuse, extending the characterization to cover Islamic civilization as a whole. In his *The Truth about Muhammad: Founder of the World's Most Intolerant Religion* (2006), Robert Spencer—front man for Jihad Watch and grand pooh-bah of the legion of American Islamophobes—qualifies the accusation of pedophilia as "a bit anachronistic" but makes an argument similar to that made by Barham a century earlier about the Laws of Manu. Under the provocative subtitle "Pedophile Prophet?" Spencer points out that although child marriage did not bother anyone at the time, its existence in Muslim communities today can be blamed on the insistence that Muhammad's model is to be literally followed.[129] Citing deplorable statistics about child marriage, Spencer writes: "This is the price that women have paid throughout Islamic history, and continue to pay, for Muhammad's status as 'an excellent example of conduct' (Qur'an 33:21)."

With this view of child marriage, which circulated in online polemics about Muhammad a decade before Spencer's book, we move from hierarchical rankings of societies, where some persist in primitive practices, to pedophilia. However, rather than viewing pedophilia as an individual perversion, all of Islam and every Muslim is tainted because Muhammad is the perpetrator. Pedophilia is not (as polygamy once was) merely sensuality or lustfulness unrestrained, nor is it (as polygamy came to be) an indication of women's low status or the broader oppressiveness of Muhammad and Islam toward females. Here Muhammad's practice is viewed as justification for evil, meaning that in order to progress, one must reject his legacy.

Muhammad's marriage to Aisha has become, for contemporary polemicists, evidence of pedophilia not as a medical diagnosis but as an archaic and evil force. Sodomy had served, both in the early modern period and the Renaissance era, as a similar device.[130] As the historian Nabil Matar writes, "No other accusation needed less explanation or demonstration than sodomy. To mention it was to confirm it and to condemn the perpetrator; sodomy was a self-explanatory judgment, a cognitive keyword that proved that Muslims had no family structure, no 'natural' sexuality, and therefore no place in the civilized world."[131] Because the point being made in invoking this term is not, in fact, one about its diagnostic accuracy, a rebuttal like the one offered by Yahiya Emerick ("If *Muhammad* were a *pedophile,* he would not have waited for A'ishah to reach puberty before completing the marriage, nor would he have stopped at only one marriage to a young girl") is utterly ineffective.[132]

Deepak Chopra's attempt, in his fictionalized biography, to address concerns about Aisha's age in an afterword is neither quite so combative nor quite so hateful as Spencer's approach, but it draws equally false causal links between prophetic precedent and Muslim practice.[133] Chopra notes that on certain issues, Muslim perspectives differ from those of non-Muslims. He singles out, and thereby connects, two issues that have caused a great deal of consternation to contemporary observers: the reprisal against the

Banu Qurayza and the marriage to Aisha. The former is accepted by Muslim historians: "After his death, the ranks closed around absolute truth, which meant that it was a test of faith to turn any act by the Prophet, even the beheading of his enemies, into something right and good." He then continues:

> On this point, the critics of Muhammad cite his marriage to Aisha. She was the youngest daughter of Abu Bakr. . . . At the age of six Aisha was betrothed to a husband, until Muhammad had a revelation that she was meant for him. The prospective groom was persuaded to give her up. The marriage to Muhammad took place but wasn't consummated until Aisha was nine. Beyond Islam, this episode is more than distasteful. Within the faith, however, it is praised. None of Muhammad's other wives were virgins, and the rationale is that Aisha served as a kind of Virgin Mary, made all the more pure because she was so young. To the outside world, this is a prescription for blind fanaticism.[134]

Many things about Chopra's statement cry out for analysis, beginning with the link between a mass beheading and Aisha's age. The two are also intertwined in a biography by Adil Salahi, published by the UK-based Islamic Foundation. Originally published in 1995, the 2008 edition of *Muhammad: Man and Prophet* contains major changes in precisely these two sections. In the first, Salahi rejects Ibn Ishaq's version and thereby reports "a certain event . . . in a new light that totally negates what has been held as true by most people, including the present author." He also adds an appendix treating Aisha's age at marriage. In the case of the

Banu Qurayza, he acknowledges that his current view runs counter to his previous belief. With regard to Aisha's age, however, he explains, "I have always felt that the common notion concerning her age is wrong."[135]

Returning to Chopra and the comparison he draws between Aisha and Mary: If any one woman is parallel to Mary in Muslim tradition, it is Muhammad's daughter Fatima, who pious Shi'a call "the virgin," her offspring by Ali having been born, it is said, from her side or thigh; she was also exempt from menstruation. Alternately, some have drawn a parallel between Mary and Muhammad himself, each made into a pristine vessel to receive the Word of God.[136] Chopra is correct about the concern with purity (connected in South Asian texts with her youth), though it is probably asserted so forcefully because it was questioned so vigorously. Chopra writes, "The bald fact is that we cannot identify with customs that exist across such a yawning abyss."[137] To the contrary, it is precisely our acute preoccupation with the sexualization of young girls and the sexual abuse of children that leads to recent worry over Aisha's age.

Although Chopra makes a strange bedfellow for contemporary right-wing and evangelical figures who treat Islam as "an evil and wicked religion,"[138] he, like them, avoids notions of backwardness and progress and appeals instead to earlier notions of Truth and Error. Yet none of these figures merely re-creates medieval distinctions. In associating "pedophile" and "pervert" with demonic characterizations, they medicalize and pathologize religious valuations. In doing so, they draw on decidedly modern discourses about both illness and children. Contemporary polemics about Muhammad's marriages then draw from an unwieldy jumble of incompatible discourses, which have in common mostly that they can provide a language with which to denigrate Others.[139]

Women Writing Women's *Lives*

Let me close with a brief foray into fiction, which provides an important window onto historical events. Modern Muslim women writing about marriage and celebrating Muhammad's precedent-setting example as a feminist have typically chosen to write about Khadija, seeing this marriage as the crucial model. For those writers interested in Muhammad's life and the issue of women's authority, however, Aisha figures much more prominently, including in several novels.

Chapter 4 noted how Mahfouz's allegorical novel *Children of the Alley* deals with the relationship between Muhammad/Qassem and Khadija/Qamar. The same novel contains an Aisha figure, a girl named Badriya, whom Mahfouz introduces in an erotic though chaste encounter when she brings Qassem coffee. He is thinking of Qamar then. "Between sips their smiling eyes meet." (Mahfouz coyly deflects the question of her age: "'How old are you, Badriya?' She bit her lip. 'I don't know,' she murmured.")[140] Qassem then reflects on his life, acknowledging a spectrum of emotions. No confusion appears between his paternal emotions and his sexual needs:

> His lasting happiness was Ihsan [his daughter by Qamar] when he played with her, rocked her, and sang to her, but this was not the case when she reminded him of his late wife; those

occasions immersed him in gloom and the hot sighs of yearning. She had been taken from him at the outset of the journey, and left him prey to terrible depression whenever he was alone, to regret, as when he had been on the mountainside, the day he drank the coffee, the day of the shy smile, as soft as an afternoon breeze.[141]

His "tormented depression and insomnia" lead him out to walk, where he encounters one of his men; Qassem confesses, "Sometimes I can't stand being alone," and his companion notes, "Most of your men are married or have families. . . . They're never lonely."[142] He advises Qassem: "Someone like you cannot do without a woman."[143] Qassem is divided: "'Marry, after Qamar?' The objection in his voice was as strong as his feeling that the man was right."

Sexual energy pulses through Mahfouz's prose. The thought of remarrying leaves him "disturbed," as it would seem to be a betrayal "after her love and caring." At the same time, he is left with "hot sighs of yearning" and roiling with "excitement." Whatever conflict this collision of emotional residue and passionate impulses produces for him, it does not make his followers anxious, even as he marries several more wives. Qassem likes women, and his community finds his obvious virility a source of pride rather than a black mark on his character.

This is a far cry from the insistent disclaimer of any sexual motive to his marriage to Aisha or other marriages prominent in more recent apologetics. These attempts to explain Muhammad's conjugal relationships in terms that make him an indulgent husband and an ideal companion, focusing on friendly feelings (or gratitude, in

Khadija's case), render him unlike either the classical Arabic tradition of prophetic biography, which celebrates his virility, or the Western model that Haykal, among others, outwardly deplores and nonetheless emulates.[144] Aisha 'Abd al-Rahman had criticized Haykal for his apologetic stance on Muhammad's polygyny; in her view, Muhammad's wives were lucky: better to have only a fraction of the attention of a great man than all the attention of a lesser one.[145]

More recent female authors have tended to spend less time on polygyny, even if they treat the wives as a collective. More dramatically, many focus their attention on one wife, typically Aisha, who has been the chief protagonist of sprawling novels. One is the historical romance by Sherry Jones, *The Jewel of Medina* (2008), which occasioned a kerfuffle when its first publisher dropped it at the last minute, reportedly afraid of possible reprisals. Jones, who calls the tale of Muhammad and his "favorite wife" "one of the most touching love stories ever recorded," surrounds her novel with a paratext which explicitly sets up Aisha as a compelling figure.[146] She claims that Aisha was engaged at age six and "according to numerous accounts" married at nine, though "they consummated the marriage later, when she had begun her menstrual cycle. Although the tender age may seem shocking to us now, scholars generally agree that the marriage was motivated by politics." The other is Kamran Pasha's *Mother of the Believers* (2009), generally better received, whether because the author is Muslim or male, or because it fell outside the generally scorned romance genre.[147]

Neither was as critically well-regarded as their precursor. Assia Djebar (b. 1936) published *Far from Medina*, which "retold the early years from the voices of women, about women and for women," and in which Fatima and Aisha played key roles, the former "an outspoken, fighting feminist" and the latter recalling and narrating events. Djebar, in one view, "reclaim[ed] women's history of the advent of Islam . . . [seeking] out and privilege[ing] the female voices in the Islamic sources, and used her literary skill to imagine what the women of the time transmitted orally to future generations."[148] One critic, however, asserts that she gets it wrong, that she misreads the Arabic sources and, indeed, is not qualified to read them.[149] The charge is that Djebar adopts Western stereotyped images of Muslim women as silenced, and finds in the historical sources only what she intends. As much as any other perceived failing on Djebar's part, it is her critical stance toward the canonical Arabic historiographical tradition that provokes this attack.

Not quite a novel, but also a marked departure from the classical historical tradition, Nadia Yassine, a Moroccan Islamist with a complicated relationship to feminism, has written an online series of "vignettes of the life of the Prophet" in which she treads a course between minutely documented historical sources and "iconoclastic critic[ism]" of those texts, presenting a deliberately feminine perspective on the incidents she recounts.[150] She "did not challenge the authority of Muslim men—whether the classical scholars, modern authorities, or her contemporaries," although "perhaps there is a subtext" in her reimagining of Muhammad's life, "implying that Muslim men have been wanting in telling the story of the Prophet."[151] This view lies behind Tamam Kahn's *Untold*, in which she aims to join "the historical and the intuitive as respectfully as possible."[152]

These women's works rely on the same sources used by male biographers throughout the centuries, with very different results. If ʿAbd al-Rahman, as one scholar notes, "has written no 'life' of Muḥammad"—and, indeed, strikingly few Muslim women have authored *Lives* in forms typically used for the purpose—then it is worth thinking about what forms of life story count as proper biography.[153] Samira al-Zaiyyid, a scholar in the exclusively female traditionalist Qubaysiyyat network in Syria, has published a ten-volume encyclopedia, as well as a two-volume abridgment (*The Collective Epitome of Prophetic Biography*), used for teaching.[154] Her use of this format is in keeping with the Qubaysi preference for traditionalist (male) forms and norms, with the salient difference being the all-female nature of their scholarly communities. The only stand-alone biography of Muhammad I have encountered written by a Muslim woman is *The Book of Muhammad:* a small volume in English, unencumbered by scholarly apparatus, by Austrian journalist Mehru Jaffer.

A handful of other women have published English-language lives of Muhammad, including Armstrong and journalist Hazelton, whose *The First Muslim: The Story of Muhammad* appeared in 2013.[155] Women are overrepresented among authors of children's books in European languages. These books by women include Demi's lushly illustrated and generally well-received *Muhammad*, Marston's biography for secondary students, and Sarah Conover's 2013 "young adult" biography, brought out by the Unitarian Universalist publishing house. *Muhammad: The Story of a Prophet and Reformer* imaginatively reconstructs his infancy, childhood, and teen years and chronicles his early prophetic career. It closes with the emigration, avoiding controversial topics. (The issue of wives, for instance, is disposed of summarily in a way that emphasizes his monogamous bond: "He married a number of times after his wife of twenty-five years, Khadija, died."[156]) Apart from these introductory biographies, which aim at a different target audience, all recent biographies by women participate in the contemporary marketplace of ideas about spirituality, politics, and pluralism, which are the subject of Chapter 6.

Chapter 6

An Enlightened Man

On his way to see his wife Amina, Abdullah, son of 'Abd al-Muttalib, passed by the Kaaba. Though he did not realize it, a light shone from his forehead. A woman he encountered along the path tried to entice him to her bed. He declined, and continued his journey, visiting Amina and conceiving Muhammad. Returning home, he saw the woman again. She made no overture this time. When he asked why, she told him that the white light that had blazed between his eyes the previous day was gone.

This story has long been a staple of Muslim accounts of Muhammad's life. Ibn Ishaq gives two versions, which confirm that there was something special about Muhammad even before he was born. In one, the woman is the sister of Waraqa, Khadija's Christian cousin. He had told her to expect a prophet to arise from among their people; recognizing the sign, she proposes to Abdullah, even trying to sweeten the deal with one hundred camels. In the other version, the woman is another wife of Abdullah. He approaches her, but she turns him down because he needs a bath. He leaves her, bathes, and visits Amina instead. The woman's finicky attitude showed her unfit to bear God's prophet.[1] As Ibn Ishaq concludes: "So the apostle of God was the noblest of his people in birth and the greatest in honor both on his father's and on his mother's side."[2]

Muhammad's conception was unusual, marked by the transmission of the light—in some later accounts, safeguarded since creation and passed down through his ancestors—but in other respects ordinary. Unlike the conception of Jesus, which the Qur'an says took place by means of the Holy Spirit and with the intervention of an angel, both of Muhammad's parents were human, though exceptional.

What do moderns do with this story of the Muhammadan light? Some devout believers and writers still relish the tale, embellishing it and connecting it to other miraculous events surrounding Muhammad's birth and childhood, including the angel removing the black speck from his breast. These stories are told in celebrations of the Prophet's birthday. Although there has long been concern among some scholars about how precisely Muslims celebrate, in the last two centuries puritanical opposition to any commemoration has increased substantially. In a related development, tales that have long furnished material for pious devotion as well as theological elaboration about the preexistence of Muhammad and his importance to creation have become less central to Muslim accounts of Muhammad.[3]

Why this marginalization? Muir wrote, describing one such "fanciful fiction" recounting "how the Light of Mohammed, created a thousand years before the world, passed from father to son, down to the Prophet's birth," that it "forms a kind of celestial romance, the playful fantasy of an uncontrolled imagination."[4] Muir's rejection, which regards the Muhammadan light—like other supernatural elements in Muhammad's life—as an invention, garnered few direct rebuttals. Those who engaged directly with his work were more concerned with arguing for Muhammad's social and moral virtues than his cosmic status. Many Muslim authors strip miraculous occurrences and portents from Muhammad's story without any outright denial; this practice of simple omission of popular superstition, unworthy of retelling, is in keeping with a broader "desanctification of the Prophet."[5]

Stories of holy figures across religious traditions use light motifs, of course. This book has noted comparison for purposes of denigration, and comparison for purposes of exaltation, but one also finds comparison for purposes of illustrating a broader truth. Religious studies scholars have attempted to remain attentive to the specificity of stories while analyzing shared elements. Marilyn Waldman's posthumously polished and published *Prophecy and Power: Muhammad and the Qur'an in the Light of Comparison* argues for a more thorough rethinking of categories; the act of comparison ought not to be to apply a preexisting notion of prophethood or prophecy to Muhammad (or biblical figures) but to do two things. The first is to use those figures and the ways in which they have been understood to rethink the categories used for comparison. Second, and more intriguingly, is to look at the ways figures, including Muhammad, used comparison as part of their rhetorical strategies.

In addition to scholarly comparison, which attempts to understand rather than to find religious truth, one finds appreciative outsiders with devotional sensibilities who may not believe in the literal truth of such tales as the Muhammadan light but who expect to gain spiritual wisdom from the encounter with it. In similar ways to the deracinated versions of Buddhism or yoga that flourish in America, some non-Muslims approach the Muslim tradition as a source of enlightenment, and Muhammad as a spiritual teacher from whom they can learn. In her first biography of Muhammad, Karen Armstrong wrote: "In all the great religions, seers and prophets have conceived strikingly similar visions of a transcendent and ultimate reality. . . . I believe that Muhammad had such an experience and made a distinctive and valuable contribution to the spiritual experience of humanity."[6] More generally, "the Muslim interpretation of the monotheistic faith has its own special genius and has important things to teach us."[7] Fifteen years later, in her second biography, she made a similar case that Westerners need to know about Muhammad, but focused less on spirituality and more on social issues: "As a paradigmatic personality, Muhammad has important lessons, not only for Muslims but also for Western people." The example of his "tireless campaign against greed, injustice, and arrogance," his "effort to bring peace to war-torn Arabia," and his "creative effort to evolve an entirely new solution" when "the old way of thinking would no longer suffice" are vital today: "We entered another era of history on September 11, and must strive with equal intensity to develop a different outlook."[8]

Muhammad, Jesus, and the Buddha

A superficial but not unimportant difference between comparisons done in the eighteenth and nineteenth centuries and comparisons done in the twentieth and twenty-first centuries is the shift from the triad of Moses, Jesus, and Muhammad to Muhammad, Jesus, and the Buddha.[9] Whereas the early eighteenth century featured Moses, Jesus, and Muhammad as a trio of impostors—and whereas for much of the nineteenth century others were keen to join Muhammad to or separate him from biblical figures—by the late nineteenth century, the landscape had shifted: Buddhism had made its debut on the stage of world religions (as Indian author Ameer Ali acknowledged), and Moses was comparatively less important.

Today, authors often treat Muhammad, Jesus, and the Buddha in parallel. Peter Manseau's chronicle of holy relics advertises, on the inside flap, "postmortem accounts of Jesus, Buddha, Muhammad, and a crowd of other holy souls."[10] Jane Dammen McAuliffe prefaces her discussion of "prediction motifs" in "Al-Ṭabarī's Prelude to the Prophet," with nods to Buddhist biographies and Christian exegesis.[11] Jonathan Brockopp introduces his *Cambridge Companion to Muḥammad* by observing that "the popular veneration of Muḥammad is quite similar to that offered to Jesus, the Buddha, and countless other religious figures around the world."[12] In *Memories of Muhammad,* Omid Safi draws a parallel between the spiritual centrality of Muhammad's ascension and "the crucifixion of Jesus and the enlightenment of the Buddha"; he also notes that "Muslims' perceptions of the Prophet have remained no more static over the centuries than have Christians' estimations of Christ or the Buddhists' engagement with Gautama Buddha."[13]

The Enlightenment-era linkage of Moses, Jesus, and Muhammad as three impostors fraudulently claiming inspiration stands in sharp contrast to the joining of Muhammad, Jesus, and the Buddha in Deepak Chopra's Enlightenment series, a volume on each man available in a boxed set. Chopra's approach attests to their joint truthfulness, or at least usefulness. In *Muhammad,* Chopra writes of his own "fascination with the way in which consciousness rises to the level of the divine. This phenomenon links Buddha, Jesus, and Muhammad."[14] However, he still treats Muhammad differently. *Buddha: A Story of Enlightenment* and *Jesus: A Story of Enlightenment* are joined by *Muhammad: A Story of the Last Prophet.*

Though this is not Chopra's aim in his fictionalized accounts, others have attempted to find the "true" historical figures behind the legends of these three men. The archaeological and textual quest for the historical Jesus had a parallel in the Orientalist search for the man behind the statue—that is, the historical Buddha.[15] A tension between doctrine and biography meant that a distinction between the Jesus of history and the Christ of faith came to be accepted in many circles as a functional compromise. Buddhists have been less interested in the connection between the Buddha's life and his teaching, in part because that teaching downplayed the role of his own life.[16]

Muhammad is a slightly different case. Muslims have long sought guidance from records of Muhammad's human deeds, though in the modern era far more people attribute far greater weight to those acts in comparison with other elements of his role. What has changed is primarily the celebration of Muhammad's historicity, sometimes contrasted directly with the comparatively scarce evidence of other prophets' lives. In his 1925 Madras Lectures, Syed Suleman Nadvi signaled "historicity" as the first criterion by which to judge anyone's claim to be a model for humanity.[17] A related assumption is that the facts of Muhammad's life can be known independently of the authoritative and charismatic lineages of teachers and spiritual guides, and indeed apart from Muhammad's cosmic status as the jewel of creation. The historical Muhammad siphons attention from the luminous ethical exemplar: the lessons adhere in recorded facts. Very recently, moreover, some biographies written for non-Muslims have sought to connect the life and the lesson.

Where does the miraculous fit in to this picture? Scholars who quest for the historical Muhammad treat legends as "incrustations from fairyland" overlaying factual biographies.[18] Removing mythical debris, one uncovers the historical figure. Influenced by the "historical Jesus" scholarship, which sought to determine what could be precisely known of Jesus's life, Michael Edwardes introduces the London Folio Society's translation of Ibn Ishaq's *Life* with an attempt to extract a factual core from later embellishments. He distinguishes between objective facts and the "aura of the miraculous" that early biographers added, "a rich accretion of myth and miracle, mysterious portents and heavenly signs," all of which are present in the story of the "legendary Muhammad." Edwardes is confident that "behind the legendary Muhammad there lies one of the great figures of history . . . [and that] it is possible to build up the events of his real, as distinct from his symbolic life."[19]

In addition to attempting to discover the man in question, there was an attempt to understand the faith that grew up around him.

Pointing out the centrality of "the historical person of the Buddha and the incipient period of [Buddhism's] history" to early study of that tradition, historian of religion Tomoko Masuzawa gives a list of *Lives* published over the nineteenth century. They bear titles like *Buddha and His Religion; Buddha: His Life, His Doctrine, His Order;* and simply *Life of the Budd'a.* One could easily substitute "Mahomet" for "Buddha" in any of the titles. She notes, too, the "two typical, nearly requisite, means of identifying an individual religious tradition as distinct, unique, and irreducible to any other: the naming of an extraordinary yet historically genuine person as the founder and initiator of the tradition, on the one hand, and the recognition of certain ancient texts that could be claimed to hold a canonical status, on the other."[20]

Unlike with Buddhism, Muslim tradition and Western scholarship had long recognized Muhammad as this "extraordinary yet historically genuine person." Yet similar dynamics were at work. The term *Mohammedanism,* already in limited circulation, displaced loaded phrases like "the Saracen heresy" and "Arabian impostor." Scholars—occasionally the same ones who worked on Buddhist texts—sought to delimit a universe of reliable texts from which to extract the basic facts of Muhammad's biography and the Mohammedan faith.[21] (The term *Islam* would only come into its own in the twentieth century as the name for the "religion" founded by Muhammad.) The well-studied textualization of Buddhism and Hinduism in the nineteenth century—owing a great deal to the energy and labor of Orientalist scholars, whose focus on ideals and doctrines expressed in purportedly authentic texts led to the study and description of particular religions ("isms") at the expense of lived practice—had a parallel in Islam. This was neither entirely successful—people's religious practice remains messy and difficult to classify—nor a one-way imposition. The newly canonical texts were taken up by some insider elites as "true" Buddhism or Hinduism or, in this case, "Islam." Stripped-down sets of religious norms became a criterion in intra-Muslim debates, as did these desanctified biographies of Muhammad. Not everyone was so quick to jettison the mythical and symbolic elements, however.

Instead of searching for facts underneath myths, another approach sought to uncover a different sort of truth *by means of* the myths. Stories about founders conveyed something of the "person in history." John Fenton, in the late nineteenth century, applied this method to the births and awakening experiences (revelation on the one hand, enlightenment on the other) of Muhammad and the Buddha. He sought to show that, despite key differences, the myths that arose about them had universal elements. Moreover, Fenton saw both as examples of the "great man." He argued that "great men are creatures of the times which they themselves help to modify," and that by looking at myths, "we may obtain some knowledge of the man himself in history, as he appeared to his followers and contemporaries." This glimpse of the "person in history" does not correspond precisely to him as a "historic person" but as an idealized version, stripped of most of his "failings, weaknesses, peculiarities" and reenvisioned through the lens of core biographical motifs.[22] Although not factual, the mythological elements in the *Lives* of religious founders help us understand the impulses of followers, the lenses through which they seek to make sense of their towering figures. As historian of religion John Stratton Hawley notes, "Within each religion a powerful body of tradition emphasizes not codes but stories, not precepts but personalities, not lectures but lives."[23] These narratives serve a communal function, as did, in some views, the prophetic and religious impulses themselves.

Miracles, Founders, and Figureheads

Other scholars of religion were interested not in the venerating community but in how religious inspiration functioned within the psyche of extraordinary individuals. Acknowledging them as great men who did great things, these scholars sought to understand the "prophetic impulse" and its origins and effects on those who received or wielded it.

The broader transformations in ideas about religious figures that changed how Muhammad's purported miracles (or lack thereof) were viewed also made possible the attempt—rocky at first—to set such figures on a level field and judge them by the same criteria. The transition from religious polemic to "comparative religion" was halting and bumpy. Marcus Dods's 1877 book *Mohammed, Buddha, and Christ* sits at the cusp, torn between two aims. His title establishes the three men's equivalence. The contents, however, betray this superficial equality: two chapters on Mohammedanism and one on Buddhism are followed by a chapter on "The Perfect Religion." (Sometime in the last century, a reader of the University of Michigan's copy crossed out "Perfect" and wrote in "Christian"; the scribble is now digitized for posterity.)

For all that he named individuals in his title, Dods primarily used the men as metonyms for their religions. The book originated as a series of lectures to students of London's English Presbyterian College. How Islam, Buddhism, and Christianity have been and ought to be studied is one of its key concerns:

> One cannot fail to notice in the literature of the day a tendency more or less pronounced to put all religions, including the Christian, more nearly on one level, and especially to deal with them as if they were all alike outgrowths from the same root, man's religious faculty. This tendency has been stimulated by the comparative study of religions, which has brought to light the large number of resemblances existing in the various religions of the world but which has as yet been backward in detecting, analyzing, and defining essential distinctions.[24]

Dods lamented this development. Despite common impulses in Islam, Christianity, and Buddhism, the distinctions matter more.

Later authors were less wary of comparison and less willing to explicitly advocate one religion over another—even as they continued to appeal to the newfangled trinity of Muhammad, Jesus, and the Buddha. For instance, Edwardes begins by setting Muhammad in parallel to other figures: "It is always extremely difficult to be objective about the life of the founder of a great religion—his personality is inevitably blurred by an aura of the miraculous. Early biographers are preoccupied, not with historical fact, but with glorifying in every way the memory of one they believe to have been a Messenger of God or even God Himself." Edwardes lumps together a *presumed* "Messenger of God" and one *presumed* to be "God Himself" as instances of a larger category: "founder[s] of . . . great religion[s]."[25]

Edwardes implicitly sets Jesus in line with others, in sharp contrast to the Bombay Tract and Book Society's *Life of Mahomet* from the previous century, which used Jesus to illustrate Muhammad's myriad shortcomings. In nineteenth-century India, the question of Muhammad's performance of miracles was a central element of religious polemics, as was more direct comparison between Muhammad and Jesus. The missionary *Life* compares Jesus and Muhammad in its final pages. The section begins with a disclaimer about the endeavor of viewing Muhammad and Jesus side by side: "It is difficult to make a fair comparison of Mohammad with Jesus Christ. Even if religious reverence towards 'the Son of God' did not restrain us, how could we compare the licentious polygamist, the robber, the fiery warrior, the inexorable bigot, with the benevolent and majestic 'Son of Man?'"[26] Muhammad's polygamy, relatively little discussed in the book, became the first means of distinguishing the two men, perhaps because the entire passage echoes Alexander Ross's 1653 treatment of "Mahumetanisme," in which "Islam provides the foil for Ross's version of Christian Orthodoxy."[27] Despite reticence about comparing the "Son of God" with a human being, the author manages to compare on several notes: "Mohammad was a leader of Arabian plunderers: Jesus went about doing good. Mohammad became a warrior at the head of armies: Jesus was 'the Prince of peace.' Mohammad was a man of unbounded sensuality: Jesus was 'holy, harmless, undefiled, separate from sinners.' Mohammad was ambitious: Jesus was 'meek and lowly in heart.' Mohammad rested his claims on secret revelations: Jesus did 'the works which none other man did,' healing the sick, and raising the dead."[28]

Like other nineteenth-century texts, the tract is preoccupied by themes of purity and corruption. It tells of secrecy, changeability, conflict, and contradiction in Muhammad's life, in contrast to the constancy of Jesus's life. Jesus "lived and died in Judea," while Muhammad "travelled and mingled with men of varying nations, and of conflicting religions." Sameness is safe; difference is dangerous. Positing intercultural contact as inherently problematic might seem an awkward position for a British Christian living in mostly Hindu India communicating to Indian Muslims to take. Yet lest there be any doubt that commingling and contamination can lead to devastating consequences, the final sentence of the work sums it up: "Mohammad was a destroyer: Jesus is THE SAVIOUR."[29]

We find a generally similar approach delivered in a more diplomatic tone from English evangelical Thomas Patrick Hughes, who had gradually became less vociferous in his criticism of Muhammad and Islam after returning from two decades of missionary work in India. Hughes connects Muslims' defective spirituality with their inferior exemplar. If Islam "has failed in raising the hearts of men to the high level of a spiritual Christianity, it must be because it does not possess in the character of Muhammad what Christianity possesses in the character of the Divine Jesus—a living example of purity and truth."[30]

Muslim comparisons of Muhammad and Jesus take a different tack, since Muslims revere Jesus as one of God's prophets. There are, of course, anti-Christian currents in Muslim thought, but no blame accrues to Jesus himself. Jesus is a divine messenger to whom Christians have inappropriately ascribed divinity. They corrupted the Gospels he brought, but Jesus remains unsullied. Muslims tend to treat Jesus's reputation more respectfully than do many inhabitants of nominally Christian countries of the West today. However, some modern biographies venture a tentative line of argument in which Muhammad compares favorably to Jesus.[31] These involve no denigration of Jesus but they suggest that Muhammad is a better model for humanity. Since he was a man with wives, family, and worldly concerns, he can be an appropriate guide and model in a way that Jesus, who lived an *unusual* and, in particular, celibate life, cannot be.[32] As Aisha 'Abd al-Rahman observes, while Christians claim that Jesus has a divine nature, "the Islamic message has insisted upon admitting the human nature of the Prophet. . . . He is attracted to a wife, becomes involved in family life, and suffers from love and hate, desire and abstinence, fear and hope. What applies to any human applies also to him, such as daily toil, being orphaned, bereavement, disease and death." The only exception to his susceptibility to human "frailties" is in those matters directly concerning his role as prophet.[33] Here, the elements of Muhammad's life that served as fodder for criticism by earlier thinkers become the basis for his elevation. Jesus's set-apartness renders him less exemplary. In her view, Muhammad's humanity makes his role that much more meaningful: "What honour, that a Prophet carrying the Message of Heaven should be a part of mankind itself."[34]

The decades between Hughes and 'Abd al-Rahman saw extensive debates over the precise nature of Jesus's historicity and humanity. Ernest Renan's famous *Life of Jesus*, published in French in 1863—almost exactly a century prior to Edwardes's edition of Ibn

Ishaq and shortly after the Bombay Book and Tract Society's *Life*—laid a new foundation for thinking about Jesus, and therefore about comparison between him and Muhammad. Given Renan's writings on Islam, his famous declaration about Muhammad and the full light of history, and his engagement in debate with Ahmad Khan, his *Life* was not only a "critical text in the intellectual history of France" but also a milestone in Egypt and India.[35] Shortly after the book's publication, Renan spoke of Jesus publicly as "that incomparable man." A century and a half later, it is difficult to comprehend the scandal of that utterance. "Incomparable" sounds like praise. But for pious inhabitants of the nineteenth century, the key term was *man:* "incomparable" or not, to call Jesus "that . . . man" was itself offensive.

By the 1960s, things had changed dramatically in popular approaches to Jesus and in views about religious pluralism, including about the inclusion of Islam. Edwardes's introduction to the *Life* assumes this parity, even as it substitutes Buddhism for Judaism in its appeal to tradition.

Armstrong adopts a similar framing technique in *Muhammad: A Prophet for Our Time.* Her two poles, though, are not legend and fact, but "transcendent reality" and "current events in the mundane sphere." She believes in a "sacred past," neither opposed to nor circumscribed by a factual one; historicity is not the holy grail. Rather, she looks for an insider's perspective: "The faithful scrutinize the sacred past, looking for lessons that speak directly to the conditions of their lives." She continues:

> Most religions have a figurehead, an individual who expresses the ideals of the faith in human form. In contemplating the serenity of the Buddha, Buddhists see the supreme reality of

Nirvana to which each of them aspires; in Jesus, Christians glimpse the divine presence as a force for goodness and compassion in the world. These paradigmatic personalities shed light on the often dark conditions in which most of us seek salvation in our flawed world. They tell us what a human being can be.[36]

Armstrong views the Buddha and Christ as "figurehead[s]" "in human form"—"paradigmatic personalities," like Muhammad, who "tell us what a human being can be." The three figures are equivalent only insofar as one understands Jesus as a human manifestation of divine ideals. Renan's "incomparable man" begins to look utterly ordinary.

Unlike Dods, Edwardes and Armstrong presume that readers can and should evaluate Muhammad in nonconfessional terms, just as non-Christians evaluate Jesus in nonreligious terms. As W. Montgomery Watt, author of three biographies of Muhammad, puts it: "What Muslim and other non-Christians are asked to accept in this world where religions mix is this core of historical fact about the teaching and achievement of Jesus as a human being but without the theological interpretations."[37] They should extend the same courtesy to Muhammad.

Great Moral Teacher(s)?

Civic and academic discourse in purportedly secular societies of North America and Europe demands that one separate the praiseworthy historical achievements from the religious message delivered by a religious "founder" or "figurehead." Whether this is possible remains an open question. Still more fraught, however, is the question of how religious believers ought to approach competing religious claims.

Given that the issue at stake is comparison, perhaps the question can best be addressed by a comparative example. C. S. Lewis, who died in 1963, was by training a scholar of medieval literature, though he is perhaps best known as the author of the Narnia series of children's books. He was also an amateur theologian and a popular Christian apologist. His commonsensical theology includes a famous argument, which he did not invent but popularized. In *Mere Christianity,* he targets those who proclaim their admiration for Jesus as a "great moral teacher" but reject his divinity and his status as savior. This, Lewis says, is untenable. Either Jesus was telling the truth about being the Son of God or he was lying. If he was lying, either he was insane, "on a level with the man who says he is a poached egg," or he was purposefully, maliciously misleading people: "the Devil from Hell." Since one cannot, Lewis insisted, admire a madman or an evil fraud, one must either reject Jesus entirely or accept him as the Son of God and savior of humankind. What one must not do, he said, is say "the really foolish thing that people often say about Him: 'I'm ready to accept Jesus as a great moral teacher, but I don't accept His claim to be God.'"[38] Lewis's trilemma has attracted plaudits and rebuttals that do not concern us here.[39] What matters is the problem itself.

Such willingness to accept Jesus as a human moral teacher tout court would have been unintelligible to medieval Christians or nineteenth-century missionaries. It is possible because of intertwined developments in European thought. Enlightenment rationality and Romantic ideas about genius had humans seeing profound truths without any necessary Divine hand. The Enlightenment leveling of the religious playing field and the rise of academic

may include recognition of Muhammad's prophethood *for Muslims*.[42] One sign of progress is "evangelical Baptist theologian Timothy George's measured Christian conservatism regarding Islam." Rejecting other evangelicals' pronouncements that the Qur'an resulted from demon possession, George "affirmed that Muhammad's establishment of monotheism was 'in keeping with biblical faith'."[43] At the same time, he insisted that there were certain irreconcilable "truth-claims" made by each religion, particularly having to do with the nature of Jesus.[44] This awareness that there are limits to how far such recognition can proceed is absent from some Muslim writings. Ahmad Gunny, in his history of French and English depictions of Muhammad, complains that although "in 1965, Vatican Council II stressed in positive terms those aspects of his preaching that are acceptable to Christians . . . it kept silence over Muhammad's claim to divine inspiration, and there still seems to be some ambivalence towards Islam and Muhammad in Roman Catholic thinking."[45] Does the pope, the leader of a faith whose truth claims rule out Muhammad's prophethood, really err by remaining mum as to whether Islam's message is divinely inspired? (Indeed, given Pope Benedict's inflammatory 2006 remarks about Muhammad, silence seems the better option.) In contemporary Western societies, citizens widely agree on equal accommodations for religious belief and observance (or nonbelief and nonobservance) as a matter of civic law. Is it reasonable to suggest that private citizens, much less religious leaders, must go beyond tolerance to accept rival truth claims, some of which diminish or outright contradict their own beliefs?[46] Or, put a different way, "How much of the Islamic view of Muhammad can outsiders share, without becoming Muslims and ceasing to be outsiders?"[47]

These are large questions, beyond the scope of this book to answer. We may consider, however, how these questions manifest in biographical writings. There have been a few explicitly Christian attempts to grapple with Muhammad's life from a pluralist rather than a polemical perspective. One approach has been to see Muhammad as representing a kind of incomplete or inferior— in Carlyle's term, "bastard"—Christianity. Such *Lives* recognize something human and perhaps legitimately prophetic, neither deluded nor demonic. The largely unspoken view in these portraits is that he may have been connecting in some way to a divine current flowing through the universe, but he was not directly commissioned by God in the way that the Hebrew prophets were. In such attempts to explain Muhammad's religious-spiritual impulses, God is surprisingly absent. Despite their Christian origins, they often smack of broader Romantic sensibilities. Watt, for instance, disclaiming any particular theological expertise, discusses in broad terms a "creative imagination" shared by artists, in which universal themes emerge. "Prophets and prophetic religious leaders," he suggests, "share in this creative imagination" and "proclaim ideas connected with what is deepest and most central in human experience, with special reference to the particular needs of their day and generation." Watt here combines the notion of a creative current running through the universe that poets and prophets alike tap into with a sense of the social utility of their works.

Tor Andrae, a Lutheran bishop, attempts to connect the larger question of how to think about religion and religious figures with the personal story of Islam's prophet.[48] *Mohammed: The Man and His Faith* was originally published in German in 1932, the same year Haykal's first review article on Dermenghem appeared. Andrae writes:

> There was a time when it was considered in accordance with good scientific method to interpret all religious development as due to . . . social and economic factors, which operated with the simple inevitability of natural law, or to ideas and conceptions which, by their necessary and reciprocal interaction, gave rise to religious dogmas and systems. . . . No place was really left for the great, leading, creative religious personalities. To go back to the particular personal experience, or the prophetic initiative, as the source of the new religious creation, was regarded as an act of scientific bankruptcy.[49]

He argues instead for the force and impact of "the creative spiritual life" of extraordinary people: "In all religious movements whose history we can really survey the awakening power proceeded from an individual personality."[50]

In recounting Muhammad's creative shaping of what the title ambiguously calls "his faith" (is it his inner certainty or the religion he founded?), Andrae neither takes Muslim claims about revelation at face value nor assumes that Islam can be reduced to a mash-up of earlier religions:

> The development of Islam . . . presents us with yet another proof that the prophetic personality is the original source of new religious creation. . . . That the fundamental ideas of Islam were borrowed from the Biblical religions is a fact which requires no further discussion. . . . And yet it is cheap wisdom to think that this disposes of the question of Mohammed's

originality. . . . There is originality enough in Mohammed's achievement in catching up into a vital and adaptable personal synthesis the spiritual potentialities of his age.[51]

The traditional biographies allow glimpses of Muhammad's inner life, as does the Qur'an; reading it "enables us to trace a soul which wrestles with its fate, and with naïve candour reveals its aims and hopes, as well as its faults and accomplishments, its weakness and courage."[52]

In Andrae's view, "That Muhammad acted in good faith can hardly be disputed by anyone who knows the psychology of inspiration."[53] Yet this does not rule out his conscious shaping of what was "originally spontaneous inspiration."[54] For Muir, this had been the crux of the problem, the moment when Muhammad turned from spiritual seeker to grasping striver—or, as Peirce Johnstone put it, when his "sincere . . . desire to reform his countrymen" led him to take "the false, fatal step of proclaiming himself the Apostle of God," and then "to exalt his personal authority he used the Holy Name."[55] For Andrae, that "the Prophet gradually grew accustomed to think of ideas that emerged in his consciousness and decisions that matured in his soul as direct expressions of the Divine will" did not make him an impostor. Rather, Andrae concludes, "A genuine prophet is one who really has a message to deliver, one in whose soul some of the great questions of his age have stimulated a restlessness which compels him to speak and for whom the ecstasy and prophetic inspiration are but the natural and inevitable expression of a strong lasting conviction and a genuine passion."[56]

There are limitations, though, to this celebration of Muhammad's creative soul, which come in the connection between his inner resources and his outer actions, which mix, unpredictably, forbearance and violence. Andrae concludes his reflections on a less flattering note: "We Christians are inclined to compare Mohammed with the unsurpassed and exalted figure whom we meet in the Gospels, and that we cannot avoid seeing his historical personality against the background of the perfect moral ideal to which the faith of his followers tried to exalt him. And when it is measured by such a standard, what personality is not found wanting?"[57]

Native Informants?

Similar questions about the relationship between Muhammad's actions and his character arise in more recent biographies. At least a dozen English-language biographies of Muhammad aimed at general audiences have been published in the United States and United Kingdom since the turn of the twenty-first century, undoubtedly spurred in part by interest in Islam after the September 11 terrorist attacks. Their authors include academics (Jonathan Brown, Tarif Khalidi, Daniel Peterson, Omid Safi), journalists (Lesley Hazelton, Barnaby Rogerson), public intellectuals (Karen Armstrong, Tariq Ramadan), and spiritual figures (Deepak Chopra), as well as a poet (Elliott Weinberger) and a professional polemicist (Robert Spencer). These categories are inadequate: Safi has a profile as a public intellectual; Ramadan, a doctorate and an Oxford professorship; Armstrong, a growing reputation as a purveyor of spiritual advice. What they share is that they are not divided strictly by religion. With the exception of Spencer, whose books provide reasonably accurate information framed and interpreted in relentlessly negative ways, these authors give at least somewhat positive accounts of Muhammad, which combine attention to historical fact with recognition of Muhammad's spiritual agency, or initiative. They also tend to devote significant attention to the Banu Qurayza, and their diverse ways of approaching the bloodiest event of Muhammad's career are revealing.

These contemporary publications on Muhammad have mixed audiences, too. In some ways, this continues a pattern established a century and a half ago, when Muslims and non-Muslims began to regularly read one another's work. Muir aimed his biography at non-Muslims, and when Muslims read the work, it provoked anger rather than appreciation, along with extensive engagement. Yet when Zaidi aimed at correcting non-Muslim misunderstandings in his *Mothers of the Faithful* he was fooling himself; only scholars and polemicists paid heed to Muslim authors, and scholars were interested in premodern writings, the earlier the better. Since the late twentieth century, however, and in the last decade in particular, Muslim-authored works have been published to appeal to general non-Muslim audiences as well as Muslims. This shift has partly to do with the changing times and partly to do with the works themselves. Large numbers of Muslims live and write in Europe and North America, some holding academic positions and others working as journalists and public intellectuals. Works composed or published in French and, especially, English have a global reach. For some topics, books written by Muslims have additional cachet by virtue of "authenticity," but this is often true for books about women's experiences (particularly insofar as they conform to the "victim" or "escapee" model) rather than for those on topics on which one is expected to be "objective."[58]

One of the books with a legitimate claim to a crossover audience is Tariq Ramadan's *In the Footsteps of the Prophet*.[59] It is the anti-Haykal. The tone is confident, not combative; the narrative smooth, not choppy. Ramadan digresses at times to make points about

contemporary relevance but avoids direct engagement with critics. And the title itself harks back to the earlier tradition: it emphasizes Muhammad's role rather than his name and uses the imagery
of a path, which is ubiquitous in Muslim writings on spiritual and
legal conduct.[60] The appeal to non-Muslims is deliberate, with the
idea that the subtitle's "Lessons from the Life of Muhammad"—a
life that Ramadan recounts in roughly chronological fashion—
are applicable to universal human struggles. (The original French
subtitle puts it even more clearly: *Spiritual and Contemporary
Teachings.*)[61]

Ramadan interweaves accounts of key events, such as the Battle
of the Trench and the retaliation against the Banu Qurayza, with
the lessons to be learned from them. The account of the siege of
Medina is embedded in a chapter titled "Tricks and Treason"—
both terms of which refer to Muhammad's enemies. When the
chapter opens, Muhammad and his community are facing a "difficult" situation. Their defeat by the Quraysh at Uhud a few years
earlier had led their opponents to believe them "vulnerable." Muhammad was able, sporadically, to ward off "planned attacks on
Medina," but they were facing Meccans who "desire[d] to eradicate
the Muslim community from the peninsula" and made alliances to
that end.[62] All of these descriptors portray Muhammad's community as beleaguered and him as, alternately, a capable leader using
his men to best advantage and someone forced reluctantly by circumstance into using military means of communal self-defense.[63]

Ramadan rejects the view of Muhammad as weak in Mecca,
strong in Medina.[64] Rather than emphasizing Muhammad's
strength, Ramadan illustrates Muslim vulnerability: "Many Muslims were taken prisoner during those years after falling into am-
bushes or simply being outnumbered by their enemies. They were

often tortured and dreadfully put to death, and tradition reports their courage, patience, and dignity in the face of death."[65] In this complex and treacherous milieu, the defection of allies such as the Banu Nadir tribe, "who lived inside Medina itself, made it impossible for the Muslims to set up a defense strategy."[66] Muhammad used "intuition," quick thinking, and decisive action to secure his community's safety by the "exceptional" expedient of cutting down tall palm trees. Once the tribe agreed to leave, he did not carry out "his threat to execute them" but instead let them leave with not only "their women and children" but also "a considerable amount of wealth."[67]

In similar fashion, Muhammad's next unanticipated military strategy was to ward off Meccan attackers by digging a trench to complement existing natural fortifications. In recounting Muhammad's adoption of the tactic from a Persian convert, Ramadan draws a lesson about creativity.[68] Ramadan has argued elsewhere that modern Muslims should borrow others' techniques and strategies.[69] Here, he roots such appropriations in Muhammad's precedent.

The expulsion of the Banu Nadir serves as a prelude to the bloodier story of the Banu Qurayza; the two form a thematic pair. Ramadan draws lessons from Muhammad's conduct in both. In the former, he lingers less on Muhammad's strategic vision or grasp of military tactics and more on care for the environment. About the palm trees, he writes: "Never again would the Prophet act in disrespect of creation, and he was to repeat again and again ... that such respect must be complete, even in wartime."[70] (Yahiya Emerick likewise points out Muhammad's "green" bona fides; prior to this incident, "he had always ordered his men to refrain from harming the environment in their campaigns." In this instance, though, "in order to shorten the conflict, he took the drastic step, as men in war sometimes must, of choosing expediency over principle."[71]) Ramadan is not preoccupied by strict follow-through on threats or the question of Muhammad's decisiveness and resolve; rather, as he writes in another context, beyond justice there is forbearance, "the excellence of the heart, that offers forgiveness or gives people more than their due."[72] Some of the lessons are about qualities like generosity—the Banu Nadir story is about an individual's way of being in the world—and others, like that of the Banu Qurayza, emphasize communal action.

Deepak Chopra's novelized biography *Muhammad: A Story of the Last Prophet*, told in nineteen chapters with different narrators, makes an unexpected counterpart to Ramadan's book. Like Ramadan, Chopra dispenses wisdom, and he too would probably prefer the modifier "spiritual" to "religious." One similarity is superficial: both books' covers show desert scenes, Chopra's including a distance view of a man walking through the sand. In fact, it shows footsteps, presumably representing those of the Prophet.

Chopra focuses on Muhammad's humanity: not only the things he shares with other important spiritual figures—Jesus and the Buddha—but also the things he has in common with ordinary human beings. His Muhammad, like Ramadan's, is someone from whom people can learn, not through formal dictates or the vision of his conduct preserved by Muslim jurists but by understanding his struggles in his confrontation with the Divine. However understanding Chopra is about Muhammad, he presents Islam and Muslims as particularly linked to a backward past: though every faith has its orthodoxy and fundamentalists (which he conflates), he equates Muslims in toto with "fear of the modern world."[73] As noted earlier, for him, Muhammad's conduct toward the Banu Qurayza is, like his marriage to the young Aisha, incomprehensible to non-Muslims but defended by Muslims as necessarily right and proper. (In fact, recent biographies by non-Muslims take a range of approaches to the conflict with the Banu Qurayza, from deflecting blame to signaling it as a regrettable but necessary demonstration of political will.[74] Salahi's revisionist discussion makes clear also that Muslims are not of one mind about the matter.)

British convert Muhammad Marmaduke Pickthall had already, in the concise biography which prefaced his 1930 English translation of the Qur'an, set the stage for deflecting blame for the slaughter of the "treacherous" Qurayza tribe, who were "conscious of their guilt" for having attempted to betray the Muslims. Muhammad, in a move that is described in straightforward military terms, "ordered war against" them. They "surrendered unconditionally" and "begged to be judged by a member of the Arab tribe to which they were affiliated. The Prophet granted their request and carried out the sentence of the judge: the execution of the men and the enslavement of the women and children."[75] In this account, Muhammad only acceded to the tribe's own wishes and followed through on established procedure.

In *Muhammad: A Biography of the Prophet,* Armstrong describes Muhammad's actions, contextualizing them but without exculpating him. Perhaps spurred by the desire to combat anti-Muslim sentiment in the wake of September 11, her later biography shifts blame onto the arbiter, emphasizing his responsibility for the decision to execute the men.[76] Hazelton is one of the few authors to suggest that Muhammad himself bore substantially more responsibility for the gruesome outcome. Although the arbiter made the decision, Muhammad selected him knowing he was a "militant hard-liner" who could not be expected to show clemency. In her view it was a political strategy that accomplished its purpose of instilling respect and fear among other potential defectors precisely because it was a departure from customary modes of tribal dispute resolution.[77] Whether they themselves make explicit comparisons, these authors write in awareness that readers will undoubtedly compare Muhammad with other figures—Jesus, current national leaders, Muslim religious figures. Safi's *Memories of Muhammad* brings this comparative element to the fore.[78] It is also about communal boundaries and (mis)understanding. He makes the interreligious dimensions of his project explicit, and resists the monochromatic portrait of Islam and Muslims that Chopra paints. "Difficult" passages from scripture exist in all three "Abrahamic" traditions, but he lays out a constructive and positive path. "If," he writes, "we are willing to participate in a culture of generosity that affirms that *all* of our traditions contain verses, teachings, and practices that are at first glance—and sometimes at second and third glance—profoundly problematic, and that we must come to terms with them, and that all of our traditions also contain profound beauty and wisdom, then there is a journey we can take together." That journey involves recognition of the unpleasantness in Muhammad's life but also the triumph over difficulties; it also acknowledges that one's choice of lenses through which to view any tradition affect the resulting view.

Unlike the works of Anglo-Muhammadan authors of the late nineteenth century, or Egyptian writers of the first half of the twentieth century, Muhammad's world-altering accomplishments are not the centerpiece of these books. Yes, it matters that he accomplishes remarkable things. Chopra's back cover advertises "The Revelation That Changed the World." But the acts are connected also to interior changes: Muhammad "remade the world by going inward."[79] Nasr's *Muhammad: Man of God* refers to the importance of "the spiritual dimensions . . . of the life of the person who changed human history."[80] Safi writes of the "Muhammadi revolution," in which inward transformation must precede outward change: "before there can be a social movement, there has to be a spiritual awakening."[81] The crucial elements of Muhammad's story being offered to readers in these books are not recipes for starting a socialist revolution or standing up to colonial officials or being strong in the face of religious opposition. Instead, they have to do with being an ethical person, aware of God in times of adversity, and confronting complex social and moral dilemmas with an acute sense of both responsibility and wonder. Some decades earlier, Andrae and Watt were interested in the "creative spiritual life" of prophets, these extraordinary individuals. These contemporary biographies presume that readers themselves will have creative spiritual lives and that, whether Muslim or not, Muhammad's life can serve as a resource for their individual quests to develop and enhance those inner lives.

Defying Categorization

Recent biographies defy neat division into modern and traditional, Eastern and Western, or Muslim and non-Muslim; instead, they make a hash of those categories. None does so more completely than the lyrical, minimalist *Life* by Eliot Weinberger. *Muhammad* captures far better than most recent Salafi biographies the tone, at once reverent and matter-of-fact, of premodern Muslim accounts. He draws from Tabari's *History*, *hadith* collections, the Qur'an, and a seventeenth-century Persian Sufi treatise. He resuscitates the miraculous elements that Haykal and his ilk had dispensed with, resurrecting the Muhammad of devotion.[82] He recounts the transmission of the primordial light, the splitting of the breast, the splitting of the moon, and his causing hair to grow on a bald man's head. Yet Weinberger's *Muhammad* is unmistakably modern in its organization and emphases. The first section narrates his life. The last, replete with miracles, recounts the night journey and ascension. The middle section describes his relationships with women. Though the material on wives and wonders is from traditional texts, its extraction from the quotidian details of expeditions, battles, and daily life results from an impulse toward thematic coherence indispensable to the modern biographical tradition. Weinberger sidesteps the contemporary impulse to contextualize or justify and instead merely relates; his characteristic authorial act is pruning. What is essential is the inclusion and placement of the material. Between the biography proper and the spiritual and legendary, Muhammad's relations with women are, quite literally, at the center of his story.

Conclusion

By the turn of the twentieth century, two largely separate streams of writing about Muhammad, one hagiographical and the other polemical, had converged in a single contentious body of literature. European and American portraits of the Prophet, shaped decisively by new notions of what made a man great and what counted as merit, set the agenda for Muslim depictions. Along the way, "authentic" historical sources from the first centuries of Islam became a touchstone for scholars and lay readers alike: all wanted to know the *facts* about Muhammad's life. Texts written symbolically came to be read literally. A shared rhetoric of evidence and objectivity pervaded biographies. So did a shared format—mostly narrative and chronological—and shared topics: pre-Islamic paganism, "revelation," violent encounters with hostile Meccans and Medinan Jews, and relationships with women—what Ziauddin Sardar calls "wives and warfare" and Omid Safi describes as "violence, sex, and heresy."[1] This does not mean, of course, that only one version of Muhammad appears in modern biographies. This is manifestly not the case. Both among Muslims and among non-Muslims, various approaches to the Prophet's life story coexist. Using raw materials from a handful of early Muslim texts, biographers paint diverging portraits of their subject. No matter the author's background, the results "depar[t] dramatically from—without necessarily contradicting"—the sources on which they are based.[2]

The considerable overlap among modern biographies illustrates the futility of appealing to a timeless clash of civilizations between Islam and the West. In Muhammad's own era, identities were fluid and factionalized.[3] In the fourteen hundred years since then, neither Islamic nor Western civilization has been a unified entity politically, economically, or religiously. Intra-Muslim dissension exists over everything from whether one ought to stand when reciting blessings on the Prophet, to whether one can depict Muhammad's face, to which of his wives are trustworthy as sources of information, to whom, if anyone, he designated as his successor. Much less has Christianity or the West been a cohesive unit. The idea of "Europe" is of fairly recent origin. Christianity was perhaps more brutally riven by the Reformation than Islam was by the Sunni-Shi'a divide.[4] The repeated Protestant invocation of Muhammad and the Pope as twin antichrists foils any simple Christianity-versus-Islam story.

Not only is the notion of unified Muslim and Western civilizations baseless, but so is the presumption of timelessness in ideas about Muhammad. A comparison of Humphrey Prideaux's *The True Nature of Imposture,* published at the turn of the seventeenth century, and Robert Spencer's *Muhammad: Founder of the World's Most Intolerant Religion,* published at the turn of the twenty-first, shows that they differ vastly on questions of pluralism. Prideaux asserts, from an avowedly Christian perspective, that Muhammad is an impostor; he lambastes Muhammad's lustfulness, ambition, and fabrication of revelation. Spencer paints no more flattering a portrait but proclaims Muhammad not an impostor but founder of a religion.[5] And, vitally, the main criticism of this religion is not that it is false but that it is intolerant. Prideaux would have scoffed at the idea of religious tolerance; he aimed to uphold singular religious truth.

Prideaux and Spencer differ on issues of pluralism but share an animating impulse: opposing *us* to *them*. In contrast, the Enlightenment tract *The Three Impostors* and Deepak Chopra's *Muhammad*, published around the same time, respectively, as Prideaux's and Spencer's books, assume an essential sameness of religions—the former, that all are similarly untruthful; the latter, that all contain truth.

In any survey, the choice to emphasize similarity or difference affects the end result profoundly. This study has toggled back and forth. Any body of work, looked at closely enough, reveals contradictory impulses and divergent tendencies. This is true for the views of Muhammad found in early modern English drama and Enlightenment-era French biography, late nineteenth century evangelical tracts and inter-war Egyptian *Lives*. Stepping back, one sees larger trends and patterns despite these internal variations.

A similarly irresolvable tension arises in considering continuity and change in Western approaches to Islam in general and Muhammad in particular. Two models compete. Jonathan Lyons believes that for the last millennium "the West's construction of Islam and Muslims has been essentialist, uniform, and not conducive to nuance and variation."[6] Change is minimal; positive ideas about Muhammad fail to catch on because of a pervasive "anti-Islam discourse." So powerful are recurring images of violence, backwardness, and misogyny that "the argument of any individual scholar is dissipated in the face of the overwhelming power of the broader discourse at work."[7] My experiences attest to the impotence of facts alone to change people's beliefs; as another scholar notes, "Westerners and Western intellectuals often choose what they want to believe about Islam, rather than believing what the evidence suggests they believe."[8]

Lyons's pessimism seems warranted, too, by the persistence of old accusations. In American evangelical circles, references to Muhammad as false prophet, impostor, and demonically possessed continue, giving the lie to the suggestion that "connections between premodern and modern prejudices are tenuous."[9] If such terminology faded from polite discourse by the nineteenth and twentieth centuries, it continued in certain religious contexts and has made a comeback since the September 11 attacks, as with the reverend Jerry Vines's Southern Baptist Convention speech in 2002, in which he called Muhammad "a demon-possessed pedophile."[10]

Yet contrary to Lyons, there have been significant changes. In earlier periods, insults against Muhammad were typically used for rhetorical force in attacks on other Christians. Roger Williams referred to "that stupendous Cheater Mahomet" while criticizing Quaker leader George Fox in 1676.[11] An 1851 article denigrated Mormonism's prophet-founder Joseph Smith as "The Yankee Mahomet."[12] In contrast, Vines targets Muslims directly. And new accusations piled alongside the old attest to new worries: preacher Jerry Falwell's declaration that "Muhammad was a terrorist" would have made no sense in a premodern context (though it echoes accusations of violence),[13] nor would have Vines's accusation of pedophilia (though it draws on old themes of sexual perversion).

Vines combined one of the oldest accusations with one of the newest. How he defended his charges in the firestorm that followed illustrates the common ground he and his Muslim critics stood on. When challenged, Vines cited authoritative *hadith* texts quoted in a book by putative "ex-Muslims." Rejoinders to Vines took two main forms. Some accepted the literal truth of his sources but stressed the need for historical contextualization ("things were different then"). Others insisted that these *particular* texts were not accurate, and alluded (vaguely) to different facts extractable from other texts. Thus, Vines and his Muslim critics might disagree about specific texts' reliability, but all share two presumptions. The first is that authentic early sources contain facts about what Muhammad did. The second is that by his deeds is how one judges him. In contrast to medieval emphases on personal habits or physical qualities, it is deliberate acts that matter. Medieval polemics associated objects of scorn with disgust-inducing filth; today, even the ugliest accusations hurled at Muhammad condemn his actions and not, for instance, his appearance or smell. Then, sloppy eating signaled degeneracy and animality, which were linked to violence and lust.[14] Today, it is marriage that matters, not table manners.

And yet, the accusation of pedophilia is meant to elicit not just condemnation but horror. Modern accounts are largely demythologized, written in terms of history, science, and fact as opposed to symbolism, myth, and legend.[15] In this case, though, Muhammad's sexual conduct becomes the locus for a renewed vision of Islam as an archaic and evil force. Medieval emphases on debauchery and lustfulness have become, since the colonial era, concern with oppression. Exactly which oppressive practices are singled out has also changed. William Muir, unbothered by Aisha's age, was troubled by polygamy and divorce, which, alongside slavery, debased women. Today, divorce carries little stigma in the United States and Europe, and even polygamy is quaint but unthreatening;

scripted television dramas like *Big Love* and reality shows like *Sister Wives* portray it as an exotic curiosity. On the other hand, child sexual abuse ranks with school shootings as a cause for condemnation. Sex with children is evil; thus, by implication, anyone who engages in it is evil. By the twentieth century, Muhammad had largely stopped being viewed as evil, even by people who did not much approve of him. The popularity of the pedophile epithet corresponds with a resurgence of the idea of evil, and the link between evil and Islam. Nor is it coincidental that the accusation surged after the clergy sex-abuse scandal: anti-Muslim and anti-Catholic sentiments remain connected.

Just as premodern polemics based on disgust were formulated about and by members of different communities, so, too, new conventions about sexuality and achievement are shared across communal and, increasingly, geographical boundaries. This sort of give-and-take has always been part of the Muslim biographical tradition. There was no pure "Islamic" tradition prior to the encounter with Western modernity. From the start, Muslim citizens of the late antique world borrowed from biblical and Near Eastern heroic motifs, praising Muhammad in the language of their times. Muhammad's biography included "ideational complexes whose mobility exceeded the limited reach of this or that ethnicity, linguistic group, or religious sect." This is not a question of corruption but merely a question of the circulation and interpenetration of ideas and style: certain "intellectual property was held in common" across sectarian lines.[16] This approach to Muhammad's life is not illegitimate but rather inevitable.

Yet although some authors always concerned themselves with responding to outsider claims and criticisms, and varied local traditions provided plentiful images with which to glorify Muhammad, prior to the nineteenth century, one could speak about a tradition of Muslim biography that was, in meaningful ways, coherent and self-contained. There is something qualitatively different about the ways in which Muslim and non-Muslim portraits of Muhammad intermingle and intermarry from the nineteenth century forward. Some of this has to do with power: in responding to Muir, Ahmad Khan and Ameer Ali adopted the literary conventions, the styles of argument, and quite literally the language of their opponent.[17]

Such exchanges worked both ways. Muslim writings about Muhammad have also affected the way the majority of non-Muslim authors approach his life. Deference to the main contours of the newly homogenized story, as outlined in Chapter 1, prevails; the only ones who consistently buck it are scholars sometimes too quickly anathematized as revisionists. Often, what they are revising is not "the Muslim tradition" but the small slice of it consistently presented and represented as the story of his life.

Certain sorts of material were excluded from Muhammad's life story as it developed in the seventh through ninth centuries; things got left out, written off, forgotten.[18] Another round of narrowing took place in the last two centuries. A few things Muslim tradition had marginalized got pulled back to the center of the story when Western scholars resuscitated them, such as the Satanic verses; other things simply dropped out. Sunni-centrism infects mainstream Western biography: the Prophet invariably dies with his head on Aisha's shoulder;[19] the first four caliphs are always "rightly guided"; and if Ali converts first, he is usually the first "youth" to do so, making Abu Bakr the first "man."[20] And "first" means after Khadija, who is virtually always forty when she marries Muhammad. The range of anecdotes one finds in modern biographies is strikingly narrow.

So is the cast of characters. Muhammad's wives, particularly Khadija and Aisha, displace other figures, such as Muhammad's mother or foster mother. The emphasis on conjugal rather than kin relationships grows from shifting social norms but is reinforced by research practices. As Islamic studies scholar Marion Katz observes, though they are central to the *mawlid* narratives that celebrate Muhammad's birth and infancy, "Neither Āmina nor Ḥalīma is a major figure in the mainstream historical tradition dealing with the Prophet's life."[21] Since the early biographies and chronicles are the main sources used to write Muhammad's life, Amina and Halima recede.

That authors draw from a small pool of anecdotes owes partly to an understandable desire for narrative coherence. Modern readers want the story—they do not want seven versions of the tale of Aisha's necklace that repeat or, worse, contradict each other on major points or minor details. No one wants to wade through lengthy lists of authorities and weigh the information presented according to the trustworthiness of its reporters. There are, it is true, premodern examples of this sort of writing, and presumably oral storytellers preferred continuous narration. But the prevalence of smoothed-out written accounts, which proceed mostly forward in time from a determined starting point, is recent and has led to a homogenized story. If one is going to tell an incident once, it will be the majority version. The fact that there *were* alternate versions often drops out entirely.

Texts containing competing accounts of what happened, for instance, during the night journey and ascension present a problem. So do the "divergent and contradictory" accounts of Khadija's age at her marriage to Muhammad, the number of sons she bore him, and even her date of death.[22] If Ibn Hisham presents accounts that report X *and* Y *and* Z about an event, what view does one impute to him? Modern practice treats *authors* as responsible for assessing material they report ("Ibn Hisham says"). By contrast, "traditional" readers saw compilers as responsible for collecting and presenting materials that readers, properly guided by their teachers, would assess.

Which raises the issues of reading, interpretation, and authority.

Modern Islam is a profoundly Protestant tradition.[23] Among Sunni Muslims in particular, core elements of post-Reformation Protestant textual practice enjoy widespread—though not universal—acceptance. Believers read scriptural texts in isolation from their commentarial traditions and often without expert guidance. Qur'an and *hadith* are widely translated into vernacular languages. Confronted by a difficulty or a question about religious doctrine or practice, a layperson is likely to turn to scripture—translations of the Qur'an often have a subject index, though keyword-searchable online texts are rendering other mechanisms obsolete.

These notions about texts, authority, and vernacular languages were influential in the encounters among scholars and texts which shaped interreligious and intra-Muslim debates. This does not mean that modern Islam was created by missionaries and Orientalists and imposed wholesale on hapless Muslims.[24] Reformers like Ameer Ali and Muhammad Husayn Haykal—as well as more "traditional" figures like Qasim Nanautvi—were not dupes of colonialism. Instead, they used Western texts, ideas, and strategies to present, or invent, a usable Muslim past—a past that differs in crucial respects from once-traditional visions of early Islam—and a viable Muslim future. With the *sira* movement in the Indian subcontinent and the explosion of works on Islamic topics in Egypt, prophetic biography became "a tool to combat the cultural and intellectual onslaughts of the west."[25] And, even as "Modern Muslims' obsession with how Westerners represent the Prophet is inseparable from the issues of global power, hegemony, and colonialism,"[26] the form and content of Muslim prophetic biographies have been deeply conditioned by and implicated in those onslaughts. It "is not about an encounter between 'tradition' and 'modernity,' but about a peculiarly constituted modernity in which different traditions converge."[27]

The convergence of traditions which has been the subject of this book has occurred on a stage in which British and American writers and readers loom large, as does the English language itself. When Annemarie Schimmel published an expanded English version of *And Muhammad Is His Messenger* (1985)—her landmark study of poetic and mystical veneration of the Prophet—she omitted the images of him found in the German original. She explained that even though these were part of the medieval Muslim artistic tradition, contemporary Muslims might take offense. Unspoken is that although they were not likely to encounter them in the German edition, the English edition would have a global, and partly Muslim, readership.[28]

Muhammad's life continues to be central not only for ongoing exchanges—friendly and not-so-friendly—across confessional lines, but also for intra-Muslim polemical purposes. When the current head of one Ahmadi sect blames Muslim "misfortune" in the *Innocence of Muslims* debacle on the fact that "Muslims have no unity and no leadership," he is implicitly singling out his community as, unlike the majority of Muslims, unified around a single leader.[29] Debates of this sort existed long before Western political, military, and economic supremacy decisively altered the context for thinking about Muhammad. That said, the global preeminence of a hegemonic

Western order and its effect on Muslim thinking, including about Muhammad, are undeniable. Indonesian mogul Muhammad Syafii Antonio, using a team of authors from his Tazkia (piety) Institute, recently issued a glossy eight-volume encyclopedic biography of the Prophet.[30] It bears the title *Ensiklopedia Leadership & Manajemen Muhammad SAW, "The Super Leader Super Manager."* The first portion is technically in Bahasa, though loan words are so evident that one need not bother with a translation. The abbreviation "SAW" stands for the Arabic blessing that pious Muslims attach to every mention of Muhammad.[31] The last part is in English. The title is reminiscent of Labib Riyashi's 1934 Arabic biography *Muhammad: The World's First Superman* in that it attributes to Muhammad characteristics and qualities that bear little resemblance to the facts of his life as typically told.[32] Can Muhammad be seen as a model CEO? Perhaps. After all, early Muslims wrote about him as a shepherd, because all prophets were shepherds; and mid-twentieth-century Egyptians wrote about him as a socialist reformer, because that is what they needed. Why should a businessman not write about him as the epitome of executive skill? "Leadership" and "Manajemen" are not quite the same as annunciatory dreams and miracles, but they have a cosmic reverberation all their own.

Notes

Introduction

1. Jonathan A. C. Brown, *Muhammad: A Very Short Introduction* (New York: Oxford University Press, 2010), 89–93. For an overview of these sources, see Robert G. Hoyland, "The Earliest Christian Writings on Muhammad: An Appraisal," in *The Biography of Muhammad: The Issue of the Sources,* ed. Harald Motzki (Leiden: Brill, 2000): 276–297. Michael Penn's forthcoming book on Syriac Christian reactions to the rise of Islam addresses these issues in more detail. *Imaging Islam: Syriac Christianity and the Reimagining of Christian-Muslim Relations* (Philadelphia: University of Pennsylvania Press, forthcoming).

2. Virginia Burrus, *The Sex Lives of Saints: An Erotics of Ancient Hagiography* (Philadelphia: University of Pennsylvania Press, 2004), 12.

3. New research profitably explores visual depictions of Muhammad as well as the intersections between such depictions and verbal portraits. See, for example, Avinoam Shalem, ed. *Constructing the Image of Muhammad in Europe* (Berlin. De Gruyter, 2013).

4. Abdul Hameed Siddiqui, *The Life of Muhammad (P.B.U.H.),* 2nd ed. (New Delhi: Islamic Book Service, 2002 [1975]), 340; 1st ed. 1969.

1. The Historical Muhammad

1. Tarif Khalidi's *Images of Muhammad: Narratives of the Prophet in Islam through the Centuries* (New York: Doubleday, 2009), 1–2, gives an even briefer summary of this "core story"; Matthew Dimmock's version, *Mythologies of the Prophet Muhammad in Early Modern English Culture* (Cambridge: Cambridge University Press, 2013), xiii, is shorter still.

2. John Tolan, *Sons of Ishmael: Muslims through European Eyes in the Middle Ages* (Jacksonville: University Press of Florida, 2008), 145.

3. Michelina Di Cesare, "Images of Muhammad in Western Medieval Book Culture," in *Constructing the Image of Muhammad in Europe,* ed. Avinoam Shalem (Berlin: De Gruyter, 2013), 11.

4. Nimrod Hurvitz, "Biographies and Mild Asceticism: A Study of Islamic Moral Imagination," *Studia Islamica* 85 (1997): 45; Chase Robinson,

Islamic Historiography (Cambridge: Cambridge University Press, 2002), 61–66.

5. Christian Smith, *Moral, Believing Animals: Human Personhood and Culture* (New York: Oxford University Press, 2003), 65.

6. A. Kevin Reinhart, "Juynbolliana, Gradualism, the Big Bang, and Ḥadīth Study in the Twenty-First Century," *Journal of the American Oriental Society* 130, no. 3 (July–September 2010): 413–444, at p. 416. Among Muslim biographers who incorporate this line—without citation—is Maulana Muhammad Ali; see Muhammad Ali, *Muhammad the Prophet* (Lahore: Ahmadiyya Anjuman Ishaat Lahore, 1993), 186.

7. Uri Rubin, *The Eye of the Beholder: The Life of Muhammad as Viewed by the Early Muslims; A Textual Analysis* (Princeton, NJ: Darwin, 1995), 1–3.

8. Alford T. Welch, "Muhammad's Understanding of Himself: The Koranic Data," in *Islam's Understanding of Itself,* ed. Richard G. Hovannisian and Speros Vyronis Jr. (Malibu: Undena, 1983), 15. Welch views the Qur'an as reflecting Muhammad's self-understanding, and the prophetic tradition (*ḥadīth*) and *sīra* literature as the product of the Muslim community's attempt to come to grips with Muhammad.

9. F. E. Peters, "The Quest of the Historical Muhammad," *International Journal of Middle East Studies* 23 (1991); see also his *Jesus and Muhammad: Parallel Tracks, Parallel Lives* (New York: Oxford University Press, 2011). Though pessimistic about prospects for Muhammad's biography, Peters is a great deal more optimistic about the textual history of the Qur'an. The scholarly literature on the Qur'an, even simply in relation to Muhammad's biography, is vast, and I have made no attempt to survey it here.

10. For the scholarly debate over whether Muhammad was in fact the Prophet's name, see Gabriel Said Reynolds, "Remembering Muhammad," *Numen: International Review for the History of Religions* 58, no. 2/3 (2011): 188–206. On the significance of the Prophet's name(s) for Muslims, see Annemarie Schimmel, *And Muhammad Is His Messenger: The Veneration of the Prophet in Islamic Piety* (Chapel Hill: University of North Carolina Press, 1985): 105–122.

11. Welch, "Muhammad's Understanding of Himself," 19; in Aloys Sprenger's view, "Up to his fortieth year Moḥammad devoutly worshipped the gods of his fathers." Sprenger, *The Life of Mohammad from Original Sources* (Allahabad: Presbyterian Mission Press, 1851), 94.

12. M. J. Kister, "'A Bag of Meat': A Study of an Early Ḥadīth," *Bulletin of the School of Oriental and African Studies* 33 (1970): 267–275.

13. See Fred Donner's retrospective review twenty years after *Hagarism*'s initial publication: *Middle East Studies Association Bulletin* 40, no. 2 (December 2006): 197–199.

14. Patricia Crone and Michael Cook refer to *Hagarism* as a book written "by infidels for infidels." *Hagarism: The Making of the Islamic World* (Cambridge: Cambridge University Press, 1977). Robert Spencer, *Did Muhammad Exist? An Inquiry into Islam's Obscure Origins* (Wilmington, DE: Intercollegiate Studies Institute, 2012).

15. Michael Cook, *Muhammad* (New York: Oxford University Press, 1996 [1983]), 74. Jonathan E. Brockopp notes that this book "is arguably less a biography of Muhammad than it is a study of problems facing anyone who would write such a biography." Brockopp, ed., introduction to *The Cambridge Companion to Muhammad* (Cambridge: Cambridge University Press, 2010), 13.

16. G. R. Hawting, *The Idea of Idolatry and the Emergence of Islam* (Cambridge: Cambridge University Press, 2002).

17. Fred Donner, *Muhammad and the Believers: At the Origins of Islam* (Cambridge, MA: Belknap, 2012); Donner, "Muhammad and the Debates on Islam's Origins in the Digital Age," in *Muhammad in the Digital Age,* ed. Ruqayya Y. Khan (Austin: University of Texas Press, forthcoming).

18. G. W. Bowersock, *Throne of Adulis: Red Sea Wars on the Eve of Islam* (New York: Oxford University Press, 2013).

19. At the level of mundane details, for instance, facts about Muhammad's father's death become suspiciously more specific as the tradition develops. See Cook, *Muhammad,* 63–64.

20. The term "stalemate" is Gregor Schoeler's. Schoeler, "Foundations for a New Biography of Muhammad: The Production and Evaluation of the Corpus of Traditions from 'Urwah b. al-Zubayr," in *Method and Theory in the Study of Islamic Origins,* ed. Herbert Berg (Leiden: Brill: 2003), 21–28, at p. 21.

21. Schoeler, "Foundations for a New Biography of Muhammad," 22. The phrase "salvation history" is John Wansborough's.

22. Herbert Berg, "Competing Paradigms in the Study of Islamic Origins: Qur'ān 15:89–91 and the Value of *Isnād*s," in *Method and Theory,* ed. Berg, 259–90.

23. Michael Lecker, "Glimpses of Muhammad's Medinan Decade," in *Cambridge Companion,* ed. Brockopp, 75.

24. Daniel C. Peterson, *Muhammad: Prophet of God* (Grand Rapids, MI: Wm. B. Eerdmans, 2007).

25. Stephen J. Shoemaker, *The Death of a Prophet: The End of Muhammad's Life and the Beginnings of Islam* (Philadelphia: University of Pennsylvania Press, 2012); see also Robert G. Hoyland, *Seeing Islam as Others Saw It: A Survey and Evaluation of Christian, Jewish and Zoroastrian Writings on Early Islam* (Princeton, NJ: Darwin, 1998).

26. Shoemaker, *Death of a Prophet*, 87.

27. David S. Powers, *Muhammad Is Not the Father of Any of Your Men: The Making of the Last Prophet* (Philadelphia: University of Pennsylvania Press, 2009).

28. John L. Esposito, *The Future of Islam* (New York: Oxford University Press, 2013). I quote from the reviews by Mohammed Shadman (August 20, 2010) and Andrew J. Stunich (April 1, 2010).

29. In a post-9/11 special issue of the *Message International* devoted to Muhammad, an article by "Abu Iqbal, Ph.D." refers to the centuries-long history of presenting Muhammad as an impostor. His list of recent contributions to that literature mentions Patricia Crone and Michael Cook, Tor Andrae, and Alfred Guillaume, whose *Life of Muhammad* is actually a translation of Ibn Ishāq: *The Life of Muhammad: A Translation of Ibn Ishāq's Sīrat Rasūl Allāh* (Karachi: Oxford University Press, 2003 [1955]). Abu Iqbal, "Muhammad in Rewrite," *Message International*, August–September 2002, 12–13, quotation from p. 12.

30. Nigel Hamilton, *Biography: A Brief History* (Cambridge, MA: Harvard University Press, 2008), 48.

31. Khalidi, *Images of Muhammad*, 16.

32. Hamilton Gibb, "Islamic Biographical Literature," in *Historians of the Middle East*, ed. Bernard Lewis and P. M. Holt (London: Oxford University Press, 1962), 54–58, at p. 54; see also Robinson, *Islamic Historiography*, xxiv–xxv.

33. On Ibn Sa'd's treatment of Muhammad's virtuous conduct in matters of manners and habits, see Hurvitz, "Biographies and Mild Asceticism." He notes that "the Traditionists projected onto the Prophet the behavioral patterns that they practiced or held in high esteem" (59). See also, with regard to food, Tor Andrae, *Mohammed: The Man and His Faith*, trans. Theopil Menzel, rev. ed. (New York: Harper and Row, 1960), 180.

34. There is an English translation of the entries for his wives, daughters, and female companions in Ibn Sa'd, *Women of Madina*, trans. Aisha Bewley (London: Ta-Ha Publishers, 1995).

35. Khalidi, *Images of Muhammad*, 16.

36. Dwight F. Reynolds, ed., *Interpreting the Self: Autobiography in the Arabic Literary Tradition* (Berkeley: University of California Press, 2001); see esp. pp. 38–51.

37. Leor Halevi, *Muhammad's Grave: Death Rites and the Making of Islamic Society* (New York: Columbia University Press, 2007), 50; in Halevi's view, it "reveals far too much about the concerns of Ibn Isḥāq, his informants, and his audience, even if it reveals nothing at all about the historical Muḥammad" (50–51).

38. Gordon D. Newby, *The Making of the Last Prophet: A Reconstruction of the Earliest Biography of Muhammad* (Charleston: University of South Carolina Press, 1989), 9.

39. Ibid., 2.

40. Newby, *Making of the Last Prophet*. Newby attempts to reconstruct the lost book from fragments in others' writings. On this reconstruction, see Ahmad Gunny, *The Prophet Muhammad in French and English Literature, 1650 to the Present* (Leicestershire: Islamic Foundation, 2010).

41. Uri Rubin, *The Eye of the Beholder: The Life of Muhammad as Viewed by the Early Muslims; A Textual Analysis* (Princeton, NJ: Darwin, 1995).

42. Bernard Lewis, "Gibbon on Muhammad," in "Edward Gibbon and the Decline and Fall of the Roman Empire," special issue, *Daedalus* 105, no. 3 (Summer 1976): 96.

43. Peter Matthews Wright, "Critical Approaches to the Farewell *Khuṭba* in Ibn Ishaq's Life of the Prophet," *Comparative Islamic Studies* 6, nos. 1–2 (2010): 217–249, at p. 220.

44. Ibn Ishaq, *The Life of Muhammad: Apostle of Allah*, ed. Michael Edwardes, trans. Edward Rehatsek (London: Folio Society, 1964); hereafter Ibn Ishaq, *Life of Muhammad*. A recent Dutch translation by Wim Raven, *Het leven van Mohammed: de vroegste Arabische verhalen* [The life of Muhammad: The earliest Arab stories] (Amsterdam: Bulaaq, 2000), likewise identifies the author simply as Ibn Ishaak.

45. Guillaume, *Life of Muhammad*.

46. The Arabic term is *maghāzī*. The first suggestion is Jaroslav Stetkevych, *Muḥammad and the Golden Bough: Reconstructing Arabian Myth* (Bloomington: Indiana University Press, 1996), 30; the second, S. A. A. Rizvi, "Muḥammad in South Asian Biographies: Changes in Islamic Perceptions of the Individual in Society," in *Self and Biography: Essays on the Individual and Society in Asia*, ed. Wang Gungwu (Sydney: Sydney University Press), 103. Tarif Khalidi, *Arabic Historical Thought in the Classical Period* (Cambridge: Cambridge University Press, 1996), 44, sees Wāqidī and Ibn Saʻd as "a pair." See, more broadly, pp. 44–48.

47. H. R. Idris ("Réflexions sur Ibn Ishaq," *Studia Islamica* 17 [1962]) observes that al-Wāqidī "never cites Ibn Isḥāq" and attributes this to his competing work (26); Khalidi, *Arabic Historical Thought*, 48, n. 53, disagrees, citing not Wāqidī's *Maghāzī* but Ibn Saʿd's *Ṭabaqāt al-Kubrā*'.

48. Lewis, "Gibbon on Muhammad," 95.

49. Al-Wāqidī, *The Life of Muḥammad: Al-Wāqidī's Kitāb al-Maghāzī*, ed. Rizwi Faizer, trans. Rizwi Fazier, Amal Ismail, and AbdulKader Tayob (London: Routledge, 2011), xvi.

50. Ibid.

51. Khalidi, *Images of Muhammad*, 2; see also Khalidi, *Arabic Historical Thought*, 45.

52. Schimmel, *And Muhammad Is His Messenger*, 130–131.

53. Khalidi, *Images of Muhammad*, 58. On al-Ṭabarī, see also "Al-Ṭabarī: An Introduction," in *Al-Ṭabarī: A Medieval Muslim Historian and His Work*, ed. Hugh Kennedy (Princeton, NJ: Darwin), 1–9, though it is mostly focused on his Qurʾan commentary.

54. Khalidi, *Images of Muhammad*, 17, 18.

55. Ibid., 18.

56. On this dream in Ibn Hishām, see Sarah Mirza, "Dreaming the Truth in the *Sīra* of Ibn Hishām," in *Dreams and Visions in Islamic Societies*, ed. Özgen Felek and Alexander Knysh (New York: State University of New York Press, 2012), 21.

57. Alexandra Cuffel, *Gendering Disgust in Medieval Religious Polemic* (Notre Dame, IN: University of Notre Dame Press, 2007), 13.

58. Ibid., 77.

59. Tolan, *Sons of Ishmael*, 19–34.

60. Ibid., 20; Etan Kohlberg, "Western Accounts of the Death of Muḥammad," in *L'Orient dans l'histoire religieuse de l'Europe: L'invention des origines*, ed. Mohammad Ali Amir-Moezzi and John Scheid (Turnhout: Brepols, 2000), 165–195. Cuffel reports anecdotes where Muhammad's corpse would be "devoured by swine, dogs, or in one case vultures," "making him doubly filthy—unclean because these creatures ate unclean things, and impure because the animals themselves were contaminating." Cuffel, *Gendering Disgust*, 76, 226.

61. Dimmock, *Mythologies*, 37; see also 40, 59–60. Dimmock reproduces an image of "Machomeete" being consumed by swine (32).

62. Cuffel, *Gendering Disgust*, 77. A Jewish polemic makes use of this Christian anti-Islamic material; see Cuffel, *Gendering Disgust*, 134; Cuffel also (135–136) discusses Christian polemics that denigrate Muhammad and his death through association with Jews. In "Christian

antibiographies," Muhammad's "life and smelly death . . . stood as a kind of anti-incarnation against which they could contrast that of Jesus" (154).

63. Humphrey Prideaux, *The True Nature of Imposture Fully Display'd in the Life of Mahomet*, 8th ed., corrected (London: E. Curll, 1723 [1697]), 101.

64. For these stories, see Kohlberg, "Western Accounts," and, briefly, Shoemaker, *The Death of the Prophet*, 301–302, n. 75; al-Wāqidī, *The Life of Muḥammad*, 333–334. The use of poison and the martyr's death suggest important parallels to stories of the deaths of the Shi'i Imams. See Matthew Pierce, "Remembering the Infallible Imams: Narrative and Memory in Medieval Twelver Shi'ism" (Ph.D. diss., Boston University, 2013), esp. ch. 4, "Betrayal." Alfons Teipen shows that Jewish culpability in the poisoning shifted in early Muslim biographical sources from individual responsibility to a small group of culprits to a collective guilt, reflecting an increased anti-Jewish sentiment occasioned by polemical exchanges in the eighth and ninth centuries. "The 'Poisoning Jewess' Motif in Early Muslim Biographies of Muhammad," unpublished paper, presented at the American Academy of Religion Annual Meeting, November 2013.

65. Halevi, *Muhammad's Grave*; Shoemaker, *Death of a Prophet*, 90–99.

66. Robinson, *Islamic Historiography*, 11.

67. Ibid., 11.

68. Ibid., 12.

69. Brown, *Muhammad*, 90–91.

70. Khalidi, *Images of Muhammad*, 134; Pierce, "Remembering the Infallible Imams."

71. Uri Rubin, "Muḥammad's Message in Mecca: Warnings, Signs, and Miracles," in *Cambridge Companion*, ed. Brockopp, 39–56.

72. Khalidi, *Images of Muhammad*; Omid Safi, *Memories of Muhammad: Why the Prophet Matters* (New York: Harper One, 2009); Carl Ernst, "Muḥammad as the Pole of Existence," in *Cambridge Companion*, ed. Brockopp, 123–138.

73. He argues that biographical narratives about, for instance, Muhammad's marriage to Maimuna, who is largely absent from modern biographies, were formulated in support of (or against) particular legal views. Joseph Schacht, "A Revaluation of Islamic Traditions," *Journal of the Royal Asiatic Society of Great Britain and Ireland* 81, no. 3–4 (October 1949): 143–154.

74. On the hope for Muhammad's intercession, see Schimmel, *And Muhammad Is His Messenger*, 81–104.

75. Safi, *Memories of Muhammad*, 265; Schimmel, *And Muhammad Is His Messenger*, 135–137.

76. On contemporary Muslim dreams of Muhammad, see Leah Kinberg, "Dreams Online: Contemporary Appearances of the Prophet in Dreams," in *Dreams and Visions in Islamic Societies*, ed. Özgen Felek and Alexander D. Knysh (Albany: State University of New York Press, 2012), 139–157; Amira Mittermaier, *Dreams That Matter: Egyptian Landscapes of the Imagination* (Berkeley: University of California Press, 2011). Mittermaier discusses veneration of the Prophet more generally at pp. 113–114.

77. Mittermaier, *Dreams That Matter*, 168.

78. Leah Kinberg, "The Legitimization of the *Madhāhib* through Dreams," *Arabica* 32, no. 1 (March 1985): 47–79; Mimi Hanaoka, "Visions of Muhammad in Bukhara and Tabaristan: Dreams and Their Uses in Persian Local Histories," *Iranian Studies* 47, no. 2 (March 2014): 289–303. Shahzad Bashir, "Narrating Sight: Dreaming as Visual Training in Persianate Sufi Hagiography," in *Dreams and Visions in Islamic Societies*, ed. Felek and Knysh, 233–247. Bashir notes that "dream narratives need to be treated as literary artifacts placed strategically within larger textual arrangements" (233).

79. Jonathan G. Katz, "Dreams and Their Interpretation in Sufi Thought and Practice," in *Dreams and Visions in Islamic Societies*, ed. Felek and Knysh, 181–197, at p. 190; see also Meenakshi Khanna, "The Visionaries of a *Ṭarīqa:* The Uwaysī Sufis of Shāhjahānabād," in *Dreams and Visions in Islamic Societies*, ed. Felek and Knysh, 273–96, at p. 280. Dreams raised another question about Muhammad's status. Was he alive, dead, or not really either? A core distinguishing element between the Barelvis and the Deobandis in India today has to do with the status of the Prophet and the appropriate way to show reverence for him. For a brief summary, see Clinton Bennett, *In Search of Muhammad* (London: Cassell, 1998), 184; Ernst, "Muḥammad as the Pole of Existence," 138.

80. Kinberg, "Dreams Online." Kinberg emphasizes continuities between contemporary and classical ideas about the Prophet's appearance in dreams, while noting that the rise of the Internet makes individuals' narratives about such dreams accessible in an unprecedented way. Amira Mittermaier, drawing on others' work, suggests that there may be more emphasis on appearances of the Prophet in dreams from the eighteenth century forward.

81. Some reject the great man Muhammad of recent biographies, pointing out that such depictions fail to convey something crucial about

him. See, for example, the Egyptian shaykh discussed by Mittermaier (*Dreams That Matter*, 125) and the British Muslim Timothy Winter ("Jesus and Muḥammad: New Convergences," *Muslim World* 99, no. 1 [January 2009]: 31–33).

82. Mirza, "Dreaming the Truth," 26.

83. Tolan, *Sons of Ishmael*, xiv.

84. Ibid., xiii.

85. Reginald Hyatte, trans., *The Prophet of Islam in Old French: The Romance of Muhammad (1258) and The Book of Muhammad's Ladder (1264)* (Leiden: Brill, 1997).

86. See Tolan, *Sons of Ishmael*, 46–63; Ronit Ricci, *Islam Translated: Literature, Conversion, and the Arabic Cosmopolis of South and Southeast Asia* (Chicago: University of Chicago Press, 2012), 61–65.

87. *Lex Mahumet pseudoprophete;* it is also sometimes titled *Lex saracenorum* (Law of the Saracens). See Thomas E. Burman, *Reading the Qur'an in Latin Christendom, 1140–1560* (Philadelphia: University of Pennsylvania Press, 2007); Ziad Elmarsafy, *The Enlightenment Qur'ān* (Oxford: Oneworld, 2009), 2; Jonathan Lyons, *Islam through Western Eyes: From the Crusades to the War on Terrorism* (New York: Columbia University Press, 2012), 85.

88. Dimmock, *Mythologies*, 38.

89. One exception is the *Book of Muhammad's Ladder*, a retelling of the Muslim story of Muhammad's night journey and ascent into heaven, which was little more than a translation of Muslim material. See Hyatte, *The Prophet of Islam in Old French*.

90. Tolan, *Sons of Ishmael*, 145. Tolan is remarking specifically on Pedro Pascual, but the insight holds true more broadly.

91. Marc Laureys, "History and Poetry in Philippus Meyerus's Humanist Latin Portraits of the Prophet Mohammed and Ottoman Rulers (1594)," in *Latinity and Alterity in the Early Modern Empire*, ed. Yasmin Annabel Haskell and Juanita Feros Ruys (Tempe, AZ: Arizona Center for Medieval and Rennaisance Studies; Turnhout: Brepols, 2010), 286.

92. Tolan, *Sons of Ishmael*, 134.

93. Ibid.

94. Ibid.

95. Matthew Dimmock, "'A Human Head to the Neck of a Horse': Hybridity, Monstrosity and Early Christian Conceptions of Muhammad and Islam," in *The Religions of the Book: Christian Perceptions, 1400–1600*, ed. Matthew Dimmock and Andrew Hadfield (New York: Palgrave, 2008), 66–88, at p. 67.

96. Thomas Conley, *Toward a Rhetoric of Insult* (Chicago: University of Chicago Press, 2010), 69–70.

97. John Tolan, afterword to *Contextualizing the Muslim Other in Medieval Christian Discourse,* ed. Jerold C. Frakes (New York: Palgrave, 2011), 249.

98. Jonas Otterbeck, "The Depiction of Islam in Sweden: An Historical Overview," http://inhouse.lau.edu.lb/bima/papers/Jonas_Otterbeck.pdf.

99. In French, *L'Alcoran des Cordeliers.* Thomas Conley, *Toward a Rhetoric of Insult* (Chicago: University of Chicago Press, 2010), 71.

100. Laureys, "History and Poetry," 293 n. 59.

101. Quoted in Irwin, *Dangerous Knowledge: Orientalism and Its Discontents* (New York: Overlook, 2006), 70.

102. Lyons, *Islam through Western Eyes,* 135; Elmarsafy, *Enlightenment Qur'ān,* 3–7.

103. Thomas S. Kidd's *American Christians and Islam: Evangelical Culture and Muslims from the Colonial Period to the Age of Terrorism* (Princeton, NJ: Princeton University Press, 2009) shows how American Christian thinkers from what later became the evangelical tradition used Islam in intra-Protestant debates and in anti-Catholic works, continuing to use epithets like "impostor," "false prophet," and "Antichrist." See esp. pp. 8–14, 17–18. For a rarer instance of modern Catholic linking of Protestantism and Islam, see p. 81.

104. Prideaux, *True Nature of Imposture,* 13; George Bush, *The Life of Mohammed: Founder of the Religion of Islam, and of the Empire of the Saracens* (New York: Harper and Brothers, 1837).

105. Laureys, "History and Poetry," 278. Muslims also accused Christians of sexual improprieties of various sorts. See, for example, Cuffel, *Gendering Disgust,* 148.

106. Elmarsafy, *Enlightenment Qur'ān,* ix.

107. On Bedwell, see Matthew Birchwood, "Confounding Babel: The Language of Religion in the English Revolution," in *The Religions of the Book,* ed. Dimmock and Hadfield, 142–143; Guy G. Stroumsa, *A New Science: The Discovery of Religion in the Age of Reason* (Cambridge, MA: Harvard University Press, 2010), 129.

108. Stroumsa, *A New Science,* 125, and, broadly, ch. 6 ("From Mohammedis imposturae to the Three Impostors: The Study of Islam and the Enlightenment"), 124–144.

109. Quoted in ibid., 131.

110. Ibid., 130.

111. Khalidi, *Images of Muhammad,* 200–207.

112. George Minois, *The Atheist's Bible: The Most Dangerous Book That Never Existed* (Chicago: University of Chicago Press, 2012), x.

113. Ibid., xi.

114. Jacob Lassner, *Jews, Christians, and the Abode of Islam: Modern Scholarship, Medieval Realities* (Chicago: University of Chicago Press, 2012), 239.

115. Cecilia Ferrazzi, *Autobiography of an Aspiring Saint,* ed. and trans. Anne Jacobsen Schutte (Chicago: University of Chicago Press, 1996), 15.

116. Christopher J. Walker, *Islam and the West: A Dissonant Harmony of Civilizations* (London: Sutton, 2005), 184.

117. David R. Blanks and Michael Frasetto, introduction to *Western Views of Islam in Medieval and Early Modern Europe* (New York: St. Martin's, 1999), 3.

118. Astérious Argyriou, "Éléments biographiques concernant le prophète Muhammad dans la littérature grecque des trois premiers siècles de l'Hégire," in *La vie du prophète Mahomet,* ed. Toufic Fahd (Paris: Presses universitaires de France, 1983), 159–182, at p. 168.

119. Dimmock, *Mythologies,* 9.

120. Diego Venturino, quoted in Minois, *The Atheist's Bible,* 186; Tolan, *Sons of Ishmael,* 33. This biography was Voltaire's primary source for his 1742 play *Mahomet* (Ronald W. Tobin, "The Sources of Voltaire's 'Mahomet,'" *French Review* 34, no. 4 [February 1961]: 372–378). Voltaire's play condemns Muhammad to serve an anticlerical agenda. (Voltaire's later *Essay on the Moors* is substantially more approving of Muhammad.) The singling out of specific works as exceptional, unusual, and first is a frequent act of modern scholars, drawn to what is different and unusual. For instance, Kohlberg ("Western Accounts of the Death of Muḥammad," 180) remarks that Henry Stubbe's seventeenth-century biography (published only in the early twentieth century) is "exceptionally sympathetic for his time." See Henry Stubbe, *An Account of the Rise and Progress of Mahometanism with the Life of Mahomet and a Vindication of Him and His Religion from the Calumnies of the Christians,* ed. Hafiz Mahmoud Khan Shairani (London: Luzac, 1911). The fact that it was published "under the auspices of the Islamic Society" (v) attests to the perception that it was sympathetic, or, as the editor puts it in his introduction, "he was the first Englishman to cast from himself the trammels which, with the rest of his countrymen, he had inherited from the Middle Ages. There is no trace in him of that concession to preconceived ideas and malignant notions" (xvi). See the next chapter's discussion of the idea of

avoiding prejudice. For a new edition with a useful introduction, see Nabil Matar, ed. *Henry Stubbe and the Beginnings of Islam: The Originall & Progress of Mahometanism* (New York: Columbia University Press, 2014).

121. Shaden Tageldin, *Disarming Words: Empire and the Seductions of Translation in Egypt* (Berkeley: University of California Press, 2011), 173.

122. Gunny, *The Prophet Muhammad in French and English Literature*, 251.

123. On Pococke, see Birchwood, "Confounding Babel."

124. Voltaire used Gagnier's *Life* for his *Essay on the Moors*. He also borrowed Sale's translation of the Qur'an from the Bibliothèque Royale in 1747. Tobin, "Sources of Voltaire's 'Mahomet.'"

125. Daniel J. Vitkus, "Early Modern Orientalism: Representations of Islam in Sixteenth- and Seventeenth-Century Europe," in *Western Views of Islam*, ed. Blanks and Frasetto, 209–210.

126. Christopher Tyerman, *The Crusades: A Very Short Introduction* (Oxford University Press, 2005), 137; Ketton says "fear of the Turk was being replaced by impatience, contempt, and arrogance" (56). In Tolan, *Sons of Ishmael*, after 1683, "the Turk no longer seemed a threat to western European writers. . . . It was now possible to portray the Muslim as a sympathetic if benighted 'other,' rather than a threatening one. Gibbon . . . could portray Muhammad with an inimitable mix of praise and condescension" (34).

127. Maxime Rodinson, *Europe and the Mystique of Islam* (London: I. B. Tauris, 2002 [1987]), 52.

128. Ibid., 44.

129. Ursula Wokoeck, *German Orientalism: The Study of the Middle East and Islam from 1800 to 1945* (New York: Routledge, 2009), 4–5. Wokoeck mentions but is unconvinced by Rudi Paret's contrary claim that the study of Islam was more important than Arabic. On the early modern study of religion, see also Stroumsa, *A New Science*, 30.

130. Wokoeck, *German Orientalism*, 2. Wokoeck's study, focused on "professional scholars pursuing an academic career at the university" (18) in the "minor discipline" (27) of Oriental studies, takes seriously their practices, procedures, negotiations, and strategic considerations.

131. Stuart Curran, ed., *The Cambridge Companion to British Romanticism*, 2nd ed. (Cambridge: Cambridge University Press, 2010), xi. Curran gives a narrower date range, 1785–1825.

132. From the 1985 *Oxford Companion to English Literature*, quoted by Aidan Day, introduction to *Romanticism* (New York: Routledge, 1996), 1.

133. Timothy Blanning, *The Romantic Revolution: A History* (New York: Modern Library, 2012), 27.

134. Philip Almond, *Heretic and Hero: Muhammad and the Victorians* (Wiesbaden: Otto Harrassowitz, 1989), 95.

135. Kidd, *American Christians and Islam*, 28.

2. A True Prophet

1. On this story, see, for example, Maxime Rodinson, *Mahomet* (Paris: Éditions du Seuil, 1961), 70–71; Ruth Warren, *Muhammad: Prophet of Islam* (New York: Franklin Watts, 1965), 9–10. On the doctrine of Muhammad as "seal of the prophets" (Q. 33:40), see Powers, *Muhammad Is Not the Father*, 52–55. More generally, on the supernatural in Muhammad's life, see Rebecca R. Williams, *Muhammad and the Supernatural: Medieval Arab Views* (New York: Routledge, 2013), which appeared as this book was going to press.

2. On the Syriac sources, see Krisztina Szilágyi, "Muhammad and the Monk: The Making of the Christian Bahīrā Legend," *Jerusalem Studies in Arabic and Islam* 34 (2008): 169–214; for a brief discussion of some European versions of the story, see John Tolan, *Saracens: Islam in the Medieval European Imagination* (New York: Columbia University Press, 2002), 139, including one in which the monk is Nestur. See also Stubbe, *Account of the Rise*, 144; Dimmock, *Mythologies*, 29, 45.

3. Uri Rubin, *The Eye of the Beholder: The Life of Muhammad as Viewed by the Early Muslims; A Textual Analysis* (Princeton, NJ: Darwin, 1995).

4. Marilyn Waldman, *Prophecy and Power: Muhammad and the Qur'an in the Light of Comparison*, ed. Bruce B. Lawrence, with Lindsay Jones and Robert M. Baum (Sheffield, UK: Equinox, 2013), 131–135.

5. Safi, *Memories of Muhammad*, 243. See also Robinson, *Islamic Historiography*.

6. Today, when "English is the new Latin in much of Europe" and beyond, the availability of a text in English makes it more likely that its ideas will circulate. David Northrup, *How English Became the Global Language* (New York: Palgrave, 2013), 148.

7. William Murray, trans., *The Life of Mohammed Translated from the Arabic of Abulfeda* (Elgin, Scotland: A. C. Brander, n.d.). It was also printed in London, Edinburgh, and Aberdeen.

8. Lewis, "Gibbon on Muhammad," 94.

9. Lecker, "Glimpses of Muḥammad's Medinan Decade," 63.

10. Robinson, *Islamic Historiography*, 105.

11. Ibid., 65.

12. Brown, *Muhammad*, 87. The book is the *Dalāʾil al-Khairāt* of Muḥammad ibn Sulaymān al-Jazūlī (d. 1465); on this, see also Schimmel, *And Muhammad Is His Messenger*, 86.

13. Gustav Weil, *Mohammed der Prophet, sein Leben und seine Lehre: Aus handschriftlichen Quellen und dem Koran geschöpft und dargestellt von Dr. Gustav Weil; mit Beilagen und einer Stammtafel* (Stuttgart: J. B. Metzler, 1843). Lewis, "Gibbon on Muhammad," 93.

14. On the Arabian nights, see Weil, *The Story of Ali Baba and the Forty Thieves: An Extract from Dr. Weil's German Translation of the Arabian Nights* (Boston: D.C. Heath and Co., 1889), 4.

15. In Calcutta, Alfred Kramer published in 1856 an edition of al-Wāqidī's *Book of Campaigns* as *The History of Mohammed's Campaigns by Aboo 'Abdollah Mohammad bin 'Omar al-Wakidy*. Al-Wāqidī, *Life of Muḥammad*, xiii. Julius Wellhausen published "an abbreviated translation" into German based on a different manuscript in 1882. An authoritative Arabic edition was printed in Europe some decades later.

16. Gail Minault, "Aloys Sprenger: German Orientalism's 'Gift' to Delhi College," *South Asia Research* 31 no. 1 (February 2011): 7–23.

17. The expanded German edition was published as *Das Leben und die Lehre des Moḥammad, nach bisher des grösstentheils unbenutzten Quellen bearbeitet*, 2 vols. (Berlin: Nicolaische Verlagsbuchhandlung, 1861). William Muir reviews the portion of the book that discusses his sources as "The Value of Early Mahometan Historical Sources" (1868), republished in Muir, *Mohammedan Controversy*, 103–151; on the shift to scholarly work in German, see Wokoeck, *German Orientalism*, 31; she also cites much of the extensive and growing literature on German Orientalism.

18. Khalidi, *Images of Muhammad*, 247.

19. Thomas Carlyle, *The Hero as Prophet: Mahomet; Islam (Lecture II: Heroes and Hero Worship)* (New York: Maynard, Merrill, and Co., 1882), 11.

20. Ibid.

21. On such conversions, see Umar F. Abd-Allah, *A Muslim in Victorian America: The Life of Alexander Russell Webb* (New York: Oxford University Press, 2006), 69–79.

22. Schimmel, *And Muhammad Is His Messenger*, 229.

23. Khwaja Kamal-ud-Din, *The Ideal Prophet: Aspects of the Life and Qualities of the Holy Prophet Muhammad* (Woking, UK: Ahmadiyya Anjuman Isha'at Islam Lahore, 1925), xii.

24. Ibid., 248.

25. Godfrey Higgins, *An Apology for the Life and Character of the Celebrated Prophet of Arabia, Called Mohammed, or the Illustrious* (London: Rowland Hunter, 1829).

26. Charles Eliot Norton, ed., *The Correspondence of Thomas Carlyle and Ralph Waldo Emerson, 1834–1872* (Boston: James R. Osgood, 1883), 1:293. See also Carlyle, *Hero as Prophet*, 25, where he declares Islam "a confused form of Christianity" and remarks that they share the same "soul," which is to adhere to "the great, deep Law of the World."

27. The phrase is from Khalidi's *Images of Muhammad*.

28. On Orientalism—the history of the term as well as the contests over its meaning—see Robert Irwin, *Dangerous Knowledge: Orientalism and Its Discontents* (New York: Overlook, 2006), esp. 2–8; later portions of the book are devoted to a critique of Edward Said, *Orientalism* (New York: Pantheon, 1978). See also Daniel M. Varisco, *Reading Orientalism: Said and the Unsaid* (Seattle: University of Washington Press, 2007).

29. Muir, "Biographies of Mohammed," in *Mohammedan Controversy*, 100. Avril Powell, *Scottish Orientalists and India: The Muir Brothers, Religion, Education and Empire* (Woodbridge, UK: Boydell, 2010), 94, argues that since he agreed to republish it in 1897, "it may be regarded as encapsulating views on Islam to which he had adhered from his mid-20s, throughout his Indian career and into his late 70s."

30. Muir, "The Mohammedan Controversy" and "Biographies of Mohammed," in *Mohammedan Controversy*.

31. C. J. Lyall, "Obituary Notice: Sir William Muir," *Journal of the Royal Asiatic Society of Great Britain and Ireland* 37 (1905): 875–879.

32. Jabal Muhammad Buaben, *Image of the Prophet Muḥammad in the West: A Study of Muir, Margoliouth, and Watt* (Leicester, UK: Islamic Foundation, 1996); Muhammad Mohar Ali, *Sirat al-Nabi and the Orientalists, with Special Reference to the Writings of William Muir, D. S. Margoliouth and W. Montgomery Watt*, vols. 1A and 1B (Medina: Kingdom of Saudi Arabia Ministry of Islamic Affairs, King Fahd Complex for the Printing of the Holy Qur'an, 1997).

33. Khalidi, *Images of Muhammad*, 249. Edward Said highlights this same element in Muslim readers' (or nonreaders') complaints about *The Satanic Verses*, linking them to Orientalist discourse: "Why must a Moslem . . . represent us so roughly, so expertly, and so disrespectfully to an audience already primed to excoriate our traditions, reality, history, religion, language, and origin? Why . . . must a member of our culture join

the legions of Orientalists in Orientalizing Islam so radically and unfairly?" Quoted in Wendy Steiner, *The Scandal of Pleasure: Art in an Age of Fundamentalism* (Chicago: University of Chicago Press, 1995), 107; ellipses in Steiner.

34. Alan Guenther, "The Image of the Prophet Muhammad as Found in Missionary Writings of the Late Nineteenth Century," *Muslim World* 90 (Spring 2000): 44.

35. Barbara Daly Metcalf, *Islamic Revival in British India: Deoband, 1860–1900* (New Delhi: Oxford University Press, 2002).

36. Abd-Allah, *A Muslim in Victorian America*, 61; more broadly, on his correspondence with American convert Alexander Russell Webb, see pp. 61–65. The major study on the Ahmadiyya is Yohanan Friedmann, *Prophecy Continuous: Aspects of Ahmadi Religious Thought and Its Medieval Background* (Berkeley: University of California Press, 1989).

37. For an exploration of one such process, see Teena Purohit, *The Aga Khan Case: Religion and Identity in Colonial India* (Cambridge, MA: Harvard University Press, 2012).

38. Schimmel, *And Muhammad Is His Messenger*, 157.

39. Ibid.

40. Ricci, *Islam Translated*, 57–58, 231.

41. See Ricci, *Islam Translated*, 241. At the level of popular and especially shrine culture, these intersections and overlaps continue to be negotiated. Schimmel reports (*And Muhammad Is His Messenger*, 192) that a Hyderabadi Hindu political figure from the first half of the twentieth century "expressed his love of the Prince of Medina [Muhammad] and his longing for the Rauda [part of his tomb complex], in eloquent Urdu verse."

42. Ishvarchandra Vidyasagar, *Hindu Widow Marriage: An Epochal Work on Social Reform from Colonial India*, trans. Brian A. Hatcher (New York: Columbia University Press, 2011).

43. Foreword to Kamal-ud-Din, *Ideal Prophet*.

44. For instance, the introduction to the edited volume *Honor, Violence, Women and Islam* asks: "Why are honour killings and honour-related violence (HRV) so important to understand? What do such crimes represent? And how does HRV fit in with Western views and perceptions of Islam?" Mohammad Mazher Idriss, "Honour, Violence, Women and Islam: An Introduction," in *Honour, Violence, Women and Islam*, ed. Mohammad Mazher Idriss and Tahir Abbas (Abingdon, UK: Routledge 2011), 1–15, quote on p. 1.

45. Syed Ameer Ali, *A Critical Examination of the Life and Teachings of Mohammed* (London: Williams and Norgate, 1873), viii.

46. Bulandshehri combines the two tacks: condemnation of Orientalist "propaganda" and correction of errors: "This book is also written," his final sentence declares, "keeping in view to correct our educated readers who fell pray [*sic*] to the propaganda spread by the infidels and pagans against Islam which they learn by reading the books of *seerah* written by the so-called European orientalists." Muhammad Ashiq Elahi Bulandshehri, *The Wives of the Prophet Muhammad (sallalahu alayhe wasallam): A Complete Book on the Biographies of the Wives of Holy Prophet Muhammad (sallallahu alayhe wasallam)*, trans. Mohammad Akram (Lahore: Idara-e-Islamiat, 1994), 174.

47. Powell, *Scottish Orientalists and India*, 102.

48. Susan Buck-Morss, *Thinking Past Terror: Islamism and Critical Theory on the Left* (London: Verso, 2006), viii.

49. G[eorge] Lathom Browne, *The Æra of Mahomet:* A.D. 527 to 629 (London: Society for Promoting Christian Knowledge, 1856), 174.

50. John Davenport, *An Apology for Mohammed and the Koran* (London: J. Davy and Sons, 1869), 16. Powell, *Scottish Orientalists and India*, 201, discusses their interactions, noting that in Britain, Davenport had a reputation as a plagiarist.

51. William Muir, *The Life of Mahomet from Original Sources*, 2nd ed. (London: Smith, Elder, and Co., 1878), 57.

52. Ibid.

53. Andrae, *Mohammed*, 115.

54. Quoted in Lewis, "Gibbon on Muhammad," 32. Carlyle writes, "Nothing but a sense of duty could carry any European through the Koran" (*Hero as Prophet*, 31).

55. P[eirce] De Lacy Johnstone, *Muhammad and His Power* (New York: Charles Scribner's Sons, 1908), 153; Matthew Woods, *In Spite of Epilepsy: Caesar, Mohammed, Lord Byron; The Founders Respectively of an Empire, a Religion, and a School of Poetry* (New York: Cosmopolitan Press, 1913), 184.

56. Carlyle, *Hero as Prophet*, 31, 32. See also Washington Irving, *Mahomet and His Successors*, 2 vols. (New York: G. P. Putnam and Son, 1868), 336–337.

57. Carlyle, *Hero as Prophet*, 13.

58. Timothy Blanning, *The Romantic Revolution: A History* (New York: Modern Library, 2012), 28.

59. Carlyle, *Hero as Prophet*, 13.

60. Some Muslim scholars held a more nuanced view of the process of revelation and saw some role, albeit subordinate, for Muhammad's

consciousness in the formulation of revelation. For one modern attempt to recuperate this view, see Fazlur Rahman, *Prophecy in Islam: Philosophy and Orthodoxy* (Chicago: University of Chicago Press, 2011). For the modern tendency to think of Muhammad as nothing more than a "UPS delivery man," see Omid Safi, *Memories of Muhammad: Why the Prophet Matters* (New York: Harper One, 2009), 265.

61. Prideaux had accepted that Muhammad "was in truth, what they say, an *Illiterate Barbarian*"—able neither to read nor to write, and like his countrymen doomed "to continue in the same Ignorance with which they came out of the Mothers Bellies unto their Lives end." Prideaux, *True Nature of Imposture*, 29.

62. Muir, *Life of Mahomet*, 2nd ed., 88.

63. Susannah Heschel, "German Jewish Scholarship on Islam as a Tool for De-Orientalizing Judaism," *New German Critique* 39, no. 3 (Fall 2012): 91–107, at p. 94.

64. Ibid., 91. The rational and purified Islam presented in this scholarship fed back into later Muslim attempts to present a streamlined, rational, purified Islam.

65. In addition to believing that Muhammad had teachers, including Waraqa, Sprenger thought Muhammad owned or at least had access to "a version of portions of the Scriptures, both of the genuine and some of the apocryphal works." Sprenger, *Life of Mohammad*, 100.

66. Dimmock, "Human Head," 83; Browne, *Æra of Mahomet*, iv. The biography of "Mahomet, the Fanatic" covers pp. 117–179, or about one-fourth of the book, which also includes sketches of "Justinian, the Legislator"; "Belisarius, the Conqueror"; "Gregory, the Pope"; "Augustine, the Missionary"; and "Benedict, the Monk."

67. Kidd, *American Christians and Islam*, 13.

68. Yet "he is withal, a moralist by nature"—prohibiting gambling, wine, and female infanticide. Tom Stecker, *The Man Mohammed: A Dramatic Character-Sketch* (n.p.: Co-operative Press, 1900), 15–16. He also refers to "the record of his hybrid creed, the Koran" (16).

69. Harvey Newcomb, *The False Prophet: or, An Account of the Rise and Progress of the Mohammedan Religion; Comprising the History of the Church, etc.*, 2nd ed. (Boston: Massachusetts Sabbath School Society, 1844), 105–106; Prideaux had listed Jews, Christians, and "heathen Arabs" as the sources of Muhammad's religion. Prideaux, *True Nature of Imposture*, 37–38.

70. S. W. Koelle, *Mohammed and Mohammedanism Critically Considered* (London: Rivingtons, 1889), xix.

71. Lane-Poole offers a biographical introduction to a volume of Qur'anic selections and selected hadith. *The Speeches and Table-Talk of the Prophet Mohammad* (London: Macmillan, 1882), liii–liv.

72. The overall assessment wavers: "The guidance was not perfect, we know, and there is much that is blameworthy in Mohammad; but whatever we believe of him, let it be granted that his errors were not the result of premeditated imposition, but were the mistakes of an ignorant, impressible, superstitious, but nevertheless noble and great man." Lane-Poole, *Speeches and Table-Talk*, lv.

73. Browne, *Æra of Mahomet*, 174.

74. Ibid., vol. 1, cv. See also Welch, "Muhammad's Understanding of Himself," 15: Welch declares himself "not yet prepared to render a final judgment" about the trustworthiness of hadith and *sīra* literature but expresses "confiden[ce] that the contents, although not the final arrangement, of the Koran date from the time of Muhammad, and that the Koran is utterly reliable as a historical source, if it is properly interpreted."

75. Lane-Poole, *Speeches and Table-Talk*, liv.

76. Muir, *Life of Mahomet*, 2nd ed., 603.

77. Lane-Poole, *Speeches and Table-Talk*, liv.

78. William Muir, *The Life of Mahomet from Original Sources*, 3rd ed. (London: Smith, Elder, and Company, 1894), v.

79. Powell, *Scottish Orientalists and India*, 128.

80. Schimmel, *And Muhammad Is His Messenger*, 228.

81. Syed Ahmad Khan, *A Series of Essays on the Life of Muhammad and Subjects Subsidiary Thereto* (Lahore: Premier Book House, 1968). The Urdu version was *Khutbat-i Ahmadiyya* [Essays pertaining to Ahmad]. The title is ambiguous; Ahmad can refer to Ahmad Khan but also to Muhammad. The translation was probably mostly done by his son.

82. Powell, *Scottish Orientalists and India*, 202.

83. Bruce Fudge makes a similar point. "Qur'an, Canon, and Literature," in *Sacred Tropes: Tanakh, New Testament, and Qur'an as Literature and Culture*, ed. Roberta Sterman Sabbath (Leiden: Brill, 2009), 41–52. Of the Satanic verses, he notes that they are "found in the Arabic historical tradition, present but not necessarily accepted (usually denied)" (47).

84. Shahab Ahmed, "Ibn Taymiyya and the Satanic Verses," *Studia Islamica* 87 (1998): 67–124.

85. Qur'an 53:20–23.

86. Muir, *Life of Mahomet*, 2nd ed., 88. Similarly, W. Montgomery Watt says that the story is "so strange that it must be true in essentials."

Muhammad: Prophet and Statesman (London: Oxford University Press, 1974 [1961]), 61.

87. Muir, *Mohammadan Controversy*, 123.

88. Ahmad Khan, *Series of Essays*, 221.

89. See Frederick S. Colby, *Narrating Muḥammad's Night Journey: Tracing the Development of the Ibn ʿAbbās Ascension Discourse* (Albany, NY: State University of New York Press, 2008).

90. Ahmad Khan, *Series of Essays*, esp. 347.

91. See, briefly, Schimmel, *And Muhammad Is His Messenger*, 161–162, on this question, and 159–175 on the ascension more generally.

92. Sprenger, *Life of Mohammad*, 136.

93. Colby, *Narrating Muḥammad's Night Journey*, 172–173.

94. See the thirteenth-century Old French *Book of Muhammad's Ladder*. Reginald Hyatte, trans., *The Prophet of Islam in Old French: The Romance of Muhammad (1258) and The Book of Muhammad's Ladder (1264)* (Leiden: Brill, 1997).

95. Schimmel, *And Muhammad Is His Messenger*, 174.

96. For Ahmad Khan, these events did not happen physically but were nonetheless real. On the perfect and divine nature of the Qur'an, which reports (he says) these events, see *Series of Essays*, 272.

97. Muir, "Of Moslem Tradition," in *Mohammedan Controversy*, 123.

98. Ahmad Khan, *Series of Essays*, 212.

99. Ibid., 182.

100. Ibid., vii.

101. Ibid., ix.

102. Ibid., 181.

103. Ibid., 234. Sprenger, *Life of Mohammad*, 118.

104. Timothy Mitchell, *Colonising Egypt* (Berkeley: University of California Press, 1991), 152.

105. In addition to Muir, see also Johnstone, *Muhammad and His Power*, 228–229.

106. Ahmad Khan, *Series of Essays*, 141.

107. Rubin, *Eye of the Beholder*, 66.

108. Ahmad Khan, *Series of Essays*.

109. The argument that Muhammad fulfilled biblical prophecies recurs in modern texts, including those aimed at conversion of non-Muslims to Islam. See, for example, the Ahmadi biography by Sufi Mutiur Rahman Bengalee, *The Life of Muhammad* (Chicago: Moslem Sunrise Press, 1941).

110. Alcofribas Nasier, *The Three Impostors*, trans. anon. (n.p.: privately printed, 1904), 132.

111. Ahmad Khan, *Series of Essays*, 205–206.

112. Ibid., 206.

113. Ali, *Critical Examination*.

114. Syed Ameer Ali, *The Life and Teachings of Mohammed, or the Spirit of Islam* (London: W. H. Allen, 1891).

115. David Samuel Margoliouth, *Mohammed and the Rise of Islam* (New York: G. P. Putnam's Sons, 1905), vii.

116. *Jalā al-qulūb bi dhikr al-maḥbūb*. The text dates to 1839. See Powell, *Scottish Orientalists and India*, 31; Guenther, "Response of Sayyid Aḥmad Ḥān to Sir William Muir's Evaluation of *Ḥadīt* Literature," *Oriente Moderno* 82, no. 1 (2002): 221.

117. Schimmel describes this as a reformist text (*And Muhammad Is His Messenger*, 158). On Muhammad as God's beloved, see Schimmel, *And Muhammad Is His Messenger*, 87, 109.

118. Muir, *Mohammedan Controversy*, 76.

119. Mohammad Ali Salmin, *The Holy Prophet Mohammad: The Commander of the Faithful* (Bombay: M. A. Salmin, 1930s), 134.

120. These categories are Omid Safi's. Safi, *Memories of Muhammad*, 265.

121. Salmin, *Holy Prophet Mohammad*, 2. In a similar vein, the title of Indian scholar Ashraf Ali Thanvi's pamphlet on Muhammad's polygamy bears the title *Kasrat-e-Azwaaj-le-Sahib-e-Me'raj*. See Bulandshehri, *Wives of the Prophet Muhammad*, 174.

122. I borrow the phrase "Competitive Hagiography" from Steven Judd, who applies it to early legal figures, noting that one technique for ascribing merit and holiness to them is to liken them to Muhammad. Steven C. Judd, "Competitive Hagiography in Biographies of al-Awzāʿī and Sufyān al-Thawrī," *Journal of the American Oriental Society* 122, no. 1 (2002): 25–37.

123. Diane Robinson-Dunne, *The Harem, Slavery, and British Imperial Culture: Anglo-Muslim Relations in the Late Nineteenth Century* (Manchester, UK: Manchester University Press, 2006), x; Richard King, *Orientalism and Religion: Postcolonial Theory, India, and the Mystic East* (London: Routledge, 1999). See esp. his discussion of "intercultural mimesis."

124. SherAli Tareen, "The Polemic of Shahjahanpur: Religion, Miracles, and History," *Islamic Studies* 51, no. 1 (2012): 49–67, at p. 50. On the gathering, see also Metcalf, *Islamic Revival*, 221–234.

125. Muhammad Ali, "Dottrine e attività dei musulmani Aḥmadiyya di Lahore," *Oriente Moderno* 6, no. 2 (February 1926): 122.

126. For Muhammad's own use of comparative arguments, see Waldman, *Prophecy and Power*.

127. Astérious Argyriou, "Éléments biographiques concernant le prophète Muhammad dans la littérature grecque des trois premiers siècles de l'Hégire," in *La vie du prophète Mahomet*, ed. Toufic Fahd (Paris: Presses universitaires de France, 1983), 159–182, at pp. 162–163.

128. See, for example, Tolan, *Sons of Ishmael*; Cuffel, *Gendering Disgust*.

129. Argyriou, "Éléments biographiques," 166. Note that the author uses the anachronistic category "founders of religion," which is assuredly not in the dialogue attributed to Saint John of Damascus.

130. Argyriou, "Éléments biographiques," 162.

131. Theologically, Muslims believe something different about Muhammad's nature than Christians believe about Christ's nature, but as Clinton Bennett observes, the affective connection and modes of veneration can be similar. See Bennett, *In Search of Muhammad* (London: Cassell, 1998). On polemics about Muhammad, Jesus, and the idea of prophecy, see Mona Siddiqui, *Christians, Muslims, and Jesus* (New Haven, CT: Yale University Press, 2013), 43–50.

132. Rizvi, "Muḥammad in South Asian Biographies," 114.

133. Also, see Ali Dashti, *Twenty-Three Years: A Study of the Prophetic Career of Mohammad*, trans. F. R. C. Bagley (Santa Ana, CA: Mazda, 1994), 7.

134. Higgins, *Apology for the Life*, 21.

135. Ibid., 49–50. Quite a few Egyptian authors would, over the course of the following century, raise similar objections to miracle accounts.

136. For example, Prideaux, *True Nature of Imposture*, 25, 28. Browne, *Æra of Mahomet*, 173, similarly asserts, "Of miracles he makes no claim, beyond the transmission to him of the Koran."

137. Bombay Tract and Book Society, *Life of Mahomet*, 3rd ed. (Bombay, 1856); similarly, Murray, *Life of Mohammed*, 3.

138. Koelle, *Mohammed and Mohammedanism*.

139. Ibid., viii.

140. Ibid., vii.

141. Ibid., x.

142. Ibid., 242; on the modeling of Muhammad after Jesus, see, e.g., Jane Dammen McAuliffe, "Al-Ṭabarī's Prelude to the Prophet," in *Al-Ṭabarī: A Medieval Muslim Historian and His Work*, ed. Hugh Kennedy (Princeton, NJ: Darwin, 2008), 123–126, 129.

143. Sprenger absolves Muhammad of claiming an ability to perform most sorts of miracles; his enemies were responsible for circulating some of them: "When the conservatives of Makka had at length succumbed to the arms of Mohammad, he forced his religion on them, and they found it expedient to profess that they had been convinced by miracles, and not by the sword." He was not entirely blameless, though; Sprenger thought Muhammad himself "fostered" belief in the descent of the spirit to him in the form of Gabriel, and possibly about the night journey and ascension. *Life of Mohammad,* 138.

144. Koelle, *Mohammed and Mohammedanism,* 243–44.

145. Ibid., 245.

146. Rizvi, "Muḥammad in South Asian Biographies," 113.

147. Bombay Tract and Book Society, *Life of Mahomet.*

148. Kidd, *American Christians and Islam,* 47.

149. See, for example, ibid., 54: Cyrus Hamlin, once a leader of the American Board of Commissioners for Foreign Missions in Turkey, eventually left the organization, having come to believe that "direct evangelism was unnecessary and possibly counterproductive; civilization and educational and commercial progress would, over time, necessarily bring Christianization."

150. Irvin Schick, *The Erotic Margin: Spatiality and Sexuality in Alterist Discourse* (London: Verso, 1999), 25.

151. Tomoko Masuzawa, *The Invention of World Religions, or How European Universalism Was Preserved in the Language of Pluralism* (Chicago: University of Chicago Press, 2005).

152. Ameer Ali, *Critical Examination,* 19.

153. Ibid., 18.

154. Ibid., 25.

3. Eminent Muslims

1. Schimmel, *And Muhammad Is His Messenger,* 181–187, at p. 186. The quotations from the *Burda* are pp. 186–187, translated by Arthur Jeffery. A more recent translation has been done by American Muslim Hamza Yusuf, sold with CDs of performance of the ode (in Arabic) by the Fez Singers.

2. For example, in mid-eighteenth-century America, Jonathan Edwards wrote of "Mahomet's pretences to intercourse with heaven, and his success in rapine, murder, and violence" as the foundation of Islam. Edwards, quoted in Kidd, *American Christians and Islam,* 17. See also John Tolan, "European Accounts of Muḥammad's Life," in *Cambridge*

Companion, ed. Brockopp, 226–250; Tolan, *Saracens;* Frederick Quinn, *The Sum of All Heresies: The Image of Islam in Western Thought* (New York: Oxford University Press, 2008).

3. Muir, *Life of Mahomet,* 2nd ed., 172.

4. Sprenger, *Life of Mohammad,* 174.

5. Ibid., 184.

6. Ali, *Critical Examination,* 150.

7. This spirit is reflected in M. Sharif Ahmad Amini, *Muhammad: The Most Successful Prophet* (Calcutta: Asian Printers, 1978).

8. Davenport, *Apology for Mohammed,* 54.

9. Ibid., 81.

10. Quoted in Kidd, *American Christians and Islam,* 37.

11. Fisk, quoted in ibid., 37; Irwin, *Dangerous Knowledge,* 65.

12. Kidd, *American Christians and Islam,* 46.

13. Bush, *Life of Mohammed,* 18, 19.

14. Murray, *Life of Mohammed.*

15. Bush, *Life of Mohammed,* 160–161. This is at least the second use of the phrase "roving tribes of Arabia" (18).

16. Lane-Poole, *Speeches and Table-Talk,* xxxiii–xxxiv.

17. Ibid., xi. Rodinson, *Mahomet* (77), saw a passionate and nervous temperament behind a decorous and stately façade.

18. Sprenger, *Life of Mohammed,* vii, x, xi. Having declared his intent to "acquaint" his readers with Muhammad's character, Sprenger launches into a lengthy description of his physical appearance (84), habits, and "temperament," which he pronounces, like the physician he is, "melancholic, and in the highest degree nervous" (89). In some respects, Sprenger does recognize some positive behaviors in Muhammad, but assigns the praise to others. For instance, he credits Muhammad's "extraordinary firmness and perseverance" in the face of opposition to "the endurance of his wife Khadyjah" (91).

19. Ibid., 89.

20. William Muir, "Value of Early Mahometan Historical Sources," originally published in the *Calcutta Review* (1868), republished in *Mohammedan Controversy,* quote from pp. 103–104.

21. Ibid. See xii (Arab wildness) and xiv (wives).

22. Gerald MacLean, "Milton among the Muslims," in *The Religions of the Book: Christian Perceptions, 1400–1600,* ed. Dimmock and Hadfield (New York: Palgrave, 2008), 180–194, at p. 182.

23. Ibid., 183.

24. Andrae, *Mohammed*, 12. However, Andrae objects to a certain "calculating slyness" on Muhammad's part, saying that one incident "reveals a trait of his character which is particularly uncongenial to the ideals of manliness of the Nordic races" (142).

25. Carlyle, for instance, has Muhammad threatened and vulnerable, and then "the wild Son of the Desert resolved to defend himself, like a man and an Arab." Carlyle, *Hero as Prophet*, 29.

26. Said, *Orientalism;* Schick, *Erotic Margin.* Kidd, *American Christians and Islam*, 14, writes of "the multiple uses of Muhammad in early America: He could be portrayed as an example of a graceless legalist or a wild enthusiast, depending on the rhetorical need of the moment."

27. Woods, by contrast, asserts, "If he, Mohammed, assumed a false commission, it was in order to inculcate salutary doctrines." (*In Spite of Epilepsy*, 130)

28. Muir, *Life of Mahomet*, 2nd ed., 311–312, 315–316, 318–319.

29. Johnstone, *Muhammad and His Power*, 226; similarly, Irving, *Mahomet and His Successors*, 337.

30. Muir, *Life of Mahomet*, 2nd ed., 320, 321. For instance, in the final chapter of the final volume of Muir's *Life*, "The Person and Character of Mahomet," negative traits follow positive ones. After a few headings concerned with appearance, "gait," and habits, this alternation leaves the reader with a negative impression and the sense that the presentation has been thoughtful and balanced. For instance, "Urbanity and kindness of disposition," "Friendship," and "Moderation and magnanimity" are followed by "Cruelty towards his enemies" and "Craftiness and perfidy." The section "Domestic life; polygamy" begins: "In domestic life the conduct of Mahomet, with one grave exception, was exemplary."

31. Ghulam Malik, *Muhammad: An Islamic Perspective* (Lanham, MD: University Press of America, 1996), 153–154.

32. Fakir Syed Waheed-Ud-Din, *The Benefactor*, trans. Faiz Ahmed Faiz (World Community of Islam in the West, n.d. [1964]). This edition lists the publisher as World Community of Islam in the West, the name that Warith Deen Muhammad gave his community when he reshaped the Nation of Islam in the mid-1970s. It later became the American Muslim Mission and eventually the Muslim American Society. This book was published, with translation by Faiz Ahmed Faiz, in 1964, before that name was in use; presumably it is a later printing. One online source lists the publisher for the 1964 edition as the "Lost-Found Nation of Islam." Later editions (Chicago: Kazi Publications, 1987, 1995) give the

title as *The Benefactor and the Rightly Guided,* referring to the inclusion of accounts of the first four caliphs as well. For Napoleon's own view of Muhammad, see Tolan, "European Accounts," 244–245.

33. Edward E. Curtis IV, *Black Muslim Religion in the Nation of Islam, 1960–1975* (Chapel Hill: University of North Carolina Press, 2006), 79–85; Edward Curtis, personal communication, November 2013.

34. Waheed-Ud-Din, *Benefactor,* vi. The original Urdu publication mentioned the first four caliphs in the title, as did at least one later English edition.

35. Tolan, *Sons of Ishmael,* xi, discussing ninth- to fourteenth-century Christian European polemical texts: "Such texts were only rarely addressed to readers of the rival faith: more commonly, they were meant to persuade vacillating Christians of the superiority of their religion to Islam, in order to prevent them from converting to Islam or in order to convince them of the justice and necessity of wars against Muslims."

36. On Muhammad as statesman and prophet, see Cook, *Muhammad,* 2, 51. On another set of competing identities, between "ethnic warner" and "messenger sent to restore" the pure monotheistic faith of Abraham, see Cook, *Muhammad,* 39.

37. Malik, *Muhammad,* 153–154.

38. The Qur'anic phrase is *uswa ḥasana* (Q. 33:21), also meaning "a good pattern."

39. Safi, *Memories of Muhammad,* 290.

40. Robinson-Dunn, *Harem, Slavery and British Imperial Culture,* 8.

41. Rizvi, "Muḥammad in South Asian Biographies," 121. See also Muhammad Qasim Zaman, "A Venture in Critical Islamic Historiography and the Significance of Its Failure," *Numen* 41, no. 1 (January 1994): 26–50.

42. On the role of Urdu for Indian intellectuals, see Metcalf, *Islamic Revival.*

43. Schimmel, *And Muhammad Is His Messenger,* 229.

44. On these trends, see Northrup, *How English Became;* David Bellos, *Is That a Fish in Your Ear? Translation and the Meaning of Everything* (New York: Faber and Faber, 2011).

45. Ira D. Gruber, *Books and the British Army in the Age of the American Revolution* (Chapel Hill: University of North Carolina Press, 2010), 235; Gruber's context is different, but the observation applies.

46. Charles D. Smith, *Islam and the Search for Social Order in Modern Egypt: A Biography of Muhammad Husayn Haykal* (Albany: State University of New York Press, 1983), 38.

47. Ibid., 56–57.

48. Muḥammad Ḥusayn Haykal, *Tarājim Miṣrīyah wa-gharbīyah* [Egyptian and Western biographies] (Cairo: Maṭbaʻat al-Siyāsah, 1929), 144. The portrait of Cleopatra is an image of a Western sculpture, reclining and nude. See also Smith, *Islam and the Search*, 97; Smith observes Haykal's deliberate omission of "the Islamic period," instead jumping from pre-Islamic to "the Khedive who committed Egypt to the European path."

49. Quotation from back cover of book.

50. Mitchell, *Colonising Egypt*, 131. The partial quotation is from Ḥusayn al-Marsafi's 1881 *Risālat al-kalim al-thaman*.

51. Israel Gershoni, "Theory of Crises," in *Middle Eastern Historiographies: Narrating the Twentieth Century*, ed. Israel Gershoni, Amy Singer, and Y. Hakan Erdem (Seattle: University of Washington Press, 2006), 315.

52. Muḥammad Ḥusayn Haykal, *The Life of Muḥammad*, trans. Ismail Al Faruqi (Kuala Lampur: Islamic Book Trust, 2002 [1976]), xxviii.

53. Ibid.

54. Khalidi, *Images of Muhammad*.

55. Ibid.

56. On his near contemporary al-Dhahabī (d. 1348), see Robinson, *Islamic Historiography*, 64–65.

57. Muḥammad Ḥusayn Haykal, *Al-Ṣiddīq Abū Bakr* [Abū Bakr the Righteous], 6th ed. (Egypt: Dār al-Maʻārif, 1971); *Al-Fārūq ʻUmar* [ʻUmar the Just] (Cairo: Maktabat al-Nahḍah al-Miṣrīyah, 1963–1964); *ʻUthmān ibn ʻAffān: Bayna al-khilāfah wa-al-mulk* [ʻUthmān ibn ʻAffān: Between caliphate and kingship] (Beirut: Dār al-Kutub al-ʻIlmīyah, 2007). At 141 pages, the book on ʻUthmān is less than half the length of the earlier works.

58. On this book see Hoda Elsadda, "Discourses of Women's Biographies and Cultural Identity: Twentieth Century Representations of the Life of ʻAʼisha bint Abi Bakr," *Feminist Studies* 27, no. 1 (2001): 37–64, esp. pp. 47–50. On the controversy it generated over Aisha's age, see Jonathan A. C. Brown, *Misquoting Muhammad: The Challenges and Choices of Interpreting the Prophet's Legacy* (Oxford: Oneworld, forthcoming).

59. Mervat F. Hatem, "ʻAʼisha Abdel Rahman: An Unlikely Heroine: A Post-Colonial Reading of Her Life and Some of Her Biographies of Women in the Prophetic Household," *Journal of Middle East Women's Studies* 7, no. 2 (Spring 2011): 1–26, at p. 12; Elsadda, "Discourses of Women's Biographies," 49.

60. Israel Gershoni and James P. Jankowsi, *Redefining the Egyptian Nation, 1930–1945* (Cambridge: Cambridge University Press, 2002), 59.

61. Muir, *Mohammedan Controversy,* 68.

62. Ruth Roded, "Gender in an Allegorical Life of Muḥammad: Mahfouz's *Children of Gebelawi,*" *Muslim World* 93 (January 2003): 118; also Antonie Wessels, *A Modern Arabic Biography of Muḥammad: A Critical Study of Muḥammad Ḥusayn Haykal's* Ḥayāt Muḥammad (Leiden: Brill, 1972), 1–2. On these biographies, see also E. S. Sabanegh, *Muhammad b. Abdallah, "Le Prophete": Portraits contemporains, Egypte 1930–1950* (Paris: Librairie J. Vrin, n.d.).

63. 'Ā'isha 'Abd al-Raḥmān [Bint al-Shāṭi'], *The Wives of the Prophet,* trans. Matti Moosa and D. Nicholas Ranson (Lahore: Muhammad Ashraf, 1971); Wessels, *Modern Arabic Biography,* 31; Ruth Roded, "Bint Al-Shati's 'Wives of the Prophet': Feminist or Feminine?" *British Journal of Middle Eastern Studies* 33, no. 1 (May 2006): 51–66; and Roded, "Muslim Women Reclaim the Life-Story of the Prophet: 'A'isha 'Abd al-Raḥmān, Assia Djebar, and Nadia Yassine," *Muslim World* 103, no. 3 (July 2013): 334–346; see esp. 335, n. 6, which lists relevant recent publications.

64. On Amīn, see William Shepard, *The Faith of a Modern Muslim Intellectual: The Religious Aspects and Implications of the Writings of Ahmad Amin* (New Delhi: Indian Institute of Islamic Studies/Vikas, 1982). See also his autobiography, Aḥmad Amīn, *Aḥmad Amīn: My Life,* trans. Issa J. Boullata (Leiden: Brill, 1978).

65. Gustave von Grunebaum, quoted in Issa J. Boullata, introduction to *Aḥmad Amīn,* ix.

66. Shepard, *Faith of a Modern Muslim Intellectual,* 194.

67. Boullata, introduction, xiii.

68. Amīn, *Aḥmad Amīn,* 220.

69. Boullata, introduction, xiii. Like others of his time, "by comparison of cultures, he arrived at a better understanding of his own and discovered for himself some salient areas of pride in it and others of necessary reform" (ix).

70. Afazlur Rahman, *Muhammad as a Military Leader* (London: Muslim Schools Trust, 1980), 190. A more measured assessment of Muhammad's military skills can be found in Rodgers, *The Generalship of Muhammad.*

71. Salmin, *Holy Prophet Mohammad,* 153.

72. Browne, *Æra of Mahomet,* 160.

73. Ibid., 161–162.

74. Salmin, *Holy Prophet Mohammad,* 152.

75. Ibid., 153. A studiously noncritical account of Muhammad as "military strategist and warrior" appears in Elsa Marston, *Muhammad of Mecca: Prophet of Islam* (New York: Franklin Watts, 2001), 71–73.

76. Maxime Rodinson, "A Critical Survey of Modern Studies on Muhammad," in *Studies on Islam*, ed. and trans. Merlin Swartz (New York: Oxford University Press, 1981), 23–85, at p. 27. On Dermenghem, see Gunny, *The Prophet Muhammad in French and English Literature*, 213–215.

77. Al Faruqi's 1976 English translation is just under six hundred pages of text, plus nearly one hundred pages of prefaces and additional endnotes.

78. Smith, *Islam and the Search*, 114.

79. Muḥammad Ḥusayn Haykal, *Ḥayāt Muḥammad* (Cairo: Maṭbaʿat Miṣr, 1935), 3–5.

80. Ch. Vial, "Muḥammad Ḥusayn Haykal," in *Encyclopaedia of Islam*, 2nd ed., ed. P. Bearman et al. (Leiden: Brill, 2011).

81. Muḥammad Ḥusayn Haykal, *Sirat-i Rasul*, trans. Muḥammad Vāris Kāmil. (Lahore: Maktabah-yi Kāravān, 1964). A more recent edition bears the title *Hayat-i Muhammad*.

82. On Haykal's reception in contemporary Indonesia, see Anna M. Gade, "Religious Biography of the Prophet Muḥammad in Twenty-First-Century Indonesia," in *Cambridge Companion*, ed. Brockopp, 254–258, 272–273.

83. See also Gershoni, "Theory of Crises."

84. Charles D. Smith, "*Hayat Muhammad* and the Muslim Brothers: Two Interpretations of Egyptian Islam and Their Socioeconomic Implications," *Journal of the American Research Center in Egypt* 16 (1979): 175–181, at p. 175.

85. Smith, *Islam and the Search*, 9.

86. Ibid., 41.

87. Ibid., 41–42; he refers to "wahy."

88. These have been ably sketched in Wessels, *Modern Arabic Biography*.

89. Rizvi, "Muḥammad in South Asian Biographies," 113.

90. Khalidi, *Images of Muhammad*, 248; Smith, *Islam and the Search*, 17. On the translation, see Tageldin, "Secularizing Islam: Carlyle, al-Sibāʿī, and the Translations of 'Religion' in British Egypt," *PMLA* 126, no. 1 (January 2011), 124: "Nowhere is the power of the religious to attract the Egyptian Muslim intellect to secularity more evident than in al-Sibāʿī's seminal Arabic translation of Thomas Carlyle's *On Heroes, Hero-Worship, and the Heroic in History*, published in Cairo in 1911." Also see Tageldin, *Disarming Words*.

91. Edith Grossman, *Why Translation Matters* (New Haven, CT: Yale University Press, 2010), 8.

92. See Tageldin, "Secularizing Islam."

93. Louis Awad, *The Literature of Ideas in Egypt, Pt. 1* (Atlanta: Scholars Press, 1986), 169.

94. Ibid., 186.

95. Ibid., 187.

96. Ibid.

97. Ibid., 188.

98. Yaseen Noorani, *Culture and Hegemony in the Colonial Middle East* (New York: Palgrave, 2010), 1; Mittermaier, *Dreams That Matter,* likewise points out that we are not dealing with tradition versus modernity but a very specifically shaped modernity (168–174).

99. Noorani, *Culture and Hegemony,* 2.

100. Samira Haj, *Reconfiguring Islamic Tradition: Rationality, Reform, and Modernity* (Stanford, CA: Stanford University Press, 2009), 128–136, quotation at p. 128.

101. Smith, *Islam and the Search,* 204, n. 16.

102. Pierre Bayard, *How to Talk about Books You Haven't Read,* trans. Jeffrey Mehlman (New York: Bloomsbury, 2007).

103. Wessels, *Modern Arabic Biography,* 199.

104. Ibid., 196.

105. Wessels, *Modern Arabic Biography,* 228–229.

106. Gunny, *The Prophet Muhammad in French and English Literature,* 214.

107. Bernard E. Dold, *Carlyle, Goethe, and Muhammad* (Messina, Italy: Edizioni Dott. Anotonino Sfameni, 1984), 75.

108. For Haykal's reliance on Muir, see Wessels, *Modern Arabic Biography.* Broadly on Orientalist use of Arabic sources, and vice versa, with a specific reference to Theodor Nöldeke and Jalāl al-Dīn al-Suyūṭī, see Ahmad Atif Ahmad, *Islam, Modernity, Violence, and Everyday Life* (New York: Palgrave Macmillan, 2009), 29–34.

109. On a similar "intermingling of texts," see Lyons, *Islam through Western Eyes,* 170–171.

110. Haykal, *Life of Muḥammad,* 557.

111. Smith, *Islam and the Search,* 129.

112. Haykal, *Life of Muḥammad,* 108.

113. Ibid., 105. Similarly, he rejects the story of Muhammad's marriage to Zaynab. For 'Abd al-Raḥmān's refutation of his analysis, see *Wives of*

the Prophet, 146–151. For other biographers on the marriage to Zaynab, see Chapter 4.

114. Haykal, *Life of Muḥammad*, 107.

115. This succinct formulation is Tageldin's. Tageldin, *Disarming Words*, 173.

116. ʿAbd al-ʿAziz Duri, *The Rise of Historical Writing among the Arabs* (Princeton, NJ: Princeton University Press, 1983), 8–9.

117. Smith, *Islam and the Search*, 5.

118. See Ibn Ishaq, *Life of Muhammad*, 21. Ruth Warren takes the work of shepherding as a realistic possibility while treating the "miraculous happenings" recounted during Muhammad's youth with his foster mother as "legends similar to those which grow up in afteryears [*sic*] about great religious leaders." Warren, *Muhammad: Prophet of Islam*, 8.

119. Khalidi, *Images of Muhammad*, points to this phrase or a variant repeatedly (e.g., pp. 10, 158).

120. Smith, *Islam and the Search*, 5.

121. Ibid.

122. Ibid., 6.

123. Tageldin, *Disarming Words*, 164.

4. The Wife of Muhammad

1. A sampling, by no means comprehensive, would include the following: Peterson, *Muhammad*, 44–45; Warren, *Muhammad*, 11; Feisal Abdul Rauf, *Moving the Mountain: A New Vision of Islam in America* (New York: Free Press, 2012), 108; Marston, *Muhammad of Mecca*, 24; John Bagot Glubb, *The Life and Times of Muhammad* (New York: Cooper Square Press, 2001 [1970]), 72–75; G. N. Jalbani, *Life of the Holy Prophet* (Islamabad: National Hijra Council, 1988), 13 (mentioning, unusually, M. M. Pickthall, *The Life of the Prophet Muhammad: A Brief History* [Beltsville, MD: Amana Publications, 1998], 9 [originally published in 1930 as an introduction to his Qurʾan translation]); Eliot Weinberger, *Muhammad* (New York: Verso, 2006), 29; Ziauddin Sardar, *Muhammad: All that Matters* (London: Hodder, 2012), 33–34; Rizvi, "Muḥammad in South Asian Biographies," 100; Golam W. Choudhury, *The Prophet Muhammad: His Life and Eternal Message*, 2nd ed. (Kuala Lumpur: WHS Publications 1994 [1993]), 24–25; Watt, *Muhammad*, 12–13 (of her age, he writes, "perhaps this is only a round figure, and she may have been somewhat younger"); Karen Armstrong, *Muhammad: A Prophet for Our Time* (New York: Harper One, 2007), 25–26; Malik,

Muhammad, 10–11; Brown, *Muhammad*, 11. Similar material appears in a different format in Shahid Zafar Qasmi, *Questions and Answers on the Mothers of Believers (May Allah Be Pleased with Them)*, rev. Muhammad Tahir Salafi (Riyadh: Darussalam, 1997), 9–12; Siddiqui, *Life of Muhammad*, 52–53; and Mehru Jaffer, *The Book of Muhammad* (New Delhi: Penguin Global, 2010), 63, 65–66. Jaffer gives a slightly overwrought description of the interest Khadija ("a rich widow who was forty years old and managed a booming business in import and export") developed in Muhammad: "Khadija's curiosity was killing her. She wanted to see the man whose praises she heard sung by the whole town. She asked her minions to seek Muhammad out" (63). Armstrong, *Prophet for Our Time*, 24–25, is typical in every regard except that she puts Khadija's age "probably in her late thirties" without further comment. My entry on Khadija for the *Oxford Encyclopedia of Women in World History* ("Khadija bint Khuwaylid," 2007) follows much the same approach if in slightly more detail. Earlier English-language works present similar information but not usually in such a narrowly predetermined way. See, for example, Stubbe, *Account of the Rise*, 74–76, 139; George Sale, in the preliminary discourse introducing his English translation of the Qur'an, gives a slightly different account (Sale, *The Alcoran of Mohammed*, 1:50–51). Davenport, *Apology for Mohammed*, 13, gives Muhammad's age as twenty-eight and Khadija's as forty; Bush, *Life of Mohammed*, 43–44, gives the now-familiar account of Muhammad's marriage to "a rich trading widow of his native city, who had been twice married, and whose name was CADIJAH." Newcomb, *False Prophet*, 68, echoes Bush on their respective ages: she "forty" and he "twenty-eight."

2. Russ Rodgers emphasizes this element in his account of the marriage. *The Generalship of Muhammad* (Jacksonville: University Press of Florida, 2012), 35–36.

3. M. J. Kister, "The Sons of Khadīja," *Jerusalem Studies in Arabic and Islam* 16 (1993): 69–75, surveys premodern reports about Muhammad and Khadija's male children, which are, like reports about the spouses' respective ages, "divergent and contradictory" (83). He favors the early view that Khadija bore Muhammad only one male child (85).

4. Khalidi, *Images of Muhammad*, 76.

5. The use of an intermediary, derived from Ibn Saʿd and repeated by earlier authors, appears infrequently in recent texts. Emerick, who does mention it (*Muhammad*, 44) falls into anachronism when he describes Nafisa as Khadija's "best friend"; the most recent edition of Aḥmad, *Life of Muḥammad*, 22, uses "a woman friend of hers." See also Deepak

Chopra, *Muhammad: A Story of the Last Prophet* (New York: Harper One, 2010), 98.

6. The quotation is from Sprenger, *Life of Mohammad*, 82.

7. Dimmock, *Mythologies*, 34. On the marriage to Khadija, see pp. 29, 40, 44, 46, 58–59, 62. The notion that Muhammad married Khadija seeking wealth may originate in the Iraqi Christian apology *Risālat al-Kindī*, probably from the tenth century. Tolan, "European Accounts," 233.

8. *Al-sīra al-nabawīya, Sīrat al-nabī*, or *Sīrat rasūl allāh*.

9. M. M. Bravmann, *The Spiritual Background of Early Islam: Studies in Ancient Arab Concepts* (Leiden: Brill, 2009 [1972]), 128–130; see, more generally, 123–139.

10. 'Abbās Maḥmūd al-'Aqqād, *Abqarīyat Muḥammad* [The genius of Muhammad] (Cairo: Maṭba'at al-Istiqāma, 1942), 166–70 (*al-ra'īs*), 172–219 (*al-zawj*).

11. Variables include whether one counts unconsummated marriages and whether certain women were wives or enslaved concubines.

12. Lyons, *Islam through Western Eyes*, ch. 6 and literature cited there; for a rebuttal, see Ama F. Shabazz, "The Prophet on the Treatment of Women," *Message International*, August–September 2002, 37–39. Armstrong argues for Muhammad's concern: "the emancipation of women was a project dear to the Prophet's heart," though some male Muslims "resolutely opposed" it. *Muhammad: A Prophet for Our Time*, 135. See also Fatima Mernissi, *The Veil and the Male Elite: A Feminist Interpretation of Women's Rights in Islam*, trans. Mary Jo Lakeland (New York: Perseus, 1991). For a thorough exploration of these issues, see Lila Abu Lughod, *Do Muslim Women Need Saving?* (Cambridge, MA: Harvard University Press, 2013).

13. Ibn Sa'd, *Women of Madina*.

14. Matthew Pierce, "Remembering Fāṭimah: New Means of Legitimizing Female Authority in Contemporary Shī'ī Discourse," in *Women, Leadership, and Mosques: Changes in Contemporary Islamic Authority*, ed. Masooda Bano and Hilary Kalmbach (Leiden: Brill, 2012), 345–362.

15. Ibn Hishām, *Al-Sīra al-nabawīya* (Al-Mansura, Egypt: Dar al-Ghadd al-Jadeed, 2003), 157; also Guillaume, *Life of Muhammad*, 82.

16. The story is told in Ibn Sa'd and is reported by, among others, al-Ṭabarī, *The History of al-Ṭabarī*, vol. 6, *Muhammad at Mecca*, trans. W. Montgomery Watt and M. V. McDonald (Albany: State University Press of New York, 1989), 49, who reports it on the authority of al-Wāqidī, noting that he considers it an error. See also Andrae, *Mohammed*, 41; Sprenger, *Life of Mohammad*, 83. Betty Kelen, *Muhammad: The*

Messenger of God (New York: Pocket Books, 1997), 13–15, repeats it, confusing the uncle and the father.

17. Bulandshehri, *Wives of the Prophet Muhammad*, 16.

18. Al-Ṭabarī, *History of al-Ṭabarī*, vol. 6, 47. Ibn Hishām, *Al-Sīra al-nabawīya*. See also Kister, "Sons of Khadīja," 66–69. Khalidi, *Images of Muhammad*, 75, is among the rare modern scholars who include variant ages for Khadija. Tariq Ramadan likewise makes note of it, though he, too, ignores the symbolism. *In the Footsteps of the Prophet: Lessons from the Life of Muhammad* (New York: Oxford University Press, 2007), 23. See also Glubb, *Life and Times of Muhammad*, 75.

19. Ibn Saʿd, *Women of Madina*, 9.

20. Notably, Islamic jurists set fifteen as the presumptive age by which menarche will be assumed to have been reached; it is also the age at which a boy is presumed sufficiently mature to undertake jihad—though biological signs of maturity count as well.

21. Al-Ṭabarī, *History of al-Ṭabarī*, vol. 6, 60–61. One explanation of the discrepancy is a three-year gap between the commission of prophecy (at forty) and the commencement of Qur'anic revelation (at forty-three).

22. Lawrence Conrad, "Abraha and Muḥammad: Some Observations Apropos of Chronology and Literary "Topoi" in the Early Arabic Historical Tradition," *Bulletin of the School of Oriental and African Studies, University of London* 50, no. 2 (1987): 225–240, at p. 230. For its symbolic associations, see esp. 231–232; on Khadija's age, 236. For a related point on Muhammad, Abu Bakr, and Umar's ages at death, see the "Chronology" in Rubin, *Eye of the Beholder*, 209–211. Similarly, the gospel statement "that Jesus was about thirty" was "just the conventional way of saying that he was fully adult." Garry Wills, *What Jesus Meant* (New York: Viking, 2006), 5. On the use of forty, see also Schimmel, *And Muhammad Is His Messenger*, 117; she points out that the number forty corresponds in Arabic numerology to the letter *m* for Muhammad.

23. Sprenger, *Life of Mohammad;* D. A. Spellberg, *Politics, Gender, and the Islamic Past* (New York: Columbia University Press, 1996), 216, n. 5. Betty Kelen, *Muhammad*, 15, gives the usual story and then suggests that "since she bore him seven children," she "might have been somewhat younger, perhaps in her thirties."

24. Of course, pious authors might note that divine intervention can override biological norms.

25. Safi, *Memories of Muhammad*, 100, for these three "movements." Lesley Hazelton views the Mount Hirā' encounter as "the pivotal point of his life." Hazelton, *The First Muslim: The Story of Muhammad* (New

York: Riverhead Books, 2013), 11. For the view that the *hijra* to Medina was the most significant act of Muhammad's career, see Ismail R. Al Faruqi, *The Hijrah: The Necessity of Its Iqāmat or Vergegenw'artigung* (Islamabad: National Hijra Council, 1985). Nasr, *Muhammad*, 37, refers to the ascension as "the spiritual crowning of the Blessed Prophet's life" but then emphasizes the migration as "a new phase in the life of the Blessed Prophet as leader of a human society and a person immersed in the life of action" (40).

26. Guillaume, *Life of Muhammad*, 107; the quoted phrase is Guillaume's interpolation from al-Ṭabarī.

27. Sale, *The Alcoran of Mohammed*, 1:56, gives the same general story but without any references to her comforting him; instead, she is gladdened.

28. For a polemical version of this story, see Tolan, "European Accounts," 228–229.

29. Guillaume, *Life of Muhammad*, 106–107; another version of the story is told near the section on Khadija's marriage (Ibn Hishām, *Al-Sīra al-nabawīya*, 159; Guillaume, *Life of Muhammad*, 83). For Khadija's role after the first revelation, see also al-Ṭabarī, *History of al-Ṭabarī*, vol. 6, 67–77.

30. Ibn Hishām, *Al-Sīra al-nabawīya*, 193, my translation; Guillaume, *Life of Muhammad*, 155.

31. Jalbani, *Life of the Holy Prophet*, 20.

32. Ahmad Thompson, *The Wives of the Prophet Muhammad: May the Blessings and Peace of Allah Be on Him and His Family and Companions* (London: Ta-Ha Publishers, 2004 [1993]), 1.

33. "Kānat malak raḥma." The Arabic text includes both *fatḥa*s (short vowel *a* markers) on the word *malak*. Haykal, *Ḥayāt Muḥammad*, 189; Haykal, *Life of Muḥammad*, 136.

34. Stanley Lane Poole, introduction to *Selections from the Ḳur-án*, by Edward William Lane, rev. ed. (London: Trübner, 1879), liii.

35. Syed Ameer Ali, *Spirit of Islam*, 115. The sentence "She was ever his angel of hope and consolation" appears in quotation marks but without attribution.

36. Siddiqui, *Life of Muhammad*, 53.

37. Jalbani, *Life of the Holy Prophet*, 15.

38. J. W. H. Stobart, *Islam and Its Founder* (London and New York: Society for Promoting Christian Knowledge, 1895), 57.

39. Shamim Aleem, *Prophet Muhammad (S) and His Family: A Sociological Perspective* (Bloomington, IN: AuthorHouse, 2007), 8.

40. Driss Chraibi, *L'homme du livre* (Paris: Éditions Denoël, 2011 [1995]), 16.

41. Sara Pursley, "Daughters of the Right Path: Family Law, Homosocial Publics, and the Ethics of Intimacy in the Works of Shi'i Revivalist Bint al-Huda," *Journal of Middle East Women's Studies* 8, no. 2 (Spring 2012): 51–77. Pursley points out that "the valorization of Khadija conforms to historical Shi'i evaluations of the Prophet's wives, though that may simply have made it a more effective vehicle for expressing the author's distaste for polygamy" (74, n. 7; 51–77).

42. Reynolds, *Interpreting the Self,* 79–80.

43. See, for example, al-Ṭabarī, *History of al-Ṭabarī,* vol. 39, *Biographies of the Prophet's Companions and Their Successors,* trans. Ella Landau-Tasseron, 176 (regarding Aisha and Umm Salama).

44. See David S. Powers, *Zayd* (Philadelphia: University of Pennsylvania Press, forthcoming); al-Ṭabarī, *History of al-Ṭabarī,* vol. 39, 65, n. 299.

45. Nasr, *Muhammad,* 18.

46. Muhammad Anis-ur-Rahman, *The Historical Role of the Venerable Woman,* 3rd ed., enlarged (Karachi: Faran Publications, 2007), 44, 52.

47. Ibid., 32.

48. Ibid., 86. See also 44, 57, 63.

49. Anis-ur-Rahman writes, "*The first lady of Islam should be a working woman as to give lead to the women community of the world who were to come in the fold of Islam.* So a great woman was brought by the historical forces under the command of the providence to be married to the Holy Prophet." Ibid., 74. Italics in original.

50. Ibid., 57.

51. Tamam Kahn, *Untold: A History of the Wives of Prophet Muhammad* (Rhinebeck, NY: Monkfish, 2010), 16, 29.

52. Siddiqui, *Life of Muhammad,* 52–53. Italics in original.

53. Malik, *Muhammad,* 10.

54. Davenport, *Apology for Mohammed,* 23–24; quotation at p. 24.

55. Carlyle, *Hero as Prophet,* 22; Davenport, *Apology for Mohammed,* 13.

56. Irving, *Mahomet and His Successors,* 109.

57. Rodinson, *Mahomet,* 79; *Muhammad,* 55.

58. Nasr, *Muhammad,* 18–19.

59. There is some dispute over which death occurred first, or even when they happened. See Kister, "Sons of Khadīja." See also, briefly, Brown, *Muhammad,* 22.

60. Marston, *Muhammad of Mecca,* 41.

61. Guillaume, *Life of Muhammad,* 191. Numerous authors follow this, some quite closely. See, for example, Schimmel, *And Muhammad Is His Messenger,* 13.

62. Al-Ṭabari, *History of al-Ṭabarī*, vol. 6, 115; see also vol. 39, 3–4, 161. Or, in Ibn Isḥāq, "the Quraysh began to treat him in an offensive way which they would not have dared to follow in his uncle's lifetime" (Guillaume, *Life of Muhammad*, 191). See Stecker, *Man Mohammed*, 29–30, for the deaths, followed by persecution.

63. Sale, *The Alcoran of Mohammed*, 1:60

64. Peters, "Quest of the Historical Muhammad," 307; James E. Montgomery, "Editor's Introduction," in *The Oral and the Written in Early Islam*, ed. Gregor Schoeler, Uwe Vagelpohl, and James E. Montgomery (London: Taylor and Francis, 2006), 7. Nasr, *Muhammad*, 94, calls it "the most eloquent and moving biography of the Prophet" in English and recommends it "highly to those seeking to understand how the Prophet is seen in traditional Islamic sources."

65. Choudhury, *Prophet Muhammad*, 29. Stobart had called him "a faithful and affectionate husband." *Islam and Its Founder*, 64.

66. Martin Lings, *Muhammad: His Life Based on the Earliest Sources* (Rochester, VT: Inner Traditions International, 1983), 96.

67. Nasr, *Muhammad*, 26. See, similarly, Thompson, *Wives of the Prophet Muhammad*, 7.

68. Davenport, *Apology for Mohammed*, 23–24; quotation at p. 24.

69. Prideaux, *True Nature of Imposture*, 41.

70. Ibn Hishām, *Al-Sīra al-nabawiya;* al-Ṭabarī, *History of al-Ṭabarī.* Guillaume, *Life of Muhammad*, 792, n. 918, attributes this material to Ibn Hishām and not Ibn Isḥāq.

71. Ibn Kathīr, *The Life of the Prophet Muhammad*, trans. Trevor Le Gassick (Reading, UK: Garnet, 1998), 2:92, insists that the contract with Aisha occurred before the marriage to Sawda, though he acknowledges at least one scholar who held a contrary opinion (2:97); the English translation reads, "his betrothal to 'Ā'isha preceded his marriage to Sawda." (On the particulars of this "translation," see Williams, *Muhammad and the Supernatural*, ix.) See also al-Ṭabarī, *History of al-Ṭabarī*, vol. 9, 128, which notes dispute as to which marriage occurred first, but insists that "all those knowledgeable about the Messenger of God's life agree that the Messenger of God consummated his marriage with Sawda before [consummating his marriage with] 'Ā'ishah" (brackets in original). Some traditionalist accounts, however, retain the matchmaker's intervention. See, for example, Bulandshehri, *Wives of the Prophet Muhammad*, 31–33; Thompson, *Wives of the Prophet Muhammad*, 8–10.

72. For instance, Andrae, *Mohammed*, 188.

73. Carlyle, *Hero as Prophet*, 22.

74. Dashti, *Twenty-Three Years.*

75. Watt, *Muhammad*, 79.

76. Woods, *In Spite of Epilepsy*, 136. Hostile biographers suggested that Muhammad invented the story of revelations to explain his epileptic fits so that Khadija would still marry him. For a thirteenth-century Latin example, see Tolan, "European Accounts," 228–229. For early modern English examples, see Dimmock, *Mythologies*, 31.

77. Sometimes used interchangeably with motive, "interest" has a broader significance, not coterminous with ambition. In the eighteenth century, elite figures on both sides of the Atlantic used the term to mean personal "ties to men with social, political, and military power." Gruber, *Books and the British Army*, 8. In his biography of George Washington, who persistently worked to strengthen such ties, Paul Johnson explains that "interest was a connection through family ties, friendship, local ties, or clan, which put a man ahead of his immediate competitors in getting something he wanted—a place, a promotion, a contract, a favor." Paul Johnson, *George Washington: The Founding Father* (New York: Harper Collins, 2006), 12. Twenty-first-century Americans laud networking but frown on nepotism; their ancestors presumed it legitimate to draw on personal and family ties for economic and professional advancement. As a clergyman, Prideaux presumably saw "interest" less pragmatically than Washington and his British military counterparts. Yet it seems likely that Prideaux objected to Muhammad marrying to "strengthen himself" by "Alliance[s]," primarily because it was part of a larger imposture.

78. Arthur N. Wollaston, *Half-Hours with Muhammad, Being a popular Account of the Prophet of Arabia and of his more immediate Followers* (London: W.H. Allen, 1886), 48.

79. Siddiqui, *Life of Muhammad.* On this marriage, see also al-Ṭabarī, *History of al-Ṭabarī*, vol. 8, *The Victory of Islam*, trans. Michael Fishbein, 1–4.

80. Zaidi, *Mothers of the Faithful*, 1.

81. S. M. Madni Abbasi, *The Family of the Holy Prophet (S.A.W.)* (New Delhi: Adam, 2004), 67. Thompson, *Wives of the Prophet Muhammad*, 37, is unusual in mentioning—in addition to alliances, protection, or demonstration of marriage norms—that God's "decree" was the deciding factor.

82. For a treatment of this marriage in the earlier Muslim tradition, with some reference to modern Muslim thinking, see Ze'ev Maghen, "Zayd and Zaynab Revisited: Bowdlerizing the *Uswa Ḥasana*," chap. 3

in *Virtues of the Flesh: Passion and Purity in Early Islamic Jurisprudence* (Leiden: Brill, 2005), 75–110. Maghen suggests that "not only was Zayd's 'adoption by the Prophet' largely a symbolic gesture—such that we should not really think of Muḥammad as having married his adoptive *son's* wife—but marriage itself at the time could be an ephemeral affair, often failing to establish a close connection between newlywed couples—and thus we should not really think of Muḥammad as having married his adoptive son's *wife*, with all that the later title implies for us. In order to avail themselves of such a claim, however, modern Muslim apologists would have to admit that marriage among the *ṣaḥāba* did not adhere to today's ideal" (108–109, n. 80).

83. Watt, *Muhammad*, 156.

84. Siddiqui, *Life of Muhammad*, 226.

85. Wessels, *Modern Arabic Biography*, 133–141, on the marriage and some of the commentarial tradition.

86. Siddiqui, *Life of Muhammad*, 227.

87. Ibid., 225.

88. Ibid.; Thompson, *Wives of the Prophet Muhammad*, 49–52; Davenport, *Apology for Mohammed*, 35.

89. Quoted in Wessels, *Modern Arabic Biography*, 147.

90. Newcomb, *False Prophet*, 118–119.

91. Ibid., 119–120.

92. Bush, *Life of Mohammed*, 161.

93. Ibid., 162; italics in original.

94. Ibid.

95. Ibid., 163.

96. For instance, Jalbani, *Life of the Holy Prophet*, 44: "The Holy Prophet after [Khadija's] death married Saudah bint Zamʿah, one of the earliest Muslims and now a widow, so that, the minor children may be looked after with ease." See also Thompson, *Wives of the Prophet Muhammad*, 8–9; Dashti, *Twenty-Three Years*, 122–123; Qasmi, *Questions and Answers*, 24.

97. Robinson, *Islamic Historiography*, 104.

98. Salmin, *Holy Prophet Mohammad*, 122.

99. Ibid.

100. Ibid., 123.

101. Malik, *Muhammad*, 123.

102. Ibid. For Ahmad Khan, too, the links between Muhammad's polygamy and Jesus's celibacy and piety were central, but he wrote that "wives were not indicative of holiness and that Christ was holy because

he was a prophet, not because of his celibacy. Monogamy was not necessarily meritorious, and there occurred many situations in life which necessitated the practice of polygamy." Rizvi, "Muḥammad in South Asian Biographies," 115–116.

103. For a thoughtful attempt to reconcile these divergent assessments, see Kahn, *Untold,* 10–11.

104. Malik, *Muhammad,* 124.

105. Ibid.

106. Ibid., 125.

107. Sardar, *Muhammad,* 118, 120; see also Rauf, *Moving the Mountain,* 110, regarding Muhammad's marriages after he was widowed: "As was often the case in ancient times, he married for political reasons: to take care of a widow, say, or to strengthen his bond with certain key leaders. In purely religious terms, the Prophet's wives were major sources for many of the *hadiths.*"

108. Al-Ṭabarī, *History of al-Ṭabarī,* vol. 7, xviii.

109. In contrast, Rodinson (*Mahomet,* 79) suggests that Muhammad remained faithful to Khadija at significant psychological cost, given the clash between his own "erotic temperament" and his conscience, which "prevented him from satisfying his desires." (My translation; the published translation [Rodinson, *Muhammad,* 55] uses the phrase "a highly sexed man.") Sardar, *Muhammad,* 122, is also frank: "There is no doubt that Muhammad himself enjoyed the company of women and a robust sex life."

110. Thompson, *Wives of the Prophet Muhammad,* 55. Compare to al-Ṭabarī, *History of al-Ṭabarī,* vol. 39, 183.

111. Dashti, *Twenty-Three Years,* 135; discussing Zaynab, 121.

112. Ibn Hishām, *Al-sīra al-nabawīya.*

113. Abbasi, *Family of the Holy Prophet,* 67. See also Bulandshehri, *Wives of the Prophet Muhammad,* 168: "These sexually perverted people of Europe can not comprehend the sublime and exalted designs of Islam. . . . If any person with clear and impartial vision tries to evaluate the life of the Prophet Muhammad *(sallallahu alayhe wasallam),* he can not just think in the terms that he married so many wives just for sexual pleasures."

114. Abbasi, *Family of the Holy Prophet,* 67.

115. Ali, *Muhammad the Prophet,* 187.

116. Ibid.

117. Malik, *Muhammad,* 123–124.

118. Ali, *Muhammad the Prophet,* 192.

119. Ibid.

120. Siddiqui, *Life of Muhammad*, 251.

121. Ali, *Muhammad the Prophet*, 192.

122. Bulandshehri, *Wives of the Prophet Muhammad*, 170.

123. Ali, *Muhammad the Prophet*, 193.

124. Ibid.

125. Ibid.

126. An interesting case of reticence about her status as divorcee: Al-eem, *Prophet Muhammad (S)*, 105–106, includes an appendix on Muhammad's wives, including a column for marital status. Aisha is listed as a virgin; other women are listed as "W," for widow, with additional notations as to whether they have been twice or thrice married. Zaynab, in that column, has "N. A."

127. Ali, *Muhammad the Prophet*, 193.

128. Ibid., 196.

129. Nasr, *Muhammad*, 20; see also Bulandshehri, *Wives of the Prophet Muhammad*, 168–169, 170.

130. Nasr, *Muhammad*, 19.

131. Ibid., 20. See a similar argument in Higgins, *Apology for the Life*, 26; he suggests the desire for a son may have motivated his marriages.

132. Higgins, *Apology for the Life*, 26. Stubbe, *Account of the Rise*, 139, speculates that it was "perhaps out of gratitude to the raiser of his fortunes" that Muhammad did not marry again while Khadija lived.

133. Abbasi, *Family of the Holy Prophet*, 1.

134. Unusually, Qasmi, *Questions and Answers*, devotes more than twice as much space to Aisha (twenty pages) as to Khadija (nine); his work, however, is more catechism than biography.

135. Nasr, *Muhammad*, 18–19.

136. Armstrong, *Muhammad*, 75.

137. Abbasi, *Family of the Holy Prophet*, 67.

138. Chopra, *Muhammad*, 105. For Khadija's chapter, see 103–115. Other figures reflect on their marriage as well (e.g., 95–99). Emerick, *Muhammad*, 44. For an account of his conversion, see Yahiya Emerick, "Getting to Know a Friend: My Introduction to Muhammad," in *Message International*, August–September 2002, 21–25. For a different imagining of Khadija's developing love for Muhammad in a 2004 Indonesian biography, which perhaps draws on Haykal, see Gade, "Religious Biography," 261–263.

139. Emerick, *Muhammad*, 45.

140. Al-Ṭabarī, *History of al-Ṭabarī*, vol. 6, 48.

141. Emerick, *Muhammad,* 44: "An older woman . . . marrying a man fifteen years younger was unheard of in Arab society."

142. Ameer Ali, *Critical Examination,* 4–5. Note that his evidence, here, is the "Brahmanic legislator," as reported in a French history of comparative ancient criminal law; an excerpt from the Laws of Manu, published in *Tytler's Considerations on the State of India;* and a book, also French, on women in ancient India (5, n.).

143. Salmin, *Holy Prophet Mohammad,* 143; for a more recent example, see Shabazz, "Prophet on the Treatment of Women." Dashti, *Twenty-Three Years,* reports the degraded condition but does not present such a glowing portrait of Muhammad's reforms, saying only that he "blunted the edge of this savagery" (114).

144. Salmin nonsensically writes, "[He h]imself married a widow so that the remarriage of widows may not remain a taboo." But remarriage of widows in the Arabian Peninsula was not a taboo by conventional accounts which say Khadija was widowed twice—and hence remarried after being widowed—before Muhammad wed her. *Holy Prophet Mohammad,* 151. Bulandshehri makes a slightly different point in *The Wives of the Prophet,* 11: widow marriage was not sinful in the prophet's context but today "in certain nations, the re-marriage of a widow is considered as an evil. This is a colossal sin. A practice which the holy Prophet performed must not be considered wrong."

145. Sprenger, *Life of Mohammad,* 153–154.

146. *Awlād ḥāritnā* (Children of our quarter) appeared in serial form in 1959 and was first published in book form in 1967. See Roded, "Gender in an Allegorical Life," 117–134; Wessels, *Modern Arabic Biography,* 24–29.

147. For instance, Marston's *Muhammad of Mecca* discusses Khadija extensively on p. 24, throughout the next sections of the book, and then in the discussion of his family life, where Mariya, "his Egyptian concubine" (91), is mentioned; Aisha gets her own short section; and she discusses (without naming) Umm Habiba, the daughter of Abu Sufyan, because it enables her to illustrate how the marriage was for the purpose of "reconciliation" between Muhammad and her father, his "old enemy" (92–93). Wollaston mentions this marriage (*Half-Hours,* 62): "This fair matron was like all her predecessors in the apostle's harem a widow; her husband had long since died in Abyssinia, and it is conjectured that the Prophet was moved by motives of policy to add the lady to his long list of spouses, hoping that she might thereby be enabled to soften in some measure, the animosity of her father, a bitter, unrelenting, and withal power-

ful opponent to the faith of Islam." Armstrong, *Muhammad: A Prophet for Our Time,* calls this marriage "a shrewd political move" (181).

148. A sampling: Stecker, *Man Mohammed,* 37–38; Émile Dermenghem, *Life of Mahomet,* trans. Arabella Yorke (New York: Routledge, 1930), 286–287; Carlyle, *Hero as Prophet,* 26; Khalidi, *Images of Muhammad,* 75–76; Emerick, *Muhammad,* 45 (though he does not mention that it was Aisha); Andrae, *Mohammed,* 41; G. M. Draycott, *Mahomet: Founder of Islam* (New York: Dodd, Mead, and Company, 1916), 91–92; Thompson, *Wives of the Prophet Muhammad,* 6–7; Davenport, *Apology for Mohammed,* 24. Armstrong, *Muhammad: A Prophet for Our Time,* 26, writes that "after her death he used to infuriate some of his later wives by endlessly singing her praises."

149. Choudhury, *Prophet Muhammad,* 154.

5. Mother of the Faithful

1. Ibn Hishām, *Al-sīra al-nabawīya,* 668; Guillaume's version reads: "He married 'Ā'isha in Mecca when she was a child of seven and lived with her in Medina when she was nine or ten. She was the only virgin that he married" (*Life of Muhammad,* 792, n. 918). The phrase Guillaume translates as "lived with her" is *banā bihā;* the word he translates as child is *bint.*

2. Aisha's age is discussed in al-Ṭabarī, *History of al-Ṭabarī,* vol. 39, *Biographies of the Prophet's Companions and Their Successors,* trans. Ella Landau-Tasseron, 171–174, and vol. 9, *The Last Years of the Prophet,* trans. Ismail K. Poonawala, 129–131. In these accounts, she is usually six (sometimes seven) at the marriage and nine at consummation. The age at death (sixty-six) and death date (58/678) roughly corroborate this statement (39:173). In discussing whether, after Khadija's death, Muhammad married Sawda or Aisha first, al-Ṭabarī writes: "As for 'Ā'ishah, when he married her she was very young and not yet ready for consummation, whereas Sawdah was already married before" (9:128). Poonawala inserts a footnote directly after the word "consummation," in which he writes that she was six at the marriage during Shawwal, year 10, and nine when it was consummated in Shawwal. He cites Ibn Sa'd's *Ṭabaqāt* and Balādhurī's *Ansāb.* On Aisha's age, see also Brown, *Muhammad,* 24, 76–78, and al-Ṭabarī, *History of al-Ṭabarī,* vol. 39, 180.

3. Al-Ṭabarī, *History of al-Ṭabarī,* vol. 39, 180.

4. Ibid., 185.

5. Conrad, "Abraha and Muḥammad." He does not mention Aisha.

6. Spellberg, *Politics, Gender, and the Islamic Past,* 40.

7. Spellberg, *Politics, Gender, and the Islamic Past*, 197–198, n. 4.

8. One finds in Bulandshehri a rare echo of Prideaux in a discussion of Hafsa's marriage: "By this marriage, the Prophet strengthened the ties between two of his closest companions" (*Wives of the Prophet Muhammad*, 39).

9. "After the death of Khadija in 619, and while still in Mecca, he [Muhammad] married Sawda bint Zam'a, a recent widow, and Aisha, the daughter of his closest companion, Abu Bakr" (Sardar, *Muhammad*, 118). See also Nasr, *Muhammad*, 26. Siddiqui puts Sawda first, too: "After the sad demise of *Khadijah*, he again went in for a widow, this time a helpless one in great distress. She was one of the earliest converts to *Islam* who had suffered many hardships for the cause of truth." Only after that, "the Holy Prophet married *A'ishah*, the daughter of his devoted friend *Abu Bakr*. She was the only virgin wife of *Muhammad* (peace be upon him)." Siddiqui, *Life of Muhammad*, 250.

10. Prideaux, *True Nature of Imposture*, 41. Italics in original.

11. Bush, *Life of Mohammed*.

12. Ibid., 88. This passage is echoed nearly verbatim in Newcomb, *False Prophet*, 117–118. Here, Khadija's death does not serve as the lead-in. This section leads, predictably, to discussion of the degraded position of females in heathen areas.

13. Samuel Green plagiarizes this line, and much of its surrounding material, in *The Life of Mahomet: Founder of the Religion of Islamism and of the Empire of the Saracens* (London: William Tegg, 1877), 207. (Bush's *Life of Mohammed* is absent from his list of sources, vii.) Bush, in turn, borrows a great deal from Prideaux in this section.

14. Irving, *Mahomet and His Successors*, 151, 152.

15. Ibid., 109–110.

16. Davenport, *Apology for Mohammed*, 25.

17. Muir, *Life of Mahomet*, 2nd ed, 117.

18. Prideaux, *True Nature of Imposture*, 21, 85. Italics in original.

19. Muir, *Life of Mahomet*, 2nd ed, 117.

20. William Muir, *The Life of Mahomet, with Introductory Chapter on the Original Sources for the Biography of Mahomet, and on the Pre-Islamite History of Arabia* (London: Smith, Elder, 1861), 3:13, 22. Muir, *Life of Mahomet*, 2nd ed, 117, suggests that "there may have been something more than ordinarily interesting and precocious about the child." Also, Muir, *Life of Mahomet*, 2nd ed., 62: "Ayesha his daughter (born about this period, and destined while yet a girl to be the Prophet's bride)."

21. Ibid., 23.

22. Wollaston, *Half-Hours*, 42.

23. Ibid., 66–67. Italics in original. In discussing Ayesha's role at Muhammad's illness and death, Johnstone refers to her as "his best beloved, not yet twenty years old"; discusses how Muhammad "lay his weary head on Ayesha's loving breast"; and notes the "fond, faithful soothing of his young wife" (*Muhammad and His Power*, 144–146).

24. Quoted in Tolan, "European Accounts," 235–236.

25. Rizvi, "Muḥammad in South Asian Biographies," paraphrasing Shibli Numani, 117; see also Syed Suleman Nadvi [Saiyid Sulaiman Nadwi], *Muhammad: The Ideal Prophet. A Historic, Practical, Perfect Model for Humanity*, trans. Mohiuddin Ahmad (Kuala Lumpur: Islamic Book Trust, 1977 [n.d.]), 56.

26. Margoliouth, *Mohammed and the Rise of Islam*, 343.

27. Ibid., 450.

28. Ibid., 234–235.

29. Newcomb, *False Prophet*, 68.

30. Draycott, *Mahomet*, 95–96, 102, 182.

31. On the marriage to Aisha, see Lings, *Muhammad*, 105–106 (he does not use the term "betrothal"), and 132–133.

32. Glubb, *Life and Times of Muhammad*, 160.

33. Ibid., 239.

34. Sprenger also makes Muhammad a householder: "'A'yishah being only nine years of age when she married him, brought her toys into *his house;* and he occasionally played with her. She also used to race with him" (*Life of Mohammad*, 93; emphasis mine). But see, for example, Johnstone, *Muhammad and His Power*, 132.

35. Quoted in Ian Littlewood, *Sultry Climates: Travel and Sex* (Cambridge, MA: Da Capo, 2002), 52.

36. Neil Cooke, "James Burton and Slave Girls," in *Unfolding the Orient: Travellers in Egypt and the Near East*, ed. Paul and Janet Starkey (Reading, UK: Garnet, 2001), 209–217.

37. Schick, *Erotic Margin*, 137; the partial quotation is from St. John.

38. Ibid., 1.

39. On seventeenth-century British writers' views of the contribution of hot climates to "sodomitical" tendencies, see Nabil Matar, *Turks, Moors, and Englishmen in the Age of Discovery* (New York: Columbia University Press, 1999), 120. The effects of "sultry climates" are not limited to the Orient; see the discussions of tourism in Italy and Tahiti in Littlewood, *Sultry Climates;* on sexual precocity, see esp. 168, 194–196. Littlewood's occasional use or inclusion of "oriental" references—"sultanesque

fantasies," "seraglio," "bashaw" (pasha) (41, 52, 141, 156)—suggests the need for further investigation.

40. Schick, *Erotic Margin*, 108.

41. Sprenger, *Life of Mohammad*, 80.

42. Higgins, *Apology*, 34.

43. Quoted in Khan, *Essays*, 149; the ellipsis is Ahmad Khan's.

44. Newcomb, *False Prophet*, 124.

45. Ibid., 125.

46. Schick, *Erotic Margin*, 67.

47. Tolan, *Sons of Ishmael*, 144.

48. Mark Jordan, *The Ethics of Sex* (Malden, MA: Blackwell, 2002); Matar, *Turks, Moors, and Englishmen*, 112; Kidd, *American Christians and Islam*, 27.

49. Robinson-Dunn, *Harem*, 11, citing Miguel Cabrera.

50. Mrinali Sinha, *Specters of Mother India: The Global Restructuring of an Empire* (Durham, NC: Duke University Press, 2006); Schick, *Erotic Margin*, 138

51. Littlewood, *Sultry Climates*, 74.

52. Tyerman, *Crusades*, 137.

53. The relationship between overt imperial control and specific scholarship and writing is one subject to debate. See Wokoeck, *German Orientalism*.

54. Prideaux, *True Nature of Imposture*, 107.

55. Schick, *Erotic Margin*, 154.

56. Johnstone compares Islam's "enslaving women" to Christianity, which "has raised woman to her proper place as the equal of man." *Muhammad and His Power*, 159; see also: "the whole position of women was changed for the worse, and instead of the equal and help of her husband the wife was degraded to be his slave and his toy" (227).

57. Coomar Roy, with a prefatory note by Joel Benton, "Child Marriage in India," *North American Review* 147 (1888): 415–423. Though Coomar draws a number of parallels with Catholic marriage, he notably deemphasizes individual consent of spouses.

58. Mrs. Marcus B. [Jenny] Fuller, *The Wrongs of Indian Womanhood* (New York: Fleming H. Revell, 1900). "Child Marriage," 33, is followed by a chapter on widowhood. A number of authors, interestingly, connect Aisha's youth at marriage with the lengthy period she lived after Muhammad's death.

59. Fuller, *Wrongs of Indian Womanhood*, 47.

60. Sumit Sarkar and Tanika Sarkar, eds., *Women and Social Reform in Modern India: A Reader* (Bloomington: Indiana University Press, 2008), 464–465 and elsewhere; Sinha, *Specters of Mother India*.

61. Fuller, *Wrongs of Indian Womanhood*, 47.

62. Department of Commerce and Labor, Bureau of the Census, *Special Reports: Marriage and Divorce, 1867–1906*, Pt. 1: *Summary, Laws, Foreign Statistics* (Washington, DC: Government Printing Office, 1909). "Marriage and Divorce Laws: Algeria," 359. No one has yet undertaken a study of the history of the Western presentation of Aisha as Muhammad's "best-beloved wife" (Prideaux, *True Nature of Imposture*, 42, 103).

63. C. N. Barham, "Child Marriage in India," *Westminster Review* 135, no. 2 (January–June 1891): 113–124, at p. 118.

64. Ibid.

65. Such a move runs counter to the creative work that a scholar such as Isvarchandra Vidyasagar undertook, "redeploy[ing] premodern textual sources and interpretive strategies in the service of a modern reformist cause." Vidyasagar wrote on both the *Evils of Child Marriage* (1850) and *Hindu Widow Marriage* (1855). His work, as Brian Hatcher has shown, has been attacked from all directions (Hatcher, introduction to *Hindu Widow Marriage*, by Vidyasagar, 31).

66. Barham, "Child Marriage in India," 119.

67. Beth Baron, "The Making and Breaking of Marital Bonds in Modern Egypt," in *Women in Middle Eastern History: Shifting Boundaries in Sex and Gender*, ed. Nikki R. Keddie and Beth Baron (New Haven, CT: Yale University Press, 1992), 275–291; Jonathan Brown, *Misquoting Muhammad: The Challenges and Choices of Interpreting the Prophet's Legacy* (Oneworld, forthcoming), cites a few instances where Muhammad's precedent was mentioned.

68. Procedural reforms, to close loopholes and dissuade guardians and court officials from fudging girls' age, were passed in 1931 and 1933. See Hanan Kholoussy, "The Nationalization of Marriage in Monarchical Egypt," in *Re-Envisioning Egypt, 1919–1952*, ed. Arthur Goldschmidt, Amy J. Johnson, and Barak A. Salmoni (Cairo: American University in Cairo Press, 2005), 317–350, esp. 320–324.

69. Kholoussy, "Nationalization of Marriage," 317, 318.

70. Ibid., 319.

71. She cites Beth Baron, *The Women's Awakening in Egypt: Culture, Society, and the Press* (New Haven, CT: Yale University Press, 1997), 164, and says that 1907 and 1917 census numbers show that "most females

married between the ages of twenty and twenty-nine" and less than 10 percent of females married below that age. It is unclear whether this is the age at first marriage, or the age at which all marriages during that period took place.

72. Kholoussy, "Nationalization of Marriage," 320.

73. Sinha, *Specters of Mother India*.

74. Or to ignore it. Aḥmad, *Life of Muḥammad*, mentions Aisha throughout but does not specifically discuss circumstances of the marriage to her or Sawda.

75. Syed Suleman Nadvi, *Women Companions of the Holy Prophet and Their Sacred Lives* (New Delhi: Islamic Book Service, 2001): 34–35.

76. Colin Turner, *Islam: The Basics* (New York: Routledge, 2006), 35.

77. Andrae, *Mohammed*, 162.

78. Ibn Saʻd, *Women of Madina*, 44.

79. Ibid., 54–55.

80. Thompson, *Wives of the Prophet Muhammad*, 14, is among the few who repeat the story of the portrait brought by the angel Gabriel. His collective biography of Muhammad's wives was published by the publisher of Ibn Saʻd's *The Women of Madina*.

81. Zaidi, *Mothers of the Faithful*, 37; Davenport, *Apology for Mohammed*, 25.

82. Zaidi, *Mothers of the Faithful*, 37.

83. Siddiqui, *Life of Muhammad*, 150.

84. Ibid., 151.

85. Ibid.

86. Ibid. See also Thompson, *Wives of the Prophet Muhammad*, 17. Bulandshehri, *Wives of the Prophet*, 167, provides a similar rationale for Muhammad's polygamy in a final chapter entitled "The Philosophy of Wedding So Many Wives." He writes, "There were so many intricate subjects which could only be explained to the general public, specially the women, through his wives alone. For [the] purpose of imparting information and rightly educating the public, it was very important for him to have too many wives."

87. Abbasi, *Family of the Holy Prophet*, 72–73.

88. For a discussion of how even critical works can function as sources of authority, see Tageldin, *Disarming Words*.

89. For betrothal: Abbasi, *Family of the Holy Prophet*, 72 (though he uses marriage on the same page); Nasr, *Muhammad*, 26 ("A short time later he married Sawdah and became betrothed also to the daughter of Abū Bakr, ʻĀʼishah, who was then only seven years old and whom the

Blessed Prophet was to marry when she came of age"); Thompson, *Wives of the Prophet Muhammad*, 10. For engagement, see Hafez Ghulam Sarwar, *Muhammad the Holy Prophet* (Lahore: Shaykh Muhammad Ashraf, 1980 [1961]).

90. M. V. McDonald, foreword to Al-Ṭabarī, *History of al-Ṭabarī*, vol. 7, *The Foundation of the Community*, trans. M. V. McDonald, xviii. For the marriage, see Al-Ṭabarī, *History of al-Ṭabarī*, vol. 7, 6–8, including the translators' note (6, n. 12), which says, "The original marriage . . . could be considered rather a betrothal."

91. Irving lists Weil among his sources (*Mahomet and His Successors*, vi) but makes little use of him, a point Muir notes (and for which he criticizes him). See "Biographies of Mohammed," in *Mohammedan Controversy*, 69.

92. Whether *Zaynab* counts as the "first" proper Arabic novel has been the subject of some debate; see, for example, Mohammad R. Salama, *Islam, Orientalism, and Intellectual History: Modernity and Politics of Exclusion since Ibn Khaldun* (London: I. B. Tauris, 2011), 175. Salama discusses a slightly earlier novel, Maḥmūd Ṭāhir Ḥaqqī's *The Virgin of Denshawai*, about which he states that it is "free from some of the restrictions of normal historical writing. He can be episodic and fragmentary, add or delete events altogether. This is not merely freedom from the constraints of the history of Denshawai [the town where the novel is set] but also freedom to choose and to foreground, and thus to offer an understanding that holds the immediacy of direct perception" (179). I would suggest that Salama's observation applies to both premodern and postmodern biography, as well as fiction.

93. Haykal, *Ḥayāt Muḥammad*, 311–320; Haykal, *Life of Muḥammad*, 285–298.

94. "Fa khaṭaba Abī Bakr ibnatahu ʿĀʾisha, wa limmā kānat lā tazāla ṭifla fī al-sābiʿa min ʿumrihā ʿaqada ʿalayhā wa lam yabni bihā ilā baʿd sanatayn hīn balaghat al-tāsiʿa, wa fī hadhihi al-ithnāʾ tazawwaja Sawda, armalat aḥad al-muslimīn aladhīna hājaru ilā al-ḥabasha wa ʿādū ilā Makka wa matū bihā." Haykal, *Ḥayāt Muḥammad*, 193. Compare Al Faruqi's version: "He therefore asked Abū Bakr for the hand of his daughter ʿĀʾishah. Since she was still too young to marry, the engagement was announced but the marriage was postponed for three more years until Āʾishah reached the age of eleven. In the meantime, Muḥammad married Sawdah, the widow of one of the Muslim companions who emigrated to Abysinnia but died upon his return to Makkah." Haykal, *Life of Muḥammad*, 139. I discuss this translation below.

95. "Idh dhāk banā Muḥammad ṣalla Allāhu 'alayhi wa sallam bi 'Ā'isha bint Abī Bakr, wa kānat fi'l-'āshira aw al-ḥādiya 'ashira min 'umrihā, wa kānat fatā raqīqa, ḥalwat al-qasamāt, muḥabbabat al-'ishra, wa kānat takhṭū min al-ṭufūla ilā al-ṣiban wa kānat dhāt wala' bi'l-la'ib wa'l-maraḥ wa kānat nāmīya naman ḥasanan." Haykal, *Hayāt Muḥammad*, 231. Compare Al Faruqi's translation: "At this time Muḥammad married 'Ā'ishah, daughter of Abū Bakr, who was then ten or eleven years old. She was a beautiful, delicate, and amiable young girl, emerging out of childhood and blossoming into full womanhood. Although she was fully grown, she was still quite attracted by amusement and play." Haykal, *Life of Muḥammad*, 183. I discuss this translation below.

96. Al Faruqi's translation. See also Hazelton, *First Muslim*, 215: "It was as though [Muhammad] had granted her license for girlish mischief. Much as a fond father might indulge a spoiled daughter, he seemed diverted by her sassiness and charm."

97. Muir says she was ten, "though she had been three years affianced." Muir, *Life of Mahomet*, 2nd ed., 186. Elsewhere he says she was "six or seven" when betrothed and that "the marriage took place not more than three years afterwards" (117).

98. Haykal, *Hayāt Muḥammad*, 315; Haykal, *Life of Muḥammad*, 291.

99. Émile Dermenghem, *La vie de Mahomet* (Paris: Charlot, 1950), 145–146. "Elle avoit une soixantaine d'années et pourtant son mari n'avait pas songé à lui donner une co-épouse; il lui était resté obstinément fidèle."

100. He provides these details about Sawda's husband later. Haykal, *Hayāt Muḥammad*, 315; Haykal, *Life of Muḥammad*, 290.

101. Glubb, *Life and Times of Muhammad*, also refers a few times to Aisha's virginity (e.g., 237).

102. Haykal, *Hayāt Muḥammad*, 315. Al Faruqi's version reads: "If it is true that Muḥammad did in fact love 'Ā'ishah, it must have been a love which arose after marriage, surely neither before nor at the time of marriage. He had asked her hand from her father while she was only nine years old, and did not marry her until two years later. It is contrary to logic to claim that he could have fallen in love with her while she was at this tender age." Haykal, *Life of Muḥammad*, 291.

103. Muir, *Life of Mahomet*, 2nd ed, 117.

104. Haykal, *Hayāt Muḥammad*, 315; see Haykal, *Life of Muḥammad*, 290.

105. *Zawwaja* (marry or espouse); *khaṭaba* (propose); *'aqada* (contract); *banā* (consummate).

106. John Esposito, "Ismail al-Faruqi: Muslim Scholar-Activist," in *The Muslims of America*, ed. Yvonne Haddad (New York: Oxford University Press, 1991), 65–79; also Ali Zaidi, *Islam, Modernity, and the Human Sciences* (New York: Palgrave Macmillan 2011), 67–68; Imtiyaz Yusuf, ed., *Islam and Knowledge: Al Faruqi's Concept of Religion in Islamic Thought: Essays in Honor of Isma'il Al Faruqi* (London: I. B. Tauris, 2012).

107. *Lam yabni bihā ilā baʿd sanatayn ḥīn balaghat al-tāsiʿa.*

108. Haykal, *Life of Muḥammad*, 139.

109. *Min al-ṭufūla ilā al-ṣiban.*

110. Haykal, *Life of Muḥammad*, 183–184.

111. No translation is purely conservative or additive; rather, "the two models provide the notional poles of a scale of conformity." Sukanta Chaudhuri, *The Metaphysics of Text* (Cambridge: Cambridge University Press, 2010), 180–181.

112. Aysha Hidayatullah, "Māriyya the Copt: Gender, Sex and Heritage in the Legacy of Muhammad's *Umm Walad*," *Islam and Christian–Muslim Relations* 21, no. 3 (July 2010): 229. For a brief mention in the context of recounting Muhammad's children, see Ibn Hishām, *Al-Sīra al-nabawīya*, 158.

113. Washington Irving [Wāshinjtūn Irfinj], *Ḥayāt Muḥammad*. Translated by ʿAlī Ḥusnī al-Kharbūṭlī, 2nd ed. (Egypt: Dār al-Maʿārif, 1966 [1960]), 196. For the particular issues where Haykal mentions Irving, see Wessels, *Modern Arabic Biography*, 235–237.

114. *Al-ḥubb al-shadīd.* Irving, *Ḥayāt Muḥammad*, 132.

115. *Khiṭba* (betrothal), related to the word *khaṭaba* (to propose); *zawāj* (marriage).

116. Kelen, *Muhammad*, 70.

117. Watt, *Muhammad*, 102.

118. Ruqayya Y. Khan, "Of Cyber Muslimahs: Wives of the Prophet and Muslim Women in the Digital Age" in *Muhammad in the Digital Age*, ed. Ruqayya Khan.

119. Colin Turner, *Islam: The Basics* (New York: Routledge, 2006), 34. Given the connection between maturation and nourishment, his argument about puberty seems unlikely.

120. Ibid., 34–35.

121. Hazelton, *First Muslim*, 214–215. References to Aisha as a teenager appear at 134, 216, 217, and 219.

122. Armstrong, *Muhammad: A Biography of the Prophet*, 145.

123. Ibid., 157.

124. Armstrong, *Muhammad: A Prophet for Our Time*, 92–93.

125. Ibid., 126–127.

126. Al-Ṭabarī, *History of al-Ṭabarī*, vol. 7, 7; vol. 9, 130, 131; vol. 39, 171 (implicitly).

127. "Fa-ammā 'Ā'isha fa-kānat yawm tazawwajahā ṣaghīra lā tusliḥ li'l-jimā'a." Abū Ja'far Muḥammad ibn Jarīr al-Ṭabarī, *Tārīkh al-Ṭabarī: tārīkh al-rusul wa-al-mulūk*, ed. Muḥmmad Abū al-Faḍl Ibrāhīm, 11 vols. (Egypt: Dār al-Ma'ārif, 1960–[1977]), vol. 3, 161. The English translation, which Armstrong presumably relied upon, reads: "As for 'Ā'ishah, when he married her she was very young and not yet ready for consummation." The translator's note specifies that she was six at marriage and nine at consummation. Al-Ṭabarī, *History of al-Ṭabarī*, vol. 9, 128. See also Brown, *Muhammad*, 78.

128. Al-Ṭabarī, *History of al-Ṭabarī*, vol. 7, 7; vol. 9, 131; vol. 39, 171.

129. Robert Spencer, *The Truth about Muhammad: Founder of the World's Most Intolerant Religion* (Washington, DC: Regnery, 2007), 170–172. Abdulkader Tayob, "Epilogue: Muhammad in the Future," 305, points out that "the book promises to be saying something about the Prophet, but it intends to say something more specifically about Muslims."

130. Kecia Ali, *Sexual Ethics and Islam: Feminist Reflections on Qur'an, Hadith, and Jurisprudence* (Oxford: Oneworld, 2006), 135–150; Lyons, *Islam through Western Eyes*, 11–12.

131. Matar, *Turks, Moors, and Englishmen*, 126.

132. Yahiya Emerick, *Complete Idiot's Guide to Understanding Islam*, 3rd ed. (New York: Alpha, 2011), 311; see also Emerick, *Muhammad*.

133. Though he acknowledges that violence and abuses were found throughout the ancient world, "Islam has been branded with barbarity in a unique way, in part because, in its zeal to maintain the Prophet's world as well as his word, the customs of antiquity have been preserved into modern times" (1:xi). However, he concludes on a different note: "Muhammad can be judged by the worst of his followers or the best" (Chopra, *Muhammad*, 267).

134. Ibid., 264.

135. Adil Salahi, *Muhammad, Man and Prophet: A Complete Study of the Life of the Prophet of Islam*. (Leicestershire, UK: The Islamic Foundation, 2012), iv–v. The preface in this edition was originally included in the 2008 edition.

136. See, for example, Nasr, *Muhammad*, 24–25.

137. Chopra, *Muhammad*, 264.

138. Franklin Graham, son of evangelical preacher Billy Graham. Another example is Floridian Pastor Terry D. Jones, known for his

threat, eventually carried out, to burn copies of the Qur'an. Jones published a book titled *Islam Is of the Devil* (Lake Mary, FL: Creation House, 2010), which was "largely ignored." Peter Morey and Amina Yaqin, *Framing Muslims* (Cambridge, MA: Harvard University Press, 2010), 211.

139. Schick, *The Erotic Margin*, has pointed out very clearly the merger of decidedly incompatible notions in earlier accounts of "oriental sexuality." See also Tolan, "Afterword."

140. Naguib Mahfouz, *Children of the Alley: A Novel* (New York: Anchor, 1996), 333.

141. Ibid.

142. Ibid., 334.

143. Ibid., 335.

144. Wessels, *Modern Arabic Biography*, 146; Roded, "Alternate Images of the Prophet Muhammad's Virility," in *Islamic Masculinities*, ed. Lahoucine Ouzgange (London: Zed Books, 2006); Kecia Ali, "'A Beautiful Example': The Prophet Muḥammad as a Model for Muslim Husbands," *Journal of Islamic Studies* 43, no. 2 (Summer 2004): 273–291; Powers, *Muḥammad Is Not the Father*, 49; Dashti, *Twenty-Three Years*, 66. On Muhammad as a model of masculinity and how this intersects with his marital and sexual life, see also Amanullah De Sondy, *The Crisis of Islamic Masculinities* (London: Bloomsbury, 2014), 110–115.

145. Ruth Roded, "Muslim Women Reclaim the Life-Story of the Prophet: 'A'isha 'Abd al-Raḥmān, Assia Djebar, and Nadia Yassine," *Muslim World* 103, no. 3 (July 2013): 334–346, at p. 343.

146. Sherry Jones, *The Jewel of Medina* (New York: Beaufort Books, 2008), vii. On this book, see Aysha Hidayatullah, "Behind Every Good (or Bad) Muslim Man: Representation of Muhammad's Wives after 9/11," in *Muhammad in the Digital Age*, ed. Ruqayya Khan.

147. Kamran Pasha, *Mother of the Believers: A Novel of the Birth of Islam* (New York: Washington Square, 2009). Pasha interweaves a good deal of material on sex and sexual jealousy, although he fades to black in his accounts of Aisha and Muhammad's intimate encounters. However, connecting sexual immorality with pagan unbelief, he recounts Hind's arrangement of a threesome among herself, her husband Abu Sufyan, and a fourteen-year-old dancer (89–91).

148. Roded, "Muslim Women Reclaim," 340.

149. Ibid., 342. Roded sees her acknowledgment of the help of a male poet with the Arabic texts as aimed "to cement her authority." Elsayed reads the same acknowledgment ("'Silence' and Historical Tradition,"

95) as evidence of Djebar's incapacity to properly read and interpret the texts.

150. Roded, "Muslim Women Reclaim," 334–335, 337.

151. Ibid., 340.

152. Kahn, *Untold*, 9.

153. Wessels, *Modern Arabic Biography*, 31.

154. Sara Omar, "Al-Qubaysiyyāt: Negotiating Female Religious Authority in Damascus," *Muslim World* 103, no. 3 (July 2013): 355, n. 21. I was unable to consult these works.

155. Demi, *Muhammad* (New York: Margaret K. McElderberry, 2003); Marston, *Muhammad of Mecca;* Sarah Conover, *Muhammad: The Story of a Prophet and Reformer* (Boston: Skinner House, 2013). Betty Kelen, whose 1975 biography, *Muhammad,* is discussed earlier, also published biographies of Buddha and Confucius.

156. Conover, *Muhammad,* 100.

6. An Enlightened Man

1. It may also convey another moral: do not turn down your husband when he wants sex, even if he is sweaty and dirty from work; he will visit another wife, and she will get the blessing.

2. Guillaume, *Life of Muhammad,* 69.

3. On the Muhammadan light, see Schimmel, *And Muhammad Is His Messenger,* 123–143; Marion Holmes Katz, *The Birth of the Prophet Muḥammad* (New York: Routledge, 2007), 12–15; Ernst, "Muḥammad as the Pole of Existence," 124–128. Uri Rubin, "Pre-Existence and Light: Aspects of the Concept of *Nūr Muḥammad,*" *Israel Oriental Studies* 5 (1975): 62–119, and republished in Rubin, *Muḥammad the Prophet and Arabia* (Farnham, UK: Ashgate / Variorum, 2011) remains useful.

4. Muir, *Mohammedan Controversy,* viii.

5. Abdulkader Tayob, "Epilogue: Muḥammad in the Future," in *Cambridge Companion,* ed. Brockopp, 307; see also Safi, *Memories of Muhammad,* 264–265.

6. Armstrong, *Muhammad: A Biography of the Prophet,* 14.

7. Ibid., 13.

8. Armstrong, *Muhammad: A Prophet for Our Time,* 7.

9. Giving a slightly different list, Ziauddin Sardar begins his biography of Muhammad by declaring: "Prophets are persons of renown. The greatest of them—Abraham, Moses, Buddha, Jesus, Muhammad—have indisputably changed the course of human history." *Muhammad,* 2.

10. Peter Manseau, *Rag and Bone: A Journey among the World's Holy Dead* (New York: Henry Holt, 2009).

11. McAuliffe, "Al-Ṭabarī's Prelude to the Prophet," 113.

12. Brockopp, introduction to *Cambridge Companion*, 1.

13. Safi, *Memories of Muhammad*, 115, 265. See also Waldman, *Prophecy and Power*, 77; on p. 83 she compares Moses, Jesus, Buddha, and Muhammad.

14. Chopra, *Muhammad*, xii. See also 255.

15. Whalen Lai, "The Search for the Historical Śakyamuni in Light of the Historical Jesus," *Buddhist-Christian Studies*, vol. 2 (1982), 79–91; Donald Lopez, *From Stone to Flesh: A Short History of the Buddha* (Chicago: University of Chicago Press, 2013). On the scholarly study of the Buddha, see Donald Lopez, *The Scientific Buddha: His Short and Happy Life* (New Haven, CT: Yale University Press, 2012).

16. Edward Shaner, "Biographies of the Buddha," *Philosophy East and West* 37, no. 3 (July 1987): 306–322, at p. 312. On the description of the "human Buddha" as depicted in early texts, see Lopez, *From Stone to Flesh*, 206.

17. Nadvi, *Muhammad*, 15; also chapter 3, "Historicity," 33–59.

18. John Fenton, "Biographical Myths; Illustrated from the Lives of Buddha and Muhammad," *Folk-Lore Record* 3, no. 1 (1880): 26–39, at p. 26.

19. Ibn Ishaq, *Life of Muhammad*, 5.

20. Masuzawa, *Invention of World Religions*, 132.

21. For instance, Edward Salisbury formulated an influential conception of the Buddha (Lopez, *Scientific Buddha*, 39–40) and wrote on technical aspects of Muslim *hadith* criticism.

22. Fenton, "Biographical Myths," 26.

23. John S. Hawley, "Introduction: Saints and Virtues," in *Saints and Virtues*, ed. Hawley (Berkeley: University of California Press, 1987), xi.

24. Marcus Dods, *Mohammed, Buddha, and Christ: Four Lectures on Natural and Revealed Religion* (London: Hodder and Stoughton, 1877), 189.

25. Ibn Ishaq, *Life of Muhammad*.

26. Bombay Tract and Book Society, *Life of Mahomet*, 173–174.

27. Birchwood, "Confounding Babel," 151.

28. Bombay Tract and Book Society, *Life of Mahomet*, 174.

29. Ibid. Emphasis in original.

30. Quoted in Guenther, "Image of the Prophet," 54.

31. For a discussion of Muḥammad 'Abduh on this point, see Tim Winter, "Jesus and Muḥammad: New Convergences," *Muslim World* 99 (January 2009): 21–38, at p. 24.

32. The Ahmadiyya hold that Jesus survived his crucifixion, traveled to Kashmir, married, and led a mortal life. This account is not widely accepted outside Ahmadi circles.

33. 'Abd al-Raḥmān, *Wives of the Prophet*, 4.

34. Ibid., 5.

35. Alan Pitt, "The Cultural Impact of Science in France: Ernest Renan and the Vie de Jésus," *Historical Journal* 43, no. 1 (March 2000): 79–101, at p. 79. On this life, see also Terence R. Wright, "The Letter and the Spirit: Deconstructing Renan's "Life of Jesus" and the Assumptions of Modernity," *Religion & Literature* 26, no. 2 (Summer 1994): 55–71.

36. Armstrong, *Muhammad: A Prophet for Our Time*, 1. Spencer, *Truth about Muhammad*, 6, calls this biography "hagiographical," not entirely without justification.

37. Quoted in Buaben, *Image of the Prophet Muḥammad*, 214.

38. C. S. Lewis, *Mere Christianity* (San Francisco: Harper San Francisco, 2001 [1952]), 52. For two different recent approaches to the range of ways Jesus's claims could be interpreted, see Wills, *What Jesus Meant*, and Daniel Boyarin, *The Jewish Gospels: The Story of the Jewish Christ* (New York: New Press, 2013).

39. For a discussion of an earlier, roughly parallel Muslim argument "that Mohammed must have been either a true prophet or a madman," see Muir, *Mohammedan Controversy*, 59.

40. Wills, *What Jesus Meant*, xxiv.

41. Stecker, *Man Mohammed*, 44.

42. "In truth, Muhammad was and is for persons in the Arabian world, and for many others, *the* religious reformer, lawgiver, and leader; the prophet *per se*. Basically Muhammad . . . is more to those who follow him than a prophet is to us." Quoted in Tolan, "European Accounts," 248. On this point, see also Bennett, *In Search of Muhammad*, who suggests that Muhammad is as much to his followers as Jesus is to his.

43. Kidd, *American Christians and Islam*, 152. On two nineteenth-century missionaries who wrestled with the issue of Muhammad's relationship to biblical prophecy, see Guenther, "Image of the Prophet."

44. Kidd, *American Christians and Islam*, 152.

45. Gunny, *The Prophet Muhammad in French and English Literature*, 252–253.

46. For two suggestive discussions, see Jerold C. Frakes, *Vernacular and Latin Literary Discourses of the Muslim Other in Medieval Germany* (New York: Palgrave, 2011), xi–xiv and Philip Jenkins, *God's Continent:*

Christianity, Islam, and Europe's Religious Crisis (Oxford: Oxford University Press, 2007), 267–269.

47. Bennett, *In Search of Muhammad*, 222.

48. Andrae, *Mohammed*. On Andrae, see Gunny, *The Prophet Muhammad in French and English Literature*, 215–218.

49. Andrae *Mohammed*, 10.

50. Ibid.

51. Ibid., 11.

52. Ibid., 114.

53. Ibid., 47.

54. Ibid., 52.

55. Johnstone, *Muhammad and His Power*, 150.

56. Andrae, *Mohammed*, 52.

57. Ibid., 191.

58. I owe the division of memoirs into "victim" and "escapee" to Mohja Kahf.

59. Ramadan, *In the Footsteps*.

60. For instance, *sharīʿa, ṭarīqa, madhhab, ṣirāṭ al-mustaqīm*.

61. Tariq Ramadan, *Muhammad: Vie du prophète: Les enseignements spirituels et contemporains* (Paris: Presses du Châtelet. 2006).

62. Ramadan, *In the Footsteps*, 129.

63. On Muhammad's "principles" and conduct concerning warfare, see also Aḥmad, *Life of Muhammad*, 182–186, which makes comparisons with Gandhi.

64. For instance, Nasr writes: "He was still molested and oppressed in every possible way in Makkah." Nasr, *Muhammad*, 37.

65. Ramadan, *In the Footsteps*, 130.

66. Ibid., 131.

67. Ibid., 132.

68. Sherry Jones takes creative license and attributes the tactic to Aisha. Jones, *Jewel of Medina*, 210.

69. Tariq Ramadan, *Radical Reform: Islamic Ethics and Liberation* (New York: Oxford University Press, 2008).

70. Ramadan, *In the Footsteps*, 132.

71. Emerick, *Muhammad*, 210.

72. Ramadan, *In the Footsteps*, 133.

73. I borrow the phrase from Mernissi, *Islam and Democracy*.

74. See, for example, Watt, *Muhammad*, 171–175. Brown writes that Muhammad "faced the question of the Banu Qurayza Jews," who "had betrayed their non-aggression pact with the Muslims." "Muhammad

offered them" the opportunity to convert, but nearly all declined and, eventually, "surrendered." At this point, "Muhammad allowed the chief of the Aws tribe, who had been closely allied with the Banu Qurayza before, to determine their punishment. He decided that the men should be executed and the women and children sold into slavery." *Muhammad*, 43.

75. Pickthall, *Life of the Prophet Muhammad*, 32.

76. Armstrong, *Muhammad: A Biography of the Prophet*, 206–209; Armstrong, *Muhammad: A Prophet for Our Time*, 148–152). I thank Galen Olson for calling the differences between these accounts to my attention.

77. Hazelton, *First Muslim*, 226–238.

78. It also takes Shi'i perspectives seriously, lingering on the martyrdom of Muhammad's grandson, acknowledging the contemporary Iranian fondness for iconic depictions of the Prophet, and suffusing the writing with mentions of Islam's "holy family"—Ali, Fatima, Hassan, and Husayn, the "people of the household," who have historically been a focus of Sunni devotion as well, but who get short shrift in most modern accounts, displaced in favor of Muhammad's wives (part of the turn from kin to spouses Amina bint Haydar al-Sadr, another Shi'i author, criticizes; see Chapter 4).

79. Chopra, *Muhammad*, xiii; see also Nasr, *Muhammad*, 40–41, on both individual and social change (e.g., on the imposition of Islamic law). Nasr here echoes, presumably unwittingly, the Lahori Ahmadi thinker Muhammad Ali, who wrote that "the political superiority of Islam should come after its spiritual supremacy." Ali, "Dottrine e attività," 108–123, at p. 119.

80. Nasr, *Muhammad*, 7.

81. Safi, *Memories of Muhammad*, 101.

82. Unlike Dashti, *Twenty-Three Years,* which ends with an appeal to consider Muhammad's achievements.

Conclusion

1. Sardar, *Muhammad,* 115; Safi, *Memories of Muhammad,* 6.

2. Pierce, "Remembering Fāṭimah," 355, writing about 'Ali Shariati's reworking of the classical narrative of Fatima's life.

3. Donner, *Muhammad and the Believers;* Waldman, *Prophecy and Power.*

4. For an early modern view of a "fundamental antagonism between Europe and Asia, provoked by the irreconcilable opposition between Christianity and Islam," see Laureys, "History and Poetry," 279–280.

5. The term "founder" in this sense was used by some of Prideaux's contemporaries. Stroumsa, *A New Science,* 131–134.

6. Lyons, *Islam through Western Eyes,* 9.

7. Ibid., 7–8.

8. Elmarsafy, *Enlightenment Qur'ān,* xii. Or, more simply, "bigotry rarely responds to empirical evidence." Frakes, *Vernacular and Latin Literary Discourses,* xiii.

9. David R. Blanks, "Western Views of Islam in the Premodern Period: A Brief History of Past Approaches," in *Western Views of Islam in Medieval and Early Modern Europe,* ed. David R. Blanks and Michael Frasetto (New York: St. Martin's, 1999), 11–53, at p. 16.

10. Kidd, *American Christians and Islam;* see, for example, the discussion of George Otis, 128–129. On Vines, see Ali, *Sexual Ethics and Islam,* ch. 8; Kidd, *American Christians and Islam,* 147–148.

11. Quoted in Kidd, *American Christians and Islam,* 11.

12. Kidd, *American Christians and Islam,* 26; a later writer, George Seibel, "saw Smith as even worse than Muhammad, with the former being a 'cunning impostor' and the latter 'a sincere fanatic.'"

13. Falwell made this assertion on *60 Minutes.* See Kidd, *American Christians and Islam,* 145.

14. One place where symbolic "language" remains crucial is cartoons/caricatures. On the sexual and animal nature in the cartoons added to the dossier with the Danish Jyllands-Posten cartoons, see Jytte Klausen, *The Cartoons That Shook the World* (New Haven, CT: Yale University Press, 2009), 91, 101; Lawrence Rosen, *Varieties of Muslim Experience: Encounters with Arab Political and Cultural Life* (Chicago: University of Chicago Press, 2008), 107–108.

15. For one counterexample, see Nasr, *Muhammad,* 30–31, 35–36.

16. Wright, "Critical Approaches," 245.

17. So do online authors today, engaged in a similar if more rapid direct exchange, with embedded links shuttling readers back and forth, and page titles and keywords structured to give their pages an advantage when search engines look for "Muhammad" or "Muhammad's marriages" or "Banu Qurayza." Vigorous and vicious online polemics truly have—at least in that brief moment before readers click away—a genuinely global, multireligious, mixed audience, the sort of thing that earlier texts proclaimed but seldom accomplished.

18. For instance, what of the Prophet's stepchildren? According to al-Ṭabari's history, one of Khadīja's sons from a previous marriage "lived

to see [the advent of] Islam and was converted" (vol. 39, 80; bracketed text in original). See also Kister, "Sons of Khadīja," 61.

19. And many Muslim-authored biographies as well, for example, Haykal, *Life of Muḥammad*, 502–503; Aḥmad, *Life of Muḥammad*, 291–293. An exception, which notes disputes, is Hazelton, *First Muslim*, 292.

20. For an early view that Zayd was the first convert, see Powers, *Zayd*, 30. Aḥmad (*Life of Muhammad*, 383) lists all four: Khadija is the first woman, Abu Bakr the first free man, Ali "first among children" and Zayd "first among slaves." Similarly, Waheed-Ud-Din lists Khadija as his "first follower," after which she was joined by his "friend Abu Bakr, his cousin Ali, and his freed man, Zayd" (*Benefactor*, 10–11).

21. Marion Holmes Katz, "The Prophet Muḥammad in Ritual," in *Cambridge Companion*, ed. Brockopp, 143.

22. Kister, "Sons of Khadīja."

23. Safi, *Memories of Muhammad*, 264, makes a similar point using different evidence, remarking on modernist Muslims' "rationality" rather than their textual practices: they have "flattened the cosmos, both spiritually and metaphysically."

24. Haj, *Reconfiguring Islamic Tradition;* Noorani, *Culture and Hegemony,* 16–20, argues against a clear epistemic rupture between premodern and modern, or between East and West.

25. Taiyaba Nasrin, *The Prophet Muhammad as a Man: Islamic Modernism and Sirah Literature in Egypt* (Aligarh, India: Aligarh Muslim University Press, 2008 [1992]).

26. Safi, *Memories of Muhammad*, 41.

27. Mittermaier, *Dreams That Matter,* 174.

28. Schimmel, *And Muhammad Is His Messenger,* xi–xii. On Romanization and the use of English by non-Arabic-reading Muslims, see p. 98.

29. Mirza Masroor Ahmad, *True Love for the Holy Prophet* (Silver Spring, MD: Ahmadiyya Muslim Community, 2012), 25.

30. Muhammad Syafii Antonio, *Ensiklopedia Leadership & Manajemen Muhammad SAW, "The Super Leader Super Manager"* (Jakarta: Tazkia Publishing, 2010). For additional examples of hybrid titles, see Gade, "Religious Biography," 257, 263.

31. *Ṣalla Allāhu ʿalayhi wa sallam:* "May God bless him and grant him peace," often rendered "peace be upon him" or abbreviated PBUH.

32. In the original Arabic title, the word "Superman" appears transliterated into Arabic (*subirman*). See Wessels, *Modern Arabic Biography*, 2. Riyāshī later published a two-volume study of *The Psychology* [or *Inner Life* or *Psyche*] *of the Arab Messenger*. Labīb Riyāshī, *Nafsīyat al-Rasūl al-ʿArabī* (Beirut: Maṭbaʿat al-Kashshāf, 1937).

Bibliography

In my treatment of Muhammad's *Lives* I have drawn not only on scores of biographies but also on a substantial body of secondary literature about these biographies. Readers who want to explore further should begin with *The Cambridge Companion to Muhammad,* edited by Jonathan Brockopp. Tarif Khalidi's *Images of Muhammad* is a narrative history of the Muslim biographical treatment of the Prophet. Annemarie Schimmel's *And Muhammad Is His Messenger* explores devotion to the Prophet in Muslim tradition. Marion Katz's *The Birth of the Prophet Muhammad* addresses textual and ritual celebrations of the Prophet's birthday, past and present. John Tolan's writings, especially *Saracens* and the first chapters of *Sons of Ishmael,* are essential for medieval European views of Muhammad; Philip Almond's slim but richly documented *Heretic and Hero: Muhammad and the Victorians* is a treasure.

In alphabetizing entries, I ignore the prefix al- and the letter 'ayn.

Abbasi, S. M. Madani. *Family of the Holy Prophet (S.A.W.).* New Delhi: Adam, 2004.

Abd-Allah, Umar F. *A Muslim in Victorian America: The Life of Alexander Russell Webb.* New York: Oxford University Press, 2006.

'Abd al-Raḥmān, 'Ā'isha [Bint al-Shāṭī']. *The Wives of the Prophet.* Translated by Matti Moosa and D. Nicholas Ranson. Lahore: Muhammad Ashraf, 1971.

Abu Iqbal. "Muhammad in Rewrite." *Message International,* August–September 2002, 12–13.

Abu Lughod, Lila. *Do Muslim Women Need Saving?* Cambridge, MA: Harvard University Press, 2013.

Ahmad, Atif Ahmad. *Islam, Modernity, Violence, and Everyday Life.* New York: Palgrave Macmillan, 2009.

Ahmad, Mirzā Bashīruddīn Maḥmūd. *Life of Muhammad.* Tilford, UK: Islam International Publications, 2012.

Ahmad, Mirza Masroor. *True Love for the Holy Prophet.* Silver Spring, MD: Ahmadiyya Muslim Community, 2012.

Ahmad Khan, Syed. *A Series of Essays on the Life of Muhammad and Subjects Subsidiary Thereto.* Lahore: Premier Book House, 1968. First published 1870 by Trübner.

Ahmed, Shahab. "Ibn Taymiyya and the Satanic Verses." *Studia Islamica* 87 (1998): 67–124.

Aleem, Shamim. *Prophet Muhammad (S) and His Family: A Sociological Perspective.* Bloomington, IN: AuthorHouse, 2007.

Ali, Kecia. "'A Beautiful Example': The Prophet Muḥammad as a Model for Muslim Husbands." *Journal of Islamic Studies* 43, no. 2 (Summer 2004): 273–291.

———. "Khadija bint Khuwaylid." In *The Oxford Encyclopedia of Women in World History,* vol. 3, edited by Bonnie G. Smith. Oxford: Oxford University Press, 2007.

———. *Sexual Ethics and Islam: Feminist Reflections on Qur'an, Hadith, and Jurisprudence.* Oxford: Oneworld, 2006.

Ali, Muhammad. "Dottrine e attività dei musulmani Aḥmadiyya di Lahore." *Oriente Moderno* 6, no. 2 (February 1926): 108–23.

———. *Muhammad the Prophet.* Lahore: Ahmadiyya Anjuman Ishaat Islam, 1993.

Ali, Muhammad Mohar. *Sîrat al-Nabî and the Orientalists, with Special Reference to the Writings of William Muir, D. S. Margoliouth and W. Montgomery Watt.* Vols. 1A and 1B. Medina: Kingdom of Saudi Arabia, King Fahd Complex for the Printing of the Holy Qur'an, 1997.

Ali, Syed Ameer. *A Critical Examination of the Life and Teachings of Mohammed.* London: Williams and Norgate, 1873.

———. *The Life and Teachings of Mohammed, or the Spirit of Islam.* London: W. H. Allen, 1891.

Almond, Philip. *Heretic and Hero: Muhammad and the Victorians.* Wiesbaden: Otto Harrassowitz, 1989.

Amīn, Aḥmad. *Aḥmad Amīn: My Life.* Translated by Issa J. Boullata. Leiden: Brill, 1978.

Amini, M. Sharif Ahmad. *Muhammad: The Most Successful Prophet.* Calcutta: Asian Printers, 1978.

Andrae, Tor. *Mohammed: The Man and His Faith.* Translated by Theophil Menzel. Rev. ed. New York: Harper and Row, 1960. (Original German publication 1932; first English ed. 1936, rev. ed. 1955.)

Andrea, Bernadette, and Linda McJannet, eds. *Early Modern England and Islamic Worlds.* New York: Palgrave, 2011.

Anis-ur-Rahman, Muhammad. *The Historical Role of the Venerable Woman.* 3rd ed., enlarged. Karachi: Faran Publications, 2007.

Antonio, Muhammad Syafii. *Ensiklopedia Leadership and Manajemen Muhammad SAW, "The Super Leader Super Manager."* Jakarta: Tazkia Publishing, 2010.

Al-ʿAqqād, ʿAbbās Maḥmūd. *ʿAbqariyyat Muḥammad* [The genius of Muhammad]. Cairo: Maṭbaʿat al-Istiqāma, 1942.

Argyriou, Astérious. "Éléments biographiques concernant le prophète Muhammad dans la littérature grecque des trois premiers siècles de l'Hégire." In *La vie du prophète Mahomet,* edited by Toufic Fahd, 159–182. Paris: Presses universitaires de France, 1983.

Armstrong, Karen. *Muhammad: A Biography of the Prophet.* New York: Harper, 1992.

———. *Muhammad: A Prophet for Our Time.* New York: Harper One, 2007.

Awad, George. "The Prophet Muhammad." In *The Crescent and the Couch: Cross-Currents between Islam and Psychoanalysis,* edited by Salman Akhtar. Lanham, MD: Jason Aronson, 2008.

Awad, Louis. *The Literature of Ideas in Egypt, Pt. 1.* Atlanta: Scholars Press, 1986.

Barham, C. N. "Child Marriage in India." *Westminster Review* 135, no. 2 (January–June 1891): 113–124.

Baron, Beth. "The Making and Breaking of Marital Bonds in Modern Egypt." In *Women in Middle Eastern History: Shifting Boundaries in Sex and Gender,* edited by Nikki R. Keddie and Beth Baron. New Haven, CT: Yale University Press, 1992.

———. *The Women's Awakening in Egypt: Culture, Society, and the Press.* New Haven, CT: Yale University Press, 1997.

Bashir, Shahzad. "Narrating Sight: Dreaming as Visual Training in Persianate Sufi Hagiography." In *Dreams and Visions in Islamic Societies,* edited by Özgen Felek and Alexander Knysh, 233–247. Albany: State University of New York Press, 2012.

Bayard, Pierre. *How to Talk about Books You Haven't Read.* Translated by Jeffrey Mehlman. New York: Bloomsbury, 2007.

Bellos, David. *Is That a Fish in Your Ear? Translation and the Meaning of Everything.* New York: Faber and Faber, 2011.

Bennett, Clinton. *In Search of Muhammad.* London: Cassell, 1998.

Berg, Herbert. "Competing Paradigms in the Study of Islamic Origins: Qurʾān 15:89–91 and the Value of Isnāds." In *Method and Theory in the Study of Islamic Origins,* edited by Herbert Berg, 259–290. Leiden: Brill, 2003.

Birchwood, Matthew. "Confounding Babel: The Language of Religion in the English Revolution." In *The Religions of the Book: Christian Perceptions, 1400–1600,* edited by Matthew Dimmock and Andrew Hadfield, 140–158. New York: Palgrave, 2008.

Black, Jeremy. *Culture in Eighteenth-Century England: A Subject for Taste.* Hambledon, UK: Continuum, 2005.

Blanks, David R. "Western Views of Islam in the Premodern Period: A Brief History of Past Approaches." In *Western Views of Islam in Medieval and Early Modern Europe,* edited by David R. Blanks and Michael Frasetto, 11–53. New York: St. Martin's, 1999.

Blanks, David R., and Michael Frasetto. "Introduction." In *Western Views of Islam in Medieval and Early Modern Europe,* edited by Blanks and Frasetto.

Blanning, Timothy. *The Romantic Revolution: A History.* New York: Modern Library, 2012.

Bombay Tract and Book Society. *Life of Mahomet.* 3rd. ed. Bombay: Bombay Tract and Book Society, 1856.

Boullata, Issa J. Introduction to *Aḥmad Amīn: My Life,* by Aḥmad Amīn. Translated by Issa J. Boullata. Leiden: Brill, 1978.

Bowersock, G. W. *The Throne of Adulis: Red Sea Wars on the Eve of Islam.* New York: Oxford University Press, 2013.

Boyarin, Daniel. *The Jewish Gospels: The Story of the Jewish Christ.* New York: New Press, 2013.

Bravmann, M. M. *The Spiritual Background of Early Islam: Studies in Ancient Arab Concepts.* Leiden: Brill, 2009 [1972].

Brockopp, Jonathan E., ed. *The Cambridge Companion to Muḥammad.* Cambridge: Cambridge University Press, 2010.

Brown, Jonathan A. C. *Misquoting Muhammad: The Challenges and Choices of Interpreting the Prophet's Legacy.* Oxford: Oneworld, forthcoming.

———. *Muhammad: A Very Short Introduction.* New York: Oxford University Press, 2010.

Browne, G[eorge] Lathom. *The Æra of Mahomet: A.D. 527 to 629.* London: Society for Promoting Christian Knowledge, 1856.

Buaben, Jabal Muhammad. *Image of the Prophet Muḥammad in the West: A Study of Muir, Margoliouth, and Watt.* Leicester, UK: Islamic Foundation, 1996.

Buck-Morss, Susan. *Thinking Past Terror: Islamism and Critical Theory on the Left.* London: Verso, 2006.

Bulandshehri, Muhammad Ashiq Elahi. *The Wives of the Prophet Muhammad (sallalahu alayhe wasallam): A Complete Book on the Biographies of the Wives of Holy Prophet Muhammad (sallallahu alayhe wasallam).* Translated by Mohammad Akram. Lahore: Idara-e-Islamiat, 1994.

Burman, Thomas E. *Reading the Qur'an in Latin Christendom, 1140–1560.* Philadelphia: University of Pennsylvania Press, 2007.

Burrus, Virginia. *The Sex Lives of Saints: An Erotics of Ancient Hagiography.* Philadelphia: University of Pennsylvania Press, 2004.

Bush, George. *The Life of Mohammed: Founder of the Religion of Islam, and of the Empire of the Saracens.* New York: Harper and Brothers, 1837.

Carlyle, Thomas. *The Hero as Prophet: Mahomet; Islam (Lecture II: Heroes and Hero Worship).* New York: Maynard, Merrill, and Co., 1882.

Chaudhuri, Sukanta. *The Metaphysics of Text.* Cambridge: Cambridge University Press, 2010.

Chopra, Deepak. *Buddha: A Story of Enlightenment.* New York: Harper One, 2007.

———. *Jesus: A Story of Enlightenment.* New York: Harper One, 2008.

———. *Muhammad: A Story of the Last Prophet.* New York: Harper One, 2010.

Choudhury, Golam W. *The Prophet Muhammad: His Life and Eternal Message.* 2nd ed. Kuala Lumpur: WHS Publications, 1994 [1993].

Chraibi, Driss. *L'homme du livre.* Paris: Éditions Denoël, 2011 [1995].

Colby, Frederick S. *Narrating Muḥammad's Night Journey: Tracing the Development of the Ibn 'Abbās Ascension Discourse.* Albany: State University of New York Press, 2008.

Coomar, Roy. With a prefatory note by Joel Benton. "Child Marriage in India." *North American Review* 147 (1888): 415–423.

Conley, Thomas. *Toward a Rhetoric of Insult.* Chicago: University of Chicago Press, 2010.

Conover, Sarah. *Muhammad: The Story of a Prophet and Reformer.* Boston: Skinner House, 2013.

Conrad, Lawrence. "Abraha and Muḥammad: Some Observations Apropos of Chronology and Literary 'Topoi' in the Early Arabic Historical Tradition." *Bulletin of the School of Oriental and African Studies* 50, no. 2 (1987): 225–240.

Cook, Michael. *Muhammad.* New York: Oxford University Press, 1996 [1983].

Cooke, Neil. "James Burton and Slave Girls." In *Unfolding the Orient: Travellers in Egypt and the Near East,* edited by Paul and Janet Starkey, 209–217. Reading, UK: Garnet, 2001.

Cooperson, Michael. "Images without Illustrations: The Visual Imagination in Classical Arabic Biography." In *Islamic Art and Literature*, edited by Oleg Grabar and Cynthia Robinson. Princeton, NJ: Markus Wiener, 2001.

Crone, Patricia, and Michael Cook. *Hagarism: The Making of the Islamic World*. Cambridge: Cambridge University Press, 1977.

Cuffel, Alexandra. *Gendering Disgust in Medieval Religious Polemic*. Notre Dame, IN: University of Notre Dame Press, 2007.

Curran, Stuart, ed. *Cambridge Companion to British Romanticism*. 2nd ed. Cambridge: Cambridge University Press, 2010.

Curtis, Edward E., IV. *Black Muslim Religion in the Nation of Islam, 1960–1975*. Chapel Hill: University of North Carolina Press, 2006.

Dashti, Ali. *Twenty-Three Years: A Study of the Prophetic Career of Mohammad*. Translated by F. R. C. Bagley. Santa Ana, CA: Mazda, 1994.

Davenport, John. *An Apology for Mohammed and the Koran*. London: J. Davy and Sons, 1869.

Day, Adrian. *Romanticism*. London: Routledge, 1996.

Demi. *Muhammad*. New York: Margaret K. McElderberry, 2003.

Department of Commerce and Labor, Bureau of the Census. *Special Reports: Marriage and Divorce, 1867–1906*. Pt. 1, *Summary, Laws, Foreign Statistics*. Washington, DC: Government Printing Office, 1909.

Dermenghem, Émile. *The Life of Mahomet*. Translated by Arabella Yorke. New York: Routledge, 1930.

———. *La vie de Mahomet*. Paris: Charlot, 1950.

De Sondy, Amanallah. *The Crisis of Islamic Masculinities*. London: Bloomsbury, 2014.

Di Cesare, Michelina. "Images of Muhammad in Western Medieval Book Culture." In *Constructing the Image of Muhammad in Europe*, edited by Avinoam Shalem, 9–32. Berlin: De Gruyter, 2013.

Dimmock, Matthew. "'A Human Head to the Neck of a Horse': Hybridity, Monstrosity and Early Christian Conceptions of Muhammad and Islam." In *The Religions of the Book: Christian Perceptions, 1400–1600*, edited by Matthew Dimmock and Andrew Hadfield, 66–88. New York: Palgrave, 2008.

———. *Mythologies of the Prophet Muhammad in Early Modern England*. Cambridge: Cambridge University Press, 2013.

Dods, Marcus. *Mohammed, Buddha, and Christ: Four Lectures on Natural and Revealed Religion*. London: Hodder and Stoughton, 1877.

Dold, Bernard E. *Carlyle, Goethe, and Muhammad*. Messina, Italy: Edizioni Dott. Antonino Sfameni, 1984.

Donner, Fred. *Muhammad and the Believers: At the Origins of Islam.* Cambridge, MA: Belknap, 2012.

———. "Muhammad and the Debates on Islam's Origins in the Digital Age." In *Muhammad in the Digital Age*, edited by Ruqayya Y. Khan. Austin: University of Texas Press, forthcoming.

———. *Review of Hagarism. In Middle East Studies Association Bulletin* 40, no. 2 (December 2006): 197–199.

Draycott, G. M. *Mahomet: Founder of Islam.* New York: Dodd, Mead and Company, 1916.

Duri, ʿAbd al-ʿAziz. *The Rise of Historical Writings among the Arabs.* Princeton, NJ: Princeton University Press, 1983.

Elmarsafy, Ziad. *The Enlightenment Qurʾān.* Oxford: Oneworld, 2009.

Elsadda, Hoda. "Discourses of Women's Biographies and Cultural Identity: Twentieth Century Representations of the Life of ʿAʾisha bin Abi Bakr." *Feminist Studies* 27, no. 1 (2001): 37–64.

Emerick, Yahiya. *Complete Idiot's Guide to Understanding Islam.* 3rd ed. New York: Alpha, 2011.

———. "Getting to Know a Friend: My Introduction to Muhammad." *Message International,* August–September 2002, 21–25.

———. *Muhammad.* Indianapolis: Alpha, 2002.

Ernst, Carl. "Muḥammad as the Pole of Existence." In *Cambridge Companion,* edited by Brockopp, 123–138.

Esposito, John L. "Ismail al-Faruqi: Muslim Scholar-Activist." In *The Muslims of America,* edited by Yvonne Haddad, 65–79. New York: Oxford University Press, 1991.

———. *The Future of Islam* (New York: Oxford University Press, 2013).

Al Faruqi, Ismail R. *The Hijrah: The Necessity of Its* Iqāmat *or Vergegenwʾartigung.* Islamabad: National Hijra Council, 1985.

Fenton, John. "Biographical Myths; Illustrated from the Lives of Buddha and Muhammad." *The Folk-Lore Record* 3, no. 1 (1880): 26–39.

Ferrazzi, Cecilia. *Autobiography of an Aspiring Saint.* Edited and translated by Anne Jacobsen Schutte. Chicago: University of Chicago Press, 1996.

Frakes, Jerold C., ed. *Contextualizing the Muslim Other in Medieval Christian Discourse.* New York: Palgrave, 2011.

———. *Vernacular and Latin Literary Discourses of the Muslim Other in Medieval Germany.* New York: Palgrave, 2011.

Friedmann, Yohanan. *Prophecy Continuous: Aspects of Ahmadi Religious Thought and Its Medieval Background.* Berkeley: University of California Press, 1989.

Fuller, Mrs. Marcus B. [Jenny]. *The Wrongs of Indian Womanhood*. New York: Fleming H. Revell, 1900.

Gade, Anna M. "Religious Biography of the Prophet Muḥammad in Twenty-First-Century Indonesia." In *Cambridge Companion*, edited by Brockopp, 251–273.

Gershoni, Israel. "The Reader—'Another Production': The Reception of Haykal's Biography of Muhammad and the Shift of Egyptian Intellectuals to Islamic Subjects in the 1930s." *Poetics Today* 15, no. 2 (Summer 1994): 241–277.

———. "Theory of Crises." In *Middle Eastern Historiographies: Narrating the Twentieth Century*, edited by Israel Gershoni, Amy Singer, and Y. Hakan Erdem. Seattle: University of Washington Press, 2006.

Gershoni, Israel, and James P. Jankowsi. *Redefining the Egyptian Nation, 1930–1945*. Cambridge: Cambridge University Press, 2002.

Gibb, Hamilton. "Islamic Biographical Literature." In *Historians of the Middle East*, edited by Bernard Lewis and P. M. Holt, 54–58. London: Oxford University Press, 1962.

Glubb, John Bagot. *The Life and Times of Muhammad*. New York: Cooper Square Press, 2001 [1970].

Green, Samuel. *The Life of Mahomet: Founder of the Religion of Islamism and of the Empire of the Saracens*. London: William Tegg, 1877.

Grossman, Edith. *Why Translation Matters*. New Haven, CT: Yale University Press, 2010.

Gruber, Ira D. *Books and the British Army in the Age of the American Revolution*. Chapel Hill: University of North Carolina Press, 2010.

Guenther, Alan. "The Image of the Prophet Muhammad as Found in Missionary Writings of the Late Nineteenth Century." *Muslim World* 90 (Spring 2000): 43–70.

———. "Response of Sayyid Aḥmad Ḫān to Sir William Muir's Evaluation of *Ḥadīṯ* Literature." *Oriente Moderno* 82, no. 1 (2002).

Guillaume, Alfred, trans. *The Life of Muhammad: A Translation of Ibn Isḥāq's Sīrat Rasūl Allāh*. Karachi: Oxford University Press, 2003 [1955].

Gunny, Ahmad. *The Prophet Muhammad in French and English Literature, 1650 to the Present*. Leicestershire: Islamic Foundation, 2010.

Haj, Samira. *Reconfiguring Islamic Tradition: Rationality, Reform, and Modernity*. Stanford, CA: Stanford University Press, 2009.

Halevi, Leor. *Muhammad's Grave: Death Rites and the Making of Islamic Society.* New York: Columbia University Press, 2007.

Hamilton, Nigel. *Biography: A Brief History.* Cambridge, MA: Harvard University Press, 2008.

Hanaoka, Mimi. "Visions of Muhammad in Bukhara and Tabaristan: Dreams and Their Uses in Persian Local Histories," *Iranian Studies* 47, no. 2 (March 2014): 289–303.

Hatem, Mervat F. "'A'isha Abdel Rahman: An Unlikely Heroine: A Post-Colonial Reading of Her Life and Some of Her Biographies of Women in the Prophetic Household." *Journal of Middle East Women's Studies* 7, no. 2 (Spring 2011): 1–26.

Hawley, John S. "Introduction: Saints and Virtues." In *Saints and Virtues,* edited by John Stratton Hawley. Berkeley: University of California Press, 1987.

Hawting, G. R. *The Idea of Idolatry and the Emergence of Islam.* Cambridge: Cambridge University Press, 2002.

Haykal, Muhammad Husayn. *Al-Fārūq 'Umar* ['Umar the Just]. Cairo: Maktabat al-Nahdah al-Misrīyah, 1963–1964.

———. *Hayāt Muhammad.* Cairo: Matba'at Misr, 1935.

———. *Hayāt Muhammad.* 8th ed. Cairo: Maktabat al-Nahdah al-Misrīyah, 1963.

———. *The Life of Muhammad.* Translated by Ismail Al Faruqi. Kuala Lumpur: Islamic Book Trust, 2002 [1976].

———. *Al-Siddīq Abū Bakr* [Abu Bakr the Righteous]. 6th ed. Cairo: Dār al-Ma'ārif, 1971.

———. *Sirat-i Rasul.* Translated by Muhammad Vāris Kāmil. Lahore: Maktabah-yi Kāravān, 1964.

———. *Tarājim Misrīyah wa-gharbīyah* [Egyptian and Western biographies]. Cairo: Matba'at al-Siyāsah, 1929.

———. *'Uthmān ibn 'Affān: Bayna al-khilāfah wa-al-mulk* ['Uthman ibn 'Affan: Between caliphate and kingship]. Beirut: Dār al-Kutub al-'Ilmīyah, 2007.

Hazelton, Lesley. *The First Muslim: The Story of Muhammad.* New York: Riverhead Books, 2013.

Heschel, Susannah. "German Jewish Scholarship on Islam as a Tool for De-Orientalizing Judaism." *New German Critique* 39, no. 3 (Fall 2012): 91–107.

Hidayatullah, Aysha. "Behind Every Good (or Bad) Muslim Man: Representation of Muhammad's Wives after 9/11." In *Muhammad in the Digital Age,* edited by Ruqayya Y. Khan.

———. "Māriyya the Copt: Gender, Sex and Heritage in the Legacy of Muhammad's *Umm Walad*," *Islam and Christian–Muslim Relations* 21, no. 3 (July 2010): 221–243.

Higgins, Godfrey. *An Apology for the Life and Character of the Celebrated Prophet of Arabia, Called Mohamed, or the Illustrious*. London: Rowland Hunter, 1829.

Hoyland, Robert G. "The Earliest Christian Writings on Muhammad: An Appraisal." In *The Biography of Muhammad: The Issue of the Sources*. Ed. Harald Motzki. 276–297. Leiden: Brill, 2000.

———. *Seeing Islam as Others Saw It: A Survey and Evaluation of Christian, Jewish and Zoroastrian Writings on Early Islam*. Princeton, NJ: Darwin, 1998.

Hurvitz, Nimrod. "Biographies and Mild Asceticism: A Study of Islamic Moral Imagination." *Studia Islamica* 85 (1997): 41–65.

Hyatte, Reginald, trans. *The Prophet of Islam in Old French: The Romance of Muhammad (1258) and The Book of Muhammad's Ladder (1264)*. Leiden: Brill, 1997.

Ibn Hishām, *Al-sīra al-nabawīya*. Al-Mansura, Egypt: Dar al-Ghadd al-Jadeed, 2003.

Ibn Ishaak. *Het leven van Mohammed: De vroegste Arabische verhalen*. Translated by Wim Raven. Amsterdam: Bulaaq, 2000.

Ibn Ishaq. *The Life of Muhammad: Apostle of Allah*. Edited by Michael Edwardes and translated by Edward Rehatsek. London: Folio Society, 1964.

Ibn Kathīr. *The Life of the Prophet Muhammad*. Translated by Trevor Le Gassick. Reading, UK: Garnet, 1998.

Ibn Sa'd. *Women of Madina*. Translated by Aisha Bewley. London: Ta-Ha Publishers, 1995.

Idris, H. R. "Réflexions sur Ibn Ishaq." *Studia Islamica* 17 (1962): 23–36.

Idriss, Mohammad Mazher. "Honour, Violence, Women and Islam: An Introduction." In *Honour, Violence, Women and Islam*, edited by Mohammad Mazher Idriss and Tahir Abbas, 1–15. Abingdon, UK: Routledge, 2011.

Irving, Washington [Wāshinjtūn Irfinj]. *Hayāt Muhammad*. Translated by 'Alī Husnī al-Kharbūtlī, 2nd ed. Egypt: Dār al-Ma'ārif, 1966 [1960].

———. *Mahomet and His Successors*. 2 vols. New York: G. P. Putnam and Son, 1868.

Irwin, Robert. *Dangerous Knowledge: Orientalism and Its Discontents*. New York: Overlook, 2006.

Jaffer, Mehru. *The Book of Muhammad*. New Delhi: Penguin Global, 2010.

Jalbani, G. N. *Life of the Holy Prophet.* Islamabad: National Hijra Council, 1988.

Jameelah, Maryam. *Islam and Orientalism.* Rev. ed. Lahore: Mohammad Yusuf Khan and Sons, 1981.

Jenkins, Philip. *God's Continent: Christianity, Islam, and Europe's Religious Crisis.* Oxford: Oxford University Press, 2007.

Johnson, Paul. *George Washington: The Founding Father.* New York: Harper Collins, 2006.

Johnstone, P[eirce] De Lacy. *Muhammad and His Power.* New York: Charles Scribner's Sons, 1908.

Jones, Sherry. *The Jewel of Medina.* New York: Beaufort Books, 2008.

Jones, Terry D. *Islam Is of the Devil.* Lake Mary, FL: Creation House, 2010.

Jordan, Mark. *The Ethics of Sex.* Malden, MA: Blackwell, 2002.

Judd, Steven C. "Competitive Hagiography in Biographies of al-Awzā'ī and Sufyān al-Thawrī." *Journal of the American Oriental Society* 122, no. 1 (2002): 25–37.

Kahf, Mohja. *Western Representations of the Muslim Woman: From Termagant to Odalisque.* Austin: University of Texas Press, 1999.

Kahn, Tamam. *Untold: A History of the Wives of Prophet Muhammad.* Rhinebeck, NY: Monkfish, 2010.

Kamal-ud-Din, Khwaja. *The Ideal Prophet: Aspects of the Life and Qualities of the Holy Prophet Muhammad.* Woking, UK: Ahmadiyya Anjuman Isha'at Islam Lahore, 1925.

———. *The Ideal Prophet, Incorporating a Portion of "Glimpses from the Life of the Prophet."* 4th ed. Woking, UK: Woking Muslim Mission and Literary Trust, 1956 [1925].

Katz, Jonathan G. "Dreams and Their Interpretation in Sufi Thought and Practice." In *Dreams and Visions in Islamic Societies,* edited by Felek and Knysh, 181–197.

Katz, Marion Holmes. *The Birth of the Prophet Muḥammad.* New York: Routledge, 2007.

———. "The Prophet Muḥammad in Ritual." In *Cambridge Companion,* edited by Brockopp, 139–157.

Kelen, Betty. *Muhammad: The Messenger of God.* New York: Pocket Books, 1997.

Khalek, Nancy. *Damascus after the Muslim Conquest: Text and Image in Early Islam.* New York: Oxford University Press, 2011.

Khalidi, Tarif. *Arabic Historical Thought in the Classical Period.* Cambridge: Cambridge University Press, 1996.

———. *Images of Muhammad: Narratives of the Prophet in Islam through the Centuries.* New York: Doubleday, 2009.

———. "Al-Ṭabarī: An Introduction." In *Al-Ṭabarī: A Medieval Muslim Historian and His Work,* edited by Hugh Kennedy, 1–9. Princeton, NJ: Darwin Press, 2008.

Khan, Ruqayya Y., ed. *Muhammad in the Digital Age.* Austin: University of Texas Press, forthcoming.

———. "Of Cyber Muslimahs: Wives of the Prophet and Muslim Women in the Digital Age." In *Muhammad in the Digital Age,* edited by Ruqayya Y. Khan.

Khanna, Meenakshi. "The Visionaries of a *Ṭarīqa:* The Uwaysī Sufis of Shāhjahānabād." In *Dreams and Visions in Islamic Societies,* edited by Felek and Knysh, 273–296.

Kholoussy, Hanan. *For Better, for Worse: The Marriage Crisis That Made Modern Egypt.* Stanford, CA: Stanford University Press, 2010.

———. "The Nationalization of Marriage in Monarchical Egypt." In *Re-Envisioning Egypt, 1919–1952,* edited by Arthur Goldschmidt, Amy J. Johnson, and Barak A. Salmoni, 317–350. Cairo: American University in Cairo Press, 2005.

Kidd, Thomas S. *American Christians and Islam: Evangelical Culture and Muslims from the Colonial Period to the Age of Terrorism.* Princeton, NJ: Princeton University Press, 2009.

———. "Is It Worse to Follow Mahomet Than the Devil? Early American Uses of Islam." *Church History* 72, no. 4 (December 2003): 766–790.

Kinberg, Leah. "Dreams Online: Contemporary Appearances of the Prophet in Dreams." In *Dreams and Visions in Islamic Societies,* edited by Felek and Knysh, 139–157.

———. "The Legitimization of the *Madhāhib* through Dreams." *Arabica* 32, no. 1 (March 1985): 47–79.

King, Richard. *Orientalism and Religion: Postcolonial Theory, India, and the Mystic East.* London: Routledge, 1999.

Kister, M. J. "'A Bag of Meat': A Study of an Early *Ḥadīth*." *Bulletin of the School of Oriental and African Studies* 33 (1970): 267–275.

———. "The Sons of Khadīja." *Jerusalem Studies in Arabic and Islam* 16 (1993): 59–95.

Klausen, Jytte. *The Cartoons That Shook the World.* New Haven, CT: Yale University Press, 2009.

Koelle, S. W. *Mohammed and Mohammedanism Critically Considered.* London: Rivingtons, 1889.

Kohlberg, Etan. "Western Accounts of the Death of Muḥammad." In *L'Orient dans l'histoire religieuse de l'Europe: L'invention des origines,* edited by Mohammad Ali Amir-Moezzi and John Scheid, 165–195. Turnhout: Brepols, 2000.

Lai, Whalen. "The Search for the Historical Śākyamuni in Light of the Historical Jesus." *Buddhist-Christian Studies* 2 (1982): 79–91.

Lane, Edward William. *Selections from the Ḳur-án.* Rev. ed. London: Trübner, 1879.

Lane-Poole, Stanley. *The Speeches and Table-Talk of the Prophet Mohammad.* London: Macmillan, 1882.

———. Introduction to *Selections from the Ḳur-án,* by Edward William Lane, xi–cix. Rev. ed. London: Trübner, 1879.

Lassner, Jacob. *Jews, Christians, and the Abode of Islam: Modern Scholarship, Medieval Realities.* Chicago: University of Chicago Press, 2012.

Laureys, Marc. "History and Poetry in Philippus Meyerus's Humanist Latin Portraits of the Prophet Mohammed and Ottoman Rulers (1594)." In *Latinity and Alterity in the Early Modern Empire*, edited by Yasmin Annabel Haskell and Juanita Feros Ruys, 273–299. Tempe, AZ: Arizona Center for Medieval and Rennaisance Studies; Turnhout: Brepols, 2010.

Lecker, Michael. "Glimpses of Muḥammad's Medinan Decade." In *Cambridge Companion*, edited by Brockopp, 61–79.

Lee, Hermione. *Biography: A Very Short Introduction.* Oxford: Oxford University Press, 2009.

Lewis, Bernard. "Gibbon on Muhammad." In "Edward Gibbon and the Decline and Fall of the Roman Empire." Special issue, *Daedalus* 105, no. 3 (Summer 1976): 89–101.

Lewis, C. S. *Mere Christianity.* San Francisco: Harper, 2001 [1952].

Lings, Martin. *Muhammad: His Life Based on the Earliest Sources.* Rochester, VT: Inner Traditions International, 1983.

Littlewood, Ian. *Sultry Climates: Travel and Sex.* Cambridge, MA: Da Capo, 2002.

Lopez, Donald S., Jr. *From Stone to Flesh: A Short History of the Buddha.* Chicago: University of Chicago Press, 2013.

———. *The Scientific Buddha: His Short and Happy Life.* New Haven, CT: Yale University Press, 2012.

Lyall, C. J. "Obituary Notice: Sir William Muir." *Journal of the Royal Asiatic Society of Great Britain and Ireland* 37 (1905): 875–879.

Lyons, Jonathan. *Islam through Western Eyes: From the Crusades to the War on Terrorism.* New York: Columbia University Press, 2012.

MacLean, Gerald. "Milton among the Muslims." In *The Religions of the Book: Christian Perceptions, 1400–1600*, edited by Matthew Dimmock and Andrew Hadfield. New York: Palgrave, 2008: 180–94.

Maghen, Ze'ev. *Virtues of the Flesh: Passion and Purity in Early Islamic Jurisprudence*. Leiden: Brill, 2005.

Mahfouz, Naguib. *Children of the Alley: A Novel*. New York: Anchor, 1996.

Malik, Ghulam. *Muhammad: An Islamic Perspective*. Lanham, MD: University Press of America, 1996.

Manseau, Peter. *Rag and Bone: A Journey among the World's Holy Dead*. New York: Henry Holt, 2009.

Margoliouth, David Samuel. *Mohammed and the Rise of Islam*. New York: G. P. Putnam's Sons, 1905.

Marston, Elsa. *Muhammad of Mecca: Prophet of Islam*. New York: Franklin Watts, 2001.

Masuzawa, Tomoko. *The Invention of World Religions: Or, How European Universalism Was Preserved in the Language of Pluralism*. Chicago: University of Chicago Press, 2005.

Matar, Nabil. *Turks, Moors, and Englishmen in the Age of Discovery*. New York: Columbia University Press, 1999.

———, ed. *Henry Stubbe and the Beginnings of Islam: The Originall & Progress of Mahometanism*. New York: Columbia University Press, 2014.

McAuliffe, Jane Dammen. "Al-Ṭabarī's Prelude to the Prophet." In *Al-Ṭabarī: A Medieval Muslim Historian and His Work*, edited by Hugh Kennedy, 113–129. Princeton, NJ: Darwin, 2008.

Mernissi, Fatima. *Islam and Democracy: Fear of the Modern World*. Translated by Mary Jo Lakeland. New York: Perseus, 1992.

———. *The Veil and the Male Elite: A Feminist Interpretation of Women's Rights in Islam*. Translated by Mary Jo Lakeland. New York: Perseus, 1991.

Metcalf, Barbara Daly. *Islamic Revival In British India: Deoband, 1860–1900*. New Delhi: Oxford University Press, 2002.

Minault, Gail. "Aloys Sprenger: German Orientalism's 'Gift' to Delhi College." *South Asia Research* 31, no. 1 (February 2011): 7–23.

Minois, George. *The Atheist's Bible: The Most Dangerous Book That Never Existed*. Chicago: University of Chicago Press, 2012.

Mirza, Sarah. "Dreaming the Truth in the *Sīra* of Ibn Hishām." In *Dreams and Visions in Islamic Societies*, edited by Felek and Knysh, 15–30.

Mitchell, Timothy. *Colonising Egypt*. Berkeley: University of California Press, 1991.

Mittermaier, Amira. *Dreams That Matter: Egyptian Landscapes of the Imagination.* Berkeley: University of California Press, 2011.

Monroe, James T. "The Poetry of the *Sīrah* Literature." In *The Cambridge History of Arabic Literature: Arabic Literature to the End of the Umayyad Period,* edited by A. F. L. Beeston, T. M. Johnstone, R. B. Serjeant, and G. R. Smith, 368–373. Cambridge: Cambridge University Press, 1983.

Montgomery, James E. "Editor's Introduction." In *The Oral and the Written in Early Islam,* edited by Gregor Schoeler, Uwe Vagelpohl, and James E. Montgomery. London: Taylor and Francis, 2006.

Morey, Peter, and Amina Yaqin. *Framing Muslims.* Cambridge, MA: Harvard University Press, 2010.

Muir, William. *The Life of Mahomet from Original Sources.* 2nd ed. London: Smith, Elder, 1878.

———. *The Life of Mahomet from Original Sources.* 3rd ed. London: Smith, Elder, 1894.

———. *The Life of Mahomet, with Introductory Chapter on the Original Sources for the Biography of Mahomet, and on the Pre-Islamite History of Arabia.* London: Smith, Elder, 1858 (vols. 1–2) and 1861 (vols. 3–4).

———. *The Mohammedan Controversy: Biographies of Mohammed; Sprenger on Tradition; the Indian Liturgy; and the Psalter.* Edinburgh: T. & T. Clark, 1897.

Murray, William, trans. *The Life of Mohammed Translated from the Arabic of Abulfeda.* Elgin, Scotland: A. C. Brander, n.d.

Nadvi, Syed Suleman [Saiyid Sulaiman Nadwi]. *Muhammad: The Ideal Prophet. A Historic, Practical, Perfect Model for Humanity.* Translated by Mohiuddin Ahmad. Kuala Lumpur: Islamic Book Trust, 1977 [n.d.].

———. *Women Companions of the Holy Prophet and Their Sacred Lives.* New Delhi: Islamic Book Service, 2001.

Nasier, Alcofribas, trans. *The Three Impostors.* Privately printed, 1904.

Nasr, Seyyed Hossein. *Muhammad: Man of God.* Chicago: Kazi, 1995.

Nasrin, Taiyaba. *The Prophet Muhammad as a Man: Islamic Modernism and Sirah Literature in Egypt.* Aligarh, India: Aligarh Muslim University Press, 2008 [1992].

Nazik Saba Yared. *Arab Travellers and Western Civilization.* Translated by Sumayya Damluji Shahbandar. London: Saqi Books, 1996.

Newby, Gordon D. *The Making of the Last Prophet: A Reconstruction of the Earliest Biography of Muhammad.* Charleston: University of South Carolina Press, 1989.

Newcomb, Harvey. *The False Prophet; or, An Account of the Rise and Progress of the Mohammedan Religion; Comprising the History of the Church, etc.* 2nd ed. Boston: Massachusetts Sabbath School Society, 1844.

Noorani, Yaseen. *Culture and Hegemony in the Colonial Middle East.* New York: Palgrave, 2010.

Northrup, David. *How English Became the Global Language.* New York: Palgrave, 2013.

Norton, Charles Eliot, ed. *The Correspondence of Thomas Carlyle and Ralph Waldo Emerson, 1834–1872.* 2 vols. Boston: James R. Osgood, 1883.

Omar, Sara. "Al-Qubaysiyyāt: Negotiating Female Religious Authority in Damascus." *Muslim World* 103, no. 3 (July 2013): 347–362.

Otterbeck, Jonas. "The Depiction of Islam in Sweden: An Historical Overview." http://inhouse.lau.edu.lb/bima/papers/Jonas_Otterbeck.pdf.

Pasha, Kamran. *Mother of the Believers: A Novel of the Birth of Islam.* New York: Washington Square, 2009.

Pelikan, Jaroslav. *Jesus through the Centuries: His Place in the History of Culture.* New Haven: Yale University Press, 1999 [1985].

Penn, Michael. *Imaging Islam: Syriac Christianity and the Reimagining of Christian-Muslim Relations.* Philadelphia: University of Pennyslvania Press, forthcoming.

Peters, F. E. *Jesus and Muhammad: Parallel Tracks, Parallel Lives.* New York: Oxford University Press, 2011.

———. "The Quest of the Historical Muhammad." *International Journal of Middle East Studies* 23 (1991): 291–315.

Peterson, Daniel C. *Muhammad: Prophet of God.* Grand Rapids, MI: Wm. B. Eerdmans, 2007.

Pickthall, M. M. *The Life of Muhammad: A Brief History.* Beltsville, MD: Amana, 1998.

Pierce, Matthew. "Remembering Fāṭimah: New Means of Legitimizing Female Authority in Contemporary Shīʿī Discourse." In *Women, Leadership, and Mosques: Changes in Contemporary Islamic Authority,* edited by Masooda Bano and Hilary Kalmbach, 345–362. Leiden: Brill, 2012.

———. "Remembering the Infallible Imams: Narrative and Memory in Medieval Twelver Shiʿism." Ph.D. diss., Boston University, 2013.

Pitt, Alan. "The Cultural Impact of Science in France: Ernest Renan and the Vie de Jésus." *Historical Journal* 43, no. 1 (March 2000): 79–101.

Powell, Avril A. *Scottish Orientalists and India: The Muir Brothers, Religion, Education and Empire.* Woodbridge, UK: Boydell, 2010.

Powers, David S. *Muḥammad Is Not the Father of Any of Your Men: The Making of the Last Prophet.* Philadelphia: University of Pennsylvania Press, 2009.

————. *Zayd.* Philadelphia: University of Pennsylvania Press, forthcoming.

Prideaux, Humphrey. *The True Nature of Imposture Fully Display'd in the Life of Mahomet,* 8th ed. London: E. Curll, 1723 [1697].

Prothero, Stephen. *American Jesus: How the Son of God Became a National Icon.* New York: Farrar, Straus and Giroux, 2003.

Purohit, Teena. *The Aga Khan Case: Religion and Identity in Colonial India.* Cambridge, MA: Harvard University Press, 2012.

Pursley, Sara. "Daughters of the Right Path: Family Law, Homosocial Publics, and the Ethics of Intimacy in the Works of Shiʻi Revivalist Bint al-Huda." *Journal of Middle East Women's Studies* 8, no. 2 (Spring 2012): 51–77.

Qasmi, Shahid Zafar. *Questions and Answers on the Mothers of Believers (May Allah Be Pleased with Them).* Revised and checked by Muhammad Tahir Salafi. Riyadh: Darussalam, 1997.

Quinn, Frederick. *Sum of All Heresies: The Image of Islam in Western Thought.* New York: Oxford University Press, 2008.

Rahman, Afazlur. *Muhammad as a Military Leader.* London: Muslim Schools Trust, 1980.

Rahman, Fazlur. *Prophecy in Islam: Philosophy and Orthodoxy.* Chicago: University of Chicago Press, 2011.

Ramadan, Tariq. *In the Footsteps of the Prophet: Lessons from the Life of Muhammad.* New York: Oxford University Press, 2007.

————. *Muhammad: Vie du prophète; Les enseignements spirituels et contemporains.* Paris: Presses du Châtelet. 2006.

Rauf, Imam Feisal Abdul. *Moving the Mountain: A New Vision of Islam in America.* New York: Free Press, 2012.

Reinhart, A. Kevin. "Juynbolliana, Gradualism, the Big Bang, and Ḥadīth Study in the Twenty-First Century." *Journal of the American Oriental Society* 130, no. 3 (July–September 2010): 413–444.

Reynolds, Dwight F., ed. *Interpreting the Self: Autobiography in the Arabic Literary Tradition.* Berkeley: University of California Press, 2001.

Reynolds, Gabriel Said. "Remembering Muhammad." *Numen: International Review for the History of Religions* 58, no. 2/3 (2011): 188–206.

Ricci, Ronit. *Islam Translated: Literature, Conversion, and the Arabic Cosmopolis of South and Southeast Asia.* Chicago: University of Chicago Press, 2012.

Riyāshī, Labīb. *Nafsīyat al-Rasūl al-ʿArabī.* Beirut: Maṭbaʿat al-Kashshāf, 1937.

Rizvi, S. A. A. "Muḥammad in South Asian Biographies: Changes in Islamic Perceptions of the Individual in Society." In *Self and Biography: Essays on the Individual and Society in Asia,* edited by Wang Gungwu, 99–122. Sydney: Sydney University Press, 1975.

Robinson, Chase. *Islamic Historiography.* Cambridge: Cambridge University Press, 2002.

Robinson-Dunn, Diane. *The Harem, Slavery and British Imperial Culture: Anglo-Muslim Relations in the Late Nineteenth Century.* Manchester, UK: Manchester University Press, 2006.

Roded, Ruth. "Alternate Images of the Prophet Muhammad's Virility." In *Islamic Masculinities,* edited by Lahoucine Ouzgane. London: Zed Books, 2006.

———. "Bint al-Shati's 'Wives of the Prophet': Feminist or Feminine?" *British Journal of Middle Eastern Studies* 33, no. 1 (May 2006): 51–66.

———. "Gender in an Allegorical Life of Muḥammad: Mahfouz's *Children of Gebelawi.*" *Muslim World* 93 (January 2003): 117–134.

———. "Muslim Women Reclaim the Life-Story of the Prophet: 'A'isha 'Abd al-Raḥmān, Assia Djebar, and Nadia Yassine." *Muslim World* 103, no. 3 (July 2013): 334–346.

Rodgers, Russ. *The Generalship of Muhammad.* Jacksonville: University Press of Florida, 2012.

Rodinson, Maxime. "A Critical Survey of Modern Studies on Muhammad." In *Studies on Islam,* edited and translated by Merlin Swartz, 23–85. New York: Oxford University Press, 1981.

———. *Europe and the Mystique of Islam.* London: I. B. Tauris, 2002 [1987].

———. *Mahomet.* Paris: Éditions du Seuil, 1961. Translated by Anne Carter as *Muḥammad* (New York: Pantheon, 1980 [1971]).

Rosen, Lawrence. *Varieties of Muslim Experience: Encounters with Arab Political and Cultural Life.* Chicago: University of Chicago Press, 2008.

Roy, Coomar. With a prefatory note by Joel Benton. "Child Marriage in India," *North American Review* 147 (1888): 415–423.

Rubin, Uri. *The Eye of the Beholder: The Life of Muhammad as Viewed by the Early Muslims; A Textual Analysis.* Princeton, NJ: Darwin, 1995.

———, ed. *The Life of Muḥammad.* Aldershot, UK: Ashgate / Variorum, 1998.

———. "Muḥammad's Message in Mecca: Warnings, Signs, and Miracles." In *Cambridge Companion*, edited by Brockopp, 39–56.

———. *Muhammad the Prophet and Arabia*. Farnham, UK: Ashgate / Variorum, 2011.

———. "Pre-Existence and Light: Aspects of the Concept of *Nūr Muḥammad*." *Israel Oriental Studies* 5 (1975): 62–119.

Sabanegh, E. S. *Muhammad b. Abdallah, "Le prophete": Portraits contemporains, Egypte 1930–1950*. Paris: Librairie J. Vrin, n.d.

Sabbath, Roberta Sterman, ed. *Sacred Tropes: Tanakh, New Testament, and Qur'an as Literature and Culture*. Leiden: Brill, 2009.

Safi, Omid. *Memories of Muhammad: Why the Prophet Matters*. New York: Harper One, 2009.

Said, Edward. *Orientalism*. New York: Pantheon, 1978.

Salahi, Adil. *Muhammad, Man and Prophet: A Complete Study of the Life of the Prophet of Islam*. Leicestershire, UK: Islamic Foundation, 2012.

Salama, Mohammad R. *Islam, Orientalism, and Intellectual History: Modernity and the Politics of Exclusion since Ibn Khaldun*. London: I. B. Tauris, 2011.

Sale, George, trans. *The Koran: Commonly Called the Alcoran of Mohammed*. London: L. Hawes et al., 1734.

Salmin, Muhammad Ali-Al-Haj. *The Holy Prophet Mohammad: The Commander of the Faithful*. Bombay: M. A. Salmin, 1930s.

Sardar, Ziauddin. *Muhammad: All That Matters*. London: Hodder, 2012.

Sarkar, Sumit, and Tanika Sarkar, eds. *Women and Social Reform in Modern India: A Reader*. Bloomington: Indiana University Press, 2008.

Sarwar, Hafiz Ghulam. *Muhammad: The Holy Prophet*. Lahore: Shaykh Muhamamd Ashraf, 1980 [1961].

Schacht, Joseph. "A Revaluation of Islamic Traditions." *Journal of the Royal Asiatic Society of Great Britain and Ireland* 81, no. 3–4 (October 1949): 143–154.

Schick, Irvin. *The Erotic Margin: Spatiality and Sexuality in Alterist Discourse*. London: Verso, 1999.

Schimmel, Annemarie. *And Muhammad Is His Messenger: The Veneration of the Prophet in Islamic Piety*. Chapel Hill: University of North Carolina Press, 1985.

Schoeler, Gregor. "Foundations for a New Biography of Muḥammad: The Production and Evaluation of the Corpus of Traditions from 'Urwah b. al-Zubayr." In *Method and Theory in the Study of Islamic Origins*, edited by Herbert Berg, 21–28. Leiden: Brill: 2003.

Shabazz, Ama F. "The Prophet on the Treatment of Women." *Message International,* August–September 2002, 37–39.

Shalem, Avinoam, ed. *Constructing the Image of Muhammad in Europe.* Berlin: De Gruyter, 2013.

Shaner, Edward. "Biographies of the Buddha." *Philosophy East and West* 37, no. 3 (July 1987): 306–322.

Shepard, William. *The Faith of a Modern Muslim Intellectual: The Religious Aspects and Implications of the Writings of Ahmad Amin.* New Delhi: Indian Institute of Islamic Studies / Vikas, 1982.

Shoemaker, Stephen J. *The Death of a Prophet: The End of Muhammad's Life and the Beginnings of Islam.* Philadelphia: University of Pennsylvania Press, 2012.

Siddiqui, Abdul Hameed. *The Life of Muhammad (P.B.U.H.).* 2nd ed. New Delhi: Islamic Book Service, 2002 [1975]; 1st ed. 1969.

Siddiqui, Mona. *Christians, Muslims, and Jesus.* New Haven, CT: Yale University Press, 2013.

Sinha, Mrinali. *Specters of Mother India: The Global Restructuring of an Empire.* Durham, NC: Duke University Press, 2006.

Smith, Charles D. "*Hayat Muhammad* and the Muslim Brothers: Two Interpretations of Egyptian Islam and Their Socioeconomic Implications." *Journal of the American Research Center in Egypt* 16 (1979): 175–181.

———. *Islam and the Search for Social Order in Modern Egypt: A Biography of Muhammad Husayn Haykal.* Albany: State University of New York Press, 1983.

Smith, Christian. *Moral, Believing Animals: Human Personhood and Culture.* New York: Oxford University Press, 2003.

Spellberg, D. A. *Politics, Gender, and the Islamic Past.* New York: Columbia University Press, 1996.

Spencer, Robert. *Did Muhammad Exist? An Inquiry into Islam's Obscure Origins.* Wilmington, DE: Intercollegiate Studies Institute, 2012.

———. *The Truth about Muhammad: Founder of the World's Most Intolerant Religion.* Washington, DC: Regnery, 2006.

Sprenger, Aloys. *The Life of Mohammad from Original Sources.* Allahabad: Presbyterian Mission Press, 1851. Expanded German ed.: *Das Leben und die Lehre des Moḥammad, nach bisher des grösstentheils unbenutzten Quellen bearbeitet.* 2 vols. Berlin: Nicolaische Verlagsbuchhandlung, 1861.

Stecker, Tom. *The Man Mohammed: A Dramatic Character-Sketch.* Cambridge, MA: Co-operative Press, 1900.

Steiner, Wendy. *The Scandal of Pleasure: Art in an Age of Fundamentalism.* Chicago: University of Chicago Press, 1995.

Stetkevych, Jaroslav. *Muḥammad and the Golden Bough: Reconstructing Arabian Myth.* Bloomington: Indiana University Press, 1996.

Stobart, J[ames] W[illiam] H[ampson]. *Islam and Its Founder.* London: Society for Promoting Christian Knowledge, 1895.

Stroumsa, Guy G. *A New Science: The Discovery of Religion in the Age of Reason.* Cambridge, MA: Harvard University Press, 2010.

Stubbe, Henry. *An Account of the Rise and Progress of Mahometanism with the Life of Mahomet and a Vindication of Him and His Religion from the Calumnies of the Christians.* Edited by Hafiz Mahmoud Khan Shairani. London: Luzac, 1911.

Szilágyi, Krisztina. "Muḥammad and the Monk: The Making of the Christian Baḥīrā Legend." *Jerusalem Studies in Arabic and Islam* 34 (2008): 169–214.

Al-Ṭabarī, Abū Jaʿfar Muḥammad ibn Jarīr. *Tārīkh al-Ṭabarī: tārīkh al-rusul wa-al-mulūk,* edited by Muḥmmad Abū al-Faḍl Ibrāhīm. 11 vols. Egypt: Dār al-Maʿārif, 1960–[1977].

———. *The History of al-Ṭabarī.* Various translators. 39 vols. Albany: State University of New York, 1989–1998.

Tageldin, Shaden. *Disarming Words: Empire and the Seductions of Translation in Egypt.* Berkeley: University of California Press, 2011.

———. "Secularizing Islam: Carlyle, al-Sibāʿī, and the Translations of 'Religion' in British Egypt." *PMLA* 126, no. 1 (January 2011).

Tareen, SherAli. "The Polemic at Shahjahanpur: Religion, Miracles, and History." *Islamic Studies* 51, no. 1 (2012): 49–67.

Tayob, Abdulkader. "Epilogue: Muḥammad in the Future." In *Cambridge Companion,* edited by Brockopp, 293–308.

Teipen, Alfons. "The 'Poisoning Jewess' Motif in Early Muslim Biographies of Muhammad." Unpublished paper, presented at the American Academy of Religion Annual Meeting, November 2013.

Thompson, Ahmad. *The Wives of the Prophet Muhammad: May the Blessings and Peace of Allah Be on Him and His Family and Companions.* London: Ta-Ha Publishers, 2004 [1993].

Tobin, Ronald W. "The Sources of Voltaire's 'Mahomet.'" *French Review* 34, no. 4 (February 1961): 372–378.

Tolan, John. "Afterword." In *Contextualizing the Muslim Other in Medieval Christian Discourse,* edited by Jerold Frakes, 170–177. New York: Palgrave, 2011.

———. "European Accounts of Muḥammad's Life." In *Cambridge Companion,* edited by Brockopp, 226–250.

————. *Saracens: Islam in the Medieval European Imagination.* New York: Columbia University Press, 2002.

————. *Sons of Ishmael: Muslims through European Eyes in the Middle Ages.* Jacksonville: University Press of Florida, 2008.

Turner, Colin. *Islam: The Basics.* New York: Routledge, 2006.

Tyerman, Christopher. *The Crusades: A Very Short Introduction.* Oxford: Oxford University Press, 2005.

Varisco, Daniel M. *Reading Orientalism: Said and the Unsaid.* Seattle: University of Washington Press, 2007.

Vial, Ch. "Muḥammad Ḥusayn Haykal." In *Encyclopaedia of Islam,* 2nd ed., edited by P. J. Bearman, Th. Bianquis, C. E. Bosworth, E. van Donzel, and W. P. Heinrichs. Leiden: Brill, 2011.

Vidyasagar, Ishvarchandra. *Hindu Widow Marriage: An Epochal Work on Social Reform from Colonial India.* Translated by Brian A. Hatcher. New York: Columbia University Press, 2011.

Vitkus, Daniel J. "Early Modern Orientalism: Representations of Islam in Sixteenth- and Seventeenth-Century Europe." In *Western Views of Islam in Medieval and Early Modern Europe,* edited by David R. Blanks and Michael Frasetto, 207–230. New York: St. Martin's, 1999.

Waheed-Ud-Din, Fakir Syed. *The Benefactor.* Translated by Faiz Ahmed Faiz. World Community of Islam in the West, n.d. [1964].

Waldman, Marilyn. *Prophecy and Power: Muhammad and the Qur'an in the Light of Comparison.* Edited by Bruce B. Lawrence, with Lindsay Jones and Robert M. Baum. Sheffield, UK: Equinox, 2013.

Walker, Christopher J. *Islam and the West: A Dissonant Harmony of Civilizations.* London: Sutton, 2005.

Al-Wāqidī, Muḥammad b. 'Umar. *The Life of Muḥammad: Al-Wāqidī's Kitāb al-Maghāzī.* Edited by Rizwi Faizer and translated by Rizwi Fazier, Amal Ismail, and AbdulKader Tayob. London: Routledge, 2011.

Warren, Ruth. *Muhammad: Prophet of Islam.* New York: Franklin Watts, 1965.

Watt, W. Montgomery. *Muhammad: Prophet and Statesman.* London: Oxford University Press, 1974 [1961].

Weil, Gustav. *Mohammed der Prophet, sein Leben und seine Lehre: Aus handschriftlichen Quellen und dem Koran geschöpft und dargestellt von Dr. Gustav Weil; mit Beilagen und einer Stammtafel.* Stuttgart: J. B. Metzler, 1843.

————. *The Story of Ali Baba and the Forty Thieves: An Extract from Dr. Weil's German Translation of the Arabian Nights.* Boston: D. C. Heath, 1889.

Weinberger, Eliot. *Muhammad*. New York: Verso, 2006.

Welch, Alford T. "Muhammad's Understanding of Himself: The Koranic Data." In *Islam's Understanding of Itself*, edited by Richard G. Hovannisian and Speros Vyronis Jr., 15–52. Malibu, CA: Undena, 1983.

Wessels, Antonie. *A Modern Arabic Biography of Muhammad: A Critical Study of Muhammad Husayn Haykal's* Hayāt Muhammad. Leiden: Brill, 1972.

Williams, Rebecca R. *Muhammad and the Supernatural: Medieval Arab Views*. New York: Routledge, 2013.

Wills, Garry. *What Jesus Meant*. New York: Viking, 2006.

Winter, Tim. "Jesus and Muhammad: New Convergences." *Muslim World* 99 (January 2009): 21–38.

Wokoeck, Ursula. *German Orientalism: The Study of the Middle East and Islam from 1800 to 1945*. New York: Routledge, 2009.

Wollaston, Arthur N. *Half-Hours with Muhammad, Being a popular Account of the Prophet of Arabia and of his more immediate Followers*. London: W.H. Allen, 1886.

Woods, Matthew. *In Spite of Epilepsy: Caesar, Mohammed, Lord Byron; The Founders Respectively of an Empire, a Religion, and a School of Poetry*. New York: Cosmopolitan Press, 1913.

Wright, Peter Matthews. "Critical Approaches to the Farewell *Khutba* in Ibn Ishaq's Life of the Prophet." *Comparative Islamic Studies* 6, nos. 1–2 (2010): 217–249.

Wright, Terence R. "The Letter and the Spirit: Deconstructing Renan's "Life of Jesus" and the Assumptions of Modernity." *Religion & Literature* 26, no. 2 (Summer 1994): 55–71.

Yusuf, Imtiyaz, ed. *Islam and Knowledge: Al Faruqi's Concept of Religion in Islamic Thought; Essays in Honor of Isma'il Al Faruqi*. London: I. B. Tauris, 2012.

Zaidi, Ali. *Islam, Modernity, and the Human Sciences*. New York: Palgrave Macmillan, 2011.

Zaidi, Syed M. H. *Mothers of the Faithful: Being a Discourse on Polygamy with a Biographical Sketch of the Wives of Muhammad refuting the allegations of the non-Muslims against them and the Prophet himself*. Calcutta: N. Mukherjee at the Art Press, 1935.

Zaman, Muhammad Qasim. "A Venture in Critical Islamic Historiography and the Significance of Its Failure." *Numen* 41, no. 1 (January 1994): 26–50.

Acknowledgments

As the preceding pages attest, every book is in dialogue with its predecessors; every author with her contemporaries. Many people share credit for what is valuable in this study, though none of them bears blame for its inevitable shortcomings. Colleagues and friends near and far encouraged and challenged me, responded to queries, and suggested further points of investigation. They include Leila Ahmed, Ali Asani, Jonathan Brockopp, Edward Curtis, Farid Esack, Juliane Hammer, Susannah Heschel, Aysha Hidayatullah, Marion Katz, Ruth Roded, Omid Safi, Sa'diyya Shaikh, Laury Silvers, Harvey Stark, Abdulkader Tayob, and Alfons Teipen. Kevin Fogg, Gene Garthwaite, Nasir Rana, and Sameer Sabir called my attention to biographies they thought might interest me. Jonathan Brown, Mimi Hanaoka, Ruqayya Khan, Michael Penn, and David Powers generously shared forthcoming work.

Colleagues and students at Boston University were vital interlocutors. The Muslim Studies faculty listened to an early overview; Roberta Micallef organized a conference at which I presented an early version of Chapter 3; and the Department of Religion faculty heard a draft of Chapter 2. In each case, listeners asked probing questions and suggested productive areas to explore. David Frankfurter, Deeana Klepper, Steve Prothero, and Michael Zank made time for additional conversations; Teena Purohit read two chapters in draft form and provided incisive comments. Administrators Karen Nardella and Wendy Czik kept logistics running smoothly and coffee brewing. Students in my Fall 2010 seminar on Representations of Muhammad thought through some of these issues along with me: Gerry Dunn, Galen Olson, Alix Saba, and Monsura Sirajee. Najah Ahmad brought me a book from Cairo. Eric Dorman, Andi Ogier, Matthew Pierce, and Nik Zanetti helped at various times with research tasks small and large; Matt, whose own work centrally addresses questions of biography, has also been a perceptive conversation partner throughout.

I spoke about this project as part of Arlington Community Education's Tuesday Night Conversations series and at Harvard University; the Islamic Center of Boston-Wayland; Macalester College, where I gave the 2014 Arnold Lowe Lecture; Mount Holyoke College; New York University; Transylvania University; the University of Johannesburg; the University of Cape Town; Wheaton College; and Wilson College, where I delivered the Orr Forum lectures in 2011. These audiences allowed me to field-test ideas, for which I am thankful.

Sharmila Sen at Harvard University Press went above and beyond the usual editor's duty as this book underwent twists and turns, while Heather Hughes kept the project on track. Two anonymous reviewers provided thoughtful and generous reports.

Most important, at the start and at the finish, was my family. More than ever, I am grateful beyond measure.

Index

In alphabetizing entries, I ignore the prefix al- and the letter 'ayn.

49–51, 257n33; sexuality and, 164, 166; defining religions, 207
Other ideology in Western scholarship, 164–168, 170, 191–194, 294n133
Ottoman Empire and Islam, 32, 47, 88–89, 168
Ouseley, W., 165

Paganism: *vs.* monotheism, 7, 10–11, 27–28, 76–77; morality and, 166
Pakistani scholarship, 90, 91, 121–122, 125, 147
Pascual, Pedro, 30
Pasha, Kamran, 196, 295n147
Pedophilia accusations, 187–191, 235
Persian writings, 3, 94, 229
Peters, F. E., 10, 244n9
Peterson, Daniel, 222
Peter the Venerable, 28, 32
Pfander, Karl, 50
Pickthall, Muhammad Marmaduke, 227
Piety and celibacy, 142–143, 281n102
Plato, 84
Plays on Muhammad, 106, 216–217
Pococke, Edward, 33–34, 37
Poetry, 3, 17, 52. *See also Sira* literature
"Polemical *Sira*," 20
Polishing of Hearts through Remembrance of the Beloved One, The (Ahmad Khan), 71
Polygamy: Muslim scholarship on, 107, 123, 133–135, 143–144; justification of, 130, 136, 141, 280n81, 290n86; Western scholarship on, 131–133, 136–138, 158, 191, 210; climate and, 165; and slavery, 82, 169; modern response to, 170, 196, 235–236, 278n41. *See also* Women
Pope, 31, 34, 218, 232
Pope Benedict, 218
Postel, Guillaume, 31
Powell, Avril, 61
Power as vice, 89–90
Powers, David, 13, 14
Prayer obligations of Muslims, 64, 232
Prediction motifs, 204
Presbyterian Mission Press, 46

Prideaux, Humphrey: about, 35–36, 86; on wives, 130, 131, 132, 156, 158–161; on sexuality, 164; on Aisha, 169, 178, 179; on pluralism, 232–233; on Muhammad, 260n61
Print media, 44, 53, 91, 99, 255n6
Prophecy and Power (Waldman), 202
Prophet, Muhammad as: differing viewpoints of, 5, 8; origin of, 41, 109; in Christian works, 42–43, 261n72; Muir on, 49–50, 60–61; comparison of, 62, 65–66, 73–74, 201–202, 264n131; evidence of, 68, 262n109; success of, 83–84; man *vs.*, 115–116, 131–132, 204–208, 210–212, 216–217, 226, 298n42
Prophetic traditions: of Islam, 20–21, 60, 244n8; false prophets in, 33–35, 68–69; biographies in, 94–95, 102–103, 110–111, 239–240; Haykal on, 104–105; impulse of, 208; of Islam, 261n74
Prophet's Daughters, The ('Abd al-Rahman), 100
Prophet's Mother, The ('Abd al-Rahman), 100
Prophet's Wives, The ('Abd al-Rahman), 100
Protestant Reformation, 27, 30–31, 32, 81, 85–86, 239

Qadi 'Iyad, 45
Qamar (fictional), 153, 194, 195
Qassem (fictional), 152–153, 194–195
Qubaysiyyat, 198
Qur'an: origin of, 7, 60, 218; historical accuracy of, 9–10, 244nn8–9; on Muhammad's sons, 13; on Muhammad, 24, 25, 93, 268n38; translations of, 28, 37, 38; Western scholarship on, 57–58; source reliability of, 62–63; infanticide prohibition in, 166; on women, 190; on Jesus, 201; translations of, 239; burning of, 294n138
Quraysh tribe, 6, 118, 128, 151, 224, 279n62

Rahman, Afazlur, 101
Ramadan, Tariq, 222, 223–225, 226